edited by

MARK LEVENSKY
Massachusetts Institute of Technology

HUMAN
FACTUAL
KNOWLEDGE

Prentice-Hall, Inc., Englewood Cliffs, New Jersey

Library of Congress Catalog Card Number: 75–147947

Printed in the United States of America

C 13–445031–0
P 13–445023–X

Current Printing (last digit):
10 9 8 7 6 5 4 3 2 1

PRENTICE-HALL INTERNATIONAL, INC., London
PRENTICE-HALL OF AUSTRALIA, PTY. LTD., Sydney
PRENTICE-HALL OF CANADA, LTD., Toronto
PRENTICE-HALL OF INDIA PRIVATE LIMITED, New Delhi
PRENTICE-HALL OF JAPAN, INC., Tokyo

CENTRAL ISSUES IN PHILOSOPHY SERIES

BARUCH A. BRODY
series editor

∼∼∼∼∼∼∼∼∼∼∼∼∼∼∼∼∼∼∼∼∼∼

Baruch A. Brody
MORAL RULES AND PARTICULAR CIRCUMSTANCES

Hugo A. Bedau
JUSTICE AND EQUALITY

Mark Levensky
HUMAN FACTUAL KNOWLEDGE

George I. Mavrodes
THE RATIONALITY OF BELIEF IN GOD

Robert Sleigh
NECESSARY TRUTH

David M. Rosenthal
MATERIALISM AND THE MIND BODY PROBLEM

Richard Grandy
THEORIES AND OBSERVATIONS IN SCIENCE

Gerald Dworkin
*DETERMINISM, FREE WILL, AND MORAL
RESPONSIBILITY*

David P. Gauthier
MORALITY AND RATIONAL SELF-INTEREST

Charles Landesman
THE FOUNDATIONS OF KNOWLEDGE

Adrienne and Keith Lehrer
THE THEORY OF MEANING

Foreword

The Central Issues in Philosophy series is based upon the conviction that the best way to teach philosophy to introductory students is to experience or to *do* philosophy with them. The basic unit of philosophical investigation is the particular problem, and not the area or the historical figure. Therefore, this series consists of sets of readings organised around well-defined, manageable problems. All other things being equal, problems that are of interest and relevance to the student have been chosen.

Each volume contains an introduction that clearly defines the problem and sets out the alternative positions that have been taken. The selections are chosen and arranged in such a way as to take the student through the dialectic of the problem; each reading, besides presenting a particular point of view, criticizes the points of view set out earlier.

Although no attempt has been made to introduce the student in a systematic way to the history of philosophy, classical selections relevant to the development of the problem have been included. As a side benefit, the student will therefore come to see the continuity, as well as the breaks, between classical and contemporary thought. But in no case has a selection been included merely for its historical significance; clarity of expression and systematic significance are the main criteria for selection.

BARUCH A. BRODY

Contents

INTRODUCTION   *1*

part one

CONCERNING A PERSON'S KNOWLEDGE OF PAST EVENTS IN HIS LIFE   *11*

R. F. HOLLAND
The Empiricist Theory of Memory   *13*

WILLIAM EARLE
Memory   *· 35*

E. J. FURLONG
Memory   *56*

part two

CONCERNING A PERSON'S KNOWLEDGE OF OTHER MINDS   *85*

A. J. AYER
One's Knowledge of Other Minds   *87*

C. H. WHITELEY
Behaviourism   *102*

H. H. PRICE
Our Evidence for the Existence of Other Minds   *113*

part three

CONCERNING A PERSON'S KNOWLEDGE
OF PHYSICAL OBJECTS IN HIS
IMMEDIATE VICINITY   *145*

A. J. AYER
   Phenominalism   *147*

R. J. HIRST
   The Representative Theory of Perception   *173*

C. H. WHITELEY
   Physical Objects   *204*

BIBLIOGRAPHICAL ESSAY   *213*

Introduction

The purpose of this collection of essays is to introduce the beginning reader of philosophy to a number of philosophical problems concerning human factual knowledge. By *human factual knowledge* I mean simply a person's knowledge that something is so or, to say the same thing differently, that some statement is true. One example of such knowledge is my knowledge that the statement "There are flowers on my desk" is true. Some of the philosophical problems considered in these essays can be suggested in the following way. Philosophers have generally agreed that people know the truth of all sorts of statements. And philosophers have agreed that in order for a person to know that any particular statement is true, at least three conditions must be satisfied. First, the statement must be true. A person can believe that some statement is true when, in fact, it is false. But a person cannot know that a statement is true when, in fact, the statement is false. Second, the person must believe that the statement is true. There is some dispute among philosophers as to how strong the person's belief must be. Can he just think that the statement is true, or must he be confident or sure that it is? But it is generally agreed that if the person does not believe the statement at all—if, say, his only opinion is that the statement is false, or if his only opinion about the truth or falsity of the statement is that he has no opinion—then he cannot know that the statement is true. Third, the person must have a good reason for believing the statement.[1] Some-

---

[1] Given that these three conditions are necessary conditions for human factual knowledge, are they together sufficient conditions? That is, if all three of these conditions are satisfied, does it necessarily follow that the person knows that the statement is true? Probably not.

times people believe or hope or wish or guess that a statement is true without having a good reason or any reason for believing the statement. But, philosophers argue, a person cannot know that a statement is true without having a good reason for believing the statement.[2] One thing philosophers have disagreed about is this: What is a good reason for a person's believing that some particular statement, *S*, is true and why? In particular, what is a good reason for a person's believing some statement about a past event in his life or some statement about the minds of others or some statement about a physical object in his immediate vicinity, and why? It is this last question, or better, series of questions, that will be considered in the essays that follow.

II

What is a good reason for a person's believing some statement about a past event in his life? What is a good reason for a person's believing some statement like "Once, a long time ago, I met a girl with pink hair" or "Last July I went swimming in the Tyrrhenian Sea"? Many philosophers have said that generally, if not always, a person's good reason is tied up in some way with remembering some event. Sometimes his reason is that he remembers the event in question. For example, my good reason for believing the statement "I was driving the car when it hit the garage" is that I remember being behind the wheel when the car crumpled to a halt. And sometimes a person's reason is that he remembers some other event. For example, my good reason for believing the statement "Once, as a child, I set fire to some papers in a basement near our home" is that I can still remember my mother telling me that I did.

Let's suppose that sometimes, at least, a person's good reason for believing some statement about a past event in his life is that he remembers the event in question. Why is a person's memory of a past event in his life ever a good reason for his believing some statement about the event? Here is one answer. It is just that generally a person's memory of past events in his life is reliable. Of course,

[2] Some contemporary philosophers have suggested that sometimes a person knows that a particular sort of statement is true when he does *not* have a good reason for believing the statement. For example, at the present moment I know that the statement "I am thinking about this essay" is true, but I do not have a good reason for believing this statement. What, after all, could my reason be? But those philosophers who hold the view that in order for a person to know that *any* statement is true, a person *must* have a good reason for believing the statement are content to say that in cases of this sort the person's good reason for believing the statement is just that the statement is true.

people sometimes seem to remember some past event in their lives, but later discover that the event was only a dream or a fantasy of their imagination. And in remembering one event, people sometimes get it confused with some other event they witnessed. Most people are better at remembering an event in their recent past than one in their distant past, and some people cannot rely on what they seem to remember at all. But generally a person's memory of past events in his life is reliable. Usually, if a person remembers, or seems to remember, some past happening, then it occurred more or less as he remembers it. And this is why, sometimes at least, one good reason for a person's believing some statement about a past event in his life is that he remembers the event in question.

While this account might seem reasonable enough, it leaves an important question unanswered: How can anyone know that generally a person's memory of past events in his life is reliable? For, presumably, any attempt to establish that this is so will depend, in the end, on assuming that generally a person's memory of past events is reliable. How do you know, for example, that generally your memory of past events in your life is reliable? Is it that you remember many occasions in the past when your memory of such events was reliable? But why is that a good reason for your believing what you do about the reliability of your memory? Is it that generally a person's memory of past events in his life is reliable? But that obviously won't do.

Some philosophers have tried to show that generally a person's memory of past events in his life is reliable by describing part of what occurs in a normal person's conscious experience when he remembers such an event. What does occur? Two descriptions are presented in the first group of essays that follow. R. F. Holland, in his essay "The Empiricist Theory of Memory," discusses the view that when a person remembers a past event in his life, part of what occurs is that he has an image of the event in his mind. And William Earle, in "Memory," argues that when a person remembers a past event in his life, part of what occurs is that the person experiences the event itself. Do either of these views seem right? And is it possible for you or anyone else to determine which, if either, of these views is right without assuming at some point that generally a person's memory of past events in his life is reliable? And suppose that one of these views about memory is right. Does this explain why it is that generally a person's memory of past events in his life is reliable, and, hence, why it is that sometimes a good reason for some person's believing a statement about a past event in his life is that he remembers the event? Don't be too sure.

Other philosophers have tried to show the general reliability of a person's memory of past events in his life in different ways. One such attempt is included in the first group of essays. In "Memory" E. J. Furlong argues that although it cannot be shown that usually a person's memory of past events in his life is reliable without assuming that it is, one is still justified in accepting the general reliability of this sort of memory as a tentative hypothesis. For this hypothesis is the best explanation we have of a wide variety of more or less established facts about our experience. Furlong also says a good deal about what happens in a person's conscious experience when he remembers a past event in his life. And Furlong's view of this matter is different from the view that Holland discusses and the view that Earle defends.

III

What is a good reason for a person's believing some statement about the minds of others? What is a good reason for one's believing some statement like "There are other minds" or "Riley is pleased" or "The woman is asleep"? It seems obvious that in most cases a person's good reason has something to do with the behavior or circumstances of some person or thing. For example, one of my good reasons for believing the statement "There are other minds" is that other people say things I understand. And one of my good reasons for believing the statement "My daughter is content" is that she is dry, full, warm and is talking to her doll.

But why, exactly, are these reasons ever good reasons for a person's believing some statement about other minds? Why are a person's or a thing's behavior—bodily movements, speech, sounds—and circumstances—physical condition, immediate environment—ever good reasons for another person's believing some statement to the effect that the person or thing has a mind, or that the person or thing is thinking a particular thought or experiencing a particular sensation? Philosophers have offered a variety of answers. Four such answers are included in the second group of essays. In "One's Knowledge of Other Minds," A. J. Ayer tries to explain why sometimes another person's behavior and circumstances are his (Ayer's) good reasons for believing that the person is in pain. Ayer's explanation is that in many past instances when someone was in pain, the person was in particular sorts of circumstances and behaved in particular sorts of ways. Hence, by analogy, it is probable that whenever anyone is in similar circumstances and behaves in similar ways, this person is also in pain. Is this explanation any good? How does Ayer know, for example, that in many instances in the past when some person was in pain, he was in these circumstances and behaved in these ways? Ayer knows this, he says, because he knows that in many instances in the past when *he* was in pain, *he* was in these circumstances and behaved in these ways. But, then, isn't Ayer really arguing that since something is true for him—namely, that there is a correlation between his sensations of pain and his behavior and circumstances—that this is probably true for everyone else? And is that okay? C. H. Whiteley, in his essay "Behaviourism," discusses a more radical and perhaps less plausible view. The view is that mental concepts—concepts like thinking, perceiving, being drowsy, feeling pain—are essentially behavioral. If a person is in pain, for example, this means essentially that he is behaving or is disposed to behave in certain characteristic ways. If this view is right—and Whiteley argues that it isn't—then it is easy to see why one person's behavior is sometimes a good reason for another person's believing some statement about his thoughts or feelings. What isn't easy to see at first is why anyone would think that this view is true. In "Our Evidence for the Existence of Other Minds," H. H. Price argues that one of his good reasons for believing in the existence of other minds is that other bodies emit intelligible sounds which give him new information about the world. And, according to Price, this is a good reason because the hypothesis that these other bodies do have other minds is the best available explanation of their being able to emit such sounds. This form of argument is familiar. Furlong uses it in arguing that, in general, a person's memory of past events in his life is reliable. And Price's conclusion is given some support by Whiteley in his essay "Behaviourism." But does Price's view seem right? Do any of these views seem right? Do any of them really explain why it is that a person's or a thing's behavior or circumstances are ever a good reason for another person's believing some statement about other minds? And if none of these views is satisfactory, what view is?

IV

What is a good reason for a person's believing some statement about a physical object in his immediate vicinity? What is a good reason for a person's believing some statement like "There are physical objects on top of this shelf" or "The red album cover is next to the door" or "The meat on the platter is still warm"? Again the answer seems obvious. Generally a person's good reason is connected with what he perceives or senses. Often it is that he perceives or senses—sees, hears, smells, feels, tastes—the physical object in question. For example, one of my good reasons for believing the statement "There is some cheese on my lap" is that I see and smell and feel it. And one of my good reasons for believing "There is a yellow wicker basket not far from my desk" is that I can see the basket. Sometimes a person's good reason for believing such a statement is that he perceives or senses some other physical object. For example, one of my good reasons for believing the statement "The light plug is in the socket" is that I see the lamp and it is on.

Why, exactly, are these reasons good reasons? In particular, why is a person's perceptual experience ever a good reason for his believing some statement about the existence or nature of a physical object in in his immediate vicinity? What strategy should one adopt in trying to answer this question? Some philosophers have thought that the way to proceed is first to formulate a philosophical theory of perception. But what is a philosophical theory of perception? Not all philosophers agree. Some hold it to be a description of at least part of what occurs in a normal person's conscious experience when he perceives something. Understood in this way, a philosophical theory of perception is similar in form to the theories of memory that philosophers have put forward to show why, in general, a person's memory of a past event in his life is reliable and, hence, why sometimes a person's memory of a past event in his life is his good reason for believing some statement about such an event. For other philosophers, a philosophical theory of perception is this and something more. But it is often not clear what this something more is.

Two philosophical theories of perception are presented in the last group of essays in this book. In the first, "Phenomenalism," A. J. Ayer says that when a person perceives something he never *directly* perceives a physical object. Instead, he always directly perceives something called *sense data*. Furthermore—and here it isn't clear whether what follows is a view about perception or a view about physical objects or both—every statement about a physical object is logically reducible to a statement or set of statements about actual or possible sense data. Now if both these premises are true, then it isn't difficult to understand why a person's perceptual experience is sometimes a good reason for his believing some statement about a physical object in his immediate vicinity. But why think that either premise is true? There is an obvious similarity between Ayer's views here and some of the views that Whiteley examined in "Behaviourism." For example, Ayer's view that every statement about a physical object is logically reducible to statements about sense data is like the behaviorist's view that mental concepts are essentially behavioral. There is also a similarity that is not so obvious. Ayer thinks that statements about physical objects can be reduced to statements about sense data partly because unless this is true, a person could never know that physical objects exist. And a major reason for the behaviorists Whiteley discusses thinking that mental concepts are essentially behavioral is that unless this is true, a person could never know anything at all about other minds.

R. J. Hirst, in "The Representative Theory of Perception," a chapter from his book *The Problems of Perception,* discusses a second theory of perception. On this theory it is also true that when a person perceives something he never directly perceives a physical object and always directly perceives sense data. Why have so many philosophers held this view? What has driven them to it? But on this theory it is not the case that every statement about a physical object is logically reducible to some statement or set of statements about actual or possible sense data. Instead, the relation between sense data and physical objects is causal. Sometimes physical objects are part of the cause of a person's perceiving the sense data he perceives. If, however, when a person perceives something he always perceives sense data and never physical objects, then how can he ever know that there are physical objects? And if there are physical objects, how can he ever know that they are sometimes part of the cause of his perceptual experience? And if physical objects are part of the cause of his perceptual experience on some occasions, how can he ever know whether one is part of the cause of his perceptual experience on a particular occasion? And given that this theory of perception is correct, how does it even begin to explain why a person's perceptual experience is sometimes his good reason for believing some statement about a physical object in his immediate vicinity? Hirst considers these questions and others and concludes that even in its most plausible form, the representative theory of perception is unable to answer these questions in a satisfactory way.

One other essay "Physical Objects" is included. In it C. H. Whiteley sets down his good reasons for believing in the existence of physical objects. He says that while his perceptual experience alone is not a good reason for his believing in the existence of physical objects, along with other things it is. This is because his perceptual experience—especially the regularities of his perceptual experience—and these other things can be explained only by supposing that there are physical objects. Of course, Whiteley is arguing in the way Furlong argues for the general reliability of a person's memory of past events in his life, and in the way Price does for the existence of other minds. Whiteley is also arguing in the way of some philosophers who support a representative theory of perception and who then try to show that some of their perceptual experience is a good reason for their belief in the existence of physical objects. Is Whiteley successful in using this form of argument here? And could he have used a similar argument to show that, on some occasions at least, a person's perceptual experience together with other things is a good reason for his believing that there is a physical object in his immediate vicinity, or that not only is there a physical object but also that it is long and brown and on fire?

V

In the first section of this introduction I said that many philosophers have held the view that in order for a person to know that any particular statement is true he must have a good reason for believing that the statement is true. I also said that philosophers have disagreed about the nature and justification of a person's good reasons for believing statements—in particular, statements about a past event in a person's life, statements about the minds of others, and statements about a physical object in his immediate vicinity. I have since tried to suggest what some of these disagreements are, and something about how they are dealt with in the essays included here.

One thing more. What is the point of this sort of investigation? Of course, given the connection between good reasons and human factual knowledge, if one comes to understand the nature and justification of good reasons for believing such statements, one comes to understand something about our knowledge of such statements. And our knowledge of such statements is important. But beyond that, can this sort of investigation have any real point? Can it have any practical consequences? Probably not. Suppose that no one anywhere can give a satisfactory account of the nature and justification of a person's good reasons for believing statements of this sort. What follows? It certainly doesn't follow that no one can have a good reason for believing such statements or that no one can know the truth of such statements. Do you see why? All that does follow is that, so far, no one knows as much about human factual knowledge as some philosophers would like to know. And given the kinds of questions philosophers ask about human factual knowledge, this isn't so surprising. Now suppose that some of the essays in this volume contain a full and accurate account of the nature and justification of a person's good reason for believing statements of this sort. And suppose that you come to know that this account is correct. What can you do with this knowledge? Will it make it any easier for you to come to know the truth of statements about past events in your life, or statements about the minds of others, or statements about physical objects in your immediate vicinity? Or will it make it any easier for you to come to know whether you or anyone else presently knows the truth of any such statement. It is hard to see how it could. Again, all that your knowledge of this account is likely to do is to give you a new kind, an admittedly peculiar kind, of understanding of human factual knowledge, an understanding that for all practical purposes has no consequences at all. Does this count for this sort of investigation or does this count against it?

part one

CONCERNING A PERSON'S KNOWLEDGE OF PAST EVENTS IN HIS LIFE

R. F. HOLLAND

The Empiricist Theory
of Memory

∿∿∿∿∿∿∿∿∿∿∿∿∿∿∿∿∿∿∿∿∿∿∿∿∿

Tho' the mind in its reasonings from causes or effects carries its view
beyond those objects, which it sees or remembers, it must never lose
sight of them entirely, nor reason entirely upon its own ideas, without
some mixture of impressions, or at least of ideas of the memory, which
are equivalent to impressions. When we infer effects from causes, we
must establish the existence of these causes; which we have only two
ways of doing, either by an immediate perception of our memory or
senses or by an inference from other causes; . . . 'Tis impossible for us
to carry on our inferences *ad infinitum;* and the only thing, that can
stop them, is an impression of the memory or senses, beyond which there
is no room for doubt or enquiry (*Treatise* I, Pt. III, § 4).

In speaking of the Empiricist Theory of Memory I mean to refer to
a large and variously developed body of thinking, some of whose
vertebrae may be observed in the above passage from Hume. It might
be protested that this passage is oddly chosen; for what does Hume
really have to say here about memory as such? So far from expounding
a theory of it, he does hardly more than accord it a passing mention.
But the terms in which the reference is made are pregnant with metaphysics: *Ideas of the memory which are equivalent to impressions—an
immediate perception of our memory or senses—an impression of the
memory or senses beyond which there is no room for doubt or enquiry.*
In particular, there is here the conception of remembering as a subjective experience, together with the suggestion that to this experience
belongs a kind of indubitability; and also the analogy between memory
and perception, the idea that memory and perception are two more or
less co-ordinate forms of awareness or ultimate modes of knowledge.

From R. F. Holland, "The Empiricist Theory of Memory," *Mind,* LXIII, No. 252
(1954). Reprinted by permission of the author and the editor of *Mind.*

But the Empiricist Theory of Memory is not something which belongs just to the history of philosophy nor is its persistent attractiveness felt only by those who philosophize within the august tradition of Locke, Berkeley and Hume. There is, so far as I know, scarcely any philosophical writing on memory from the time of Hume to the present day in which these conceptions, together with their ramified implications, are not to be found.

1. REMEMBERING AS A DISTINCTIVE EXPERIENCE

If examples of mental faculties are called for, 'Memory' and 'Imagination' suggest themselves as readily as anything else; and comparison is readily invited between them, so that the question: What is the difference between Memory and Imagination? provides one natural starting point for a philosophical examination of memory. If one asks oneself this question, one is most tempted to begin an answer by saying that when we remember and when we imagine, in both cases alike something comes into our minds: but in the former case whatever comes into our minds represents or refers to an actual past, whilst in the latter case it does not. But if this is said, then straight away something more has to be said. For it seems that the connexion with a past reality which distinguishes memory from imagination does not merely have to exist; it also has to announce its existence to the person who remembers at the time when he remembers. Had it existed clandestinely, as indeed it might have done, then although memory and imagination would have been different, we should never have learned to distinguish them: the difference between them would have been useless, would have meant nothing to us. So it seems necessary to add that, whenever anything comes into our minds, we must have some means of knowing in which cases the connexion with reality exists and in which cases it does not. That is to say, it seems that there must be some mark or sign whereby a remembering state of mind can be distinguished from an imagining state of mind. So that one proceeds to ask: What is this mark or sign? In what manner does the connexion with the past announce itself?

An oddly perplexing question this. But a definite answer to it has been volunteered by more than one philosophical authority. Hume wrote: "A man may indulge his fancy in feigning any past scene of adventure; nor would there be any possibility of distinguishing this from a remembrance of a like kind were not the ideas of the imagination fainter and more obscure" (*Treatise* I, Pt. III, § 5). Bertrand Russell, on the other hand, has said that memory-images, in contrast with images of the imagination, have a characteristic of familiarity, or are accompanied by a feeling of familiarity; and it is because of the presence of this characteristic, or alternatively because of the existence of this feeling, that we are able to know, whenever we remember something, that it is remembering we are engaged in and not imagining. Familiarity is "the characteristic by which we distinguish the images we trust. . . . Some images, like some sensations, feel very familiar, while others feel strange" (*Analysis of Mind,* p. 161).

Faced with these divergent pronouncements one may be inclined at first to try to adjudicate between them. In the case of Hume, an immediate difficulty arises from the fact that each of the contrasts in terms of which he proposes to differentiate between ideas of the memory and ideas of the imagination seems to be utilized already for the purpose of distinguishing some imaginings from others, or for the purpose of distinguishing some rememberings from others, or for both of these purposes. One may have recollections that are clear or unclear, faint or strong, more vivid or less vivid; one's imagination also may be vivid or not vivid, lively or not lively, weak or powerful. The suggestion that the haziest of recollections must be somehow clearer and more vivid than the most powerful products of a lively imagination seems implausible, if not senseless.

In defence of Hume it might be argued that it can still make sense to say that ideas of the imagination are *in general* fainter and so forth than ideas of the memory, just as it makes sense to speak of lead weighing heavier than cork, in spite of the fact that you can have various weights of lead and various weights of cork. A lead roof is heavier than a cork roof, a lead bath-plug heavier than a cork bath-plug; a leaden object always weighs heavier than a cork object *of a like kind.* What Hume said was that an idea of the imagination was fainter and so forth, than an idea of the memory *of a like kind.*

But this attempted defence of Hume might be answered as follows. We are able to say that a leaden object is heavier than a cork one of a similar kind because we know that the weight-ranges of these two substances are closely circumscribed and that they do not overlap; and this knowledge rests on the existence of accepted procedures for ascertaining what the weights of different substances are and within what limits they vary. In the case of ideas of the memory and ideas of the imagination there would appear to be no analogous limitation in their respective ranges of clarity etc., since we are accustomed to attribute the extremes of clarity and unclarity to each; and even if there were such a limitation, it is impossible to imagine any criterion whereby their respective clarity-ranges might be shown to stand in an analogous relationship on the scale of clarity in general to the relationship between the weight-ranges of lead and cork on the scale of weight in general. So the qualification that the ideas should be of a like kind does not render Hume's story any more plausible.

2. FAMILIARITY

Russell spoke of a familiarity which memory-images possess and images of the imagination do not; and this might seem at once to be more like the truth. For we know what it is like to come across unexpectedly a scene, face, or picture which strikes us as familiar; the feeling of familiarity which one gets in such situations is often a subject of comment: and if in recalling and visualizing some well-known scene one abstracts oneself from the process and focuses one's attention upon the image as an object something of the same feeling is apt to be produced.

But the artificiality of the situation that is here created should not be disregarded. Was I, before reading Russell and seeking to verify his assertion by making this experiment, ever *struck by* the familiarity of my memory-images? Was their familiarity ever before the subject of comment? No: but neither was the familiarity to me of this room in which I sit. I cannot say that I have ever been struck by its familiarity. Yet it certainly *is* familiar. I was about to say that because the alleged familiarity of my memory-images had never struck me they could not after all have been familiar, since it was the essence of a thing's being familiar that the familiarity should strike one. But this was a mistake. The familiarity of my memory-images could be something like the familiarity of this room.

Only, in the case of this room, the familiarity is something I can explain. The room might easily not have been familiar: it happens as a matter of fact to be so, and the reason for this is that I have spent many hours of my life in it; the furniture has always been arranged in this particular fashion, and so on. Now when I recall a scene by means of an image, my image cannot as a general rule be familiar in this sort of way. For the image is a comparatively fleeting thing: I have never had this particular image before: I may never have had another like it. Of course, the actual scene which I recall may, or may not, be a familiar scene; and if it is familiar its familiarity will be susceptible of an explanation, like the familiarity of my room.

But there are also circumstances in which to say of a thing that it is familiar would be virtually equivalent to saying that one recalls it. Thus I might revisit an art gallery after some of the pictures that were originally on display have been removed and others put in their place. As I walk round I might divide the pictures I see into the familiar and the unfamiliar, those I remember from my previous visit and those that are new. In some such circumstance as this the familiarity of a thing could serve as an indication, perhaps the first intimation, that one remembered it. It may seem that it is in the light of this family of cases that Russell's familiarity must be considered, its function being to indicate remembrance. But one now notices something very curious about the nature of the indication it is supposed to convey, namely that it is not an indication of the remembrance of the selfsame object to which the familiarity attaches. The familiarity about which Russell speaks is supposed to belong not to recollected objects, but to our images of recollected objects or to our experiences of recollecting objects. It is these that are supposed to be familiar; yet their familiarity is supposed to point beyond them to something elsewhere. How can this be possible?

There are cases where the explanation of the familiarity of a thing is to be found not in the fact that one has encountered it before, but in its resemblance to some other object. Thus the Eiffel Tower might appear familiar to the tourist at his first sight of it, if he has previously seen models or pictures of it, or if he knows Blackpool Tower. Its familiarity could here be said, perhaps, to be pointing beyond it to something elsewhere. Here, too, there is no difficulty in understanding how familiarity could function as a kind of sign-post or indicating mark; the first intimation that a resemblance exists, perhaps, or the prelude to a more explicit and self-conscious recognition of the resemblance. Obviously the alleged familiarity of our memory-images invites consideration under this category. When the question is asked: From its resemblance to what does the image acquire its familiarity? an answer is ready at hand: From its resemblance to the remembered object; from its resemblance to whatever it represents.

But is it always necessary for our images to resemble what they represent? Even if it is, will they not do so in imagining no less than in remembering?

The point is that whereas in representing to yourself, for example, an imaginary tower standing in the centre of Magdalen bridge your image is not an image of anything you have ever seen, your representation in a recollection of the actual appearance of Magdalen Tower surrounded by the college buildings is a representation of something you have seen; and it is in this that lies the source of its familiarity.

But the crux of the matter is that familiarity does not by itself indicate its own source: it does not, as it were, bear its own explanation upon its face. Your image of Magdalen Tower may be familiar: suppose that it is familiar just because you have seen Magdalen Tower and are recalling it. However your image of the imaginary tower on

Magdalen bridge might also be familiar, possibly because you have amused yourself by creating some such fanciful image as this on many occasions in the past. You may happen to know the explanation of the familiarity in both cases. But if you do not already know it, the mere familiarity by itself will not automatically indicate to you its own appropriate source.

3. REMEMBERING AND BEING CERTAIN ABOUT IT

It may now seem impossible for a characteristic or feeling of familiarity to do what Russell wished it to do. But that is not to say that some kind of Memory-Indicator cannot exist—only, perhaps, that it tends to elude description. There is still temptation to think that if Hume and Russell failed in their attempts to locate it, their failure was a failure only of a technical kind, and that *something like* what they said must surely be true. One is inclined, for instance, to argue in this way:

I can remember and know that I am remembering all in the same moment, and even in such a way that it seems impossible for me to be mistaken. Now if I can know in this immediate way that I am remembering when I am, then I must have some means of knowing. Something tells me it is not a wild flight of fancy. But what tells me? This question seems to demand an answer of the pattern: "I can tell that what I am doing is recollecting by means of *so-and-so*, rather in the way you can tell that a certain motor-car is a Rolls-Royce by the shape of the bonnet."

We often support a claim to remember by specifying some peculiar or striking feature of whatever is remembered. Thus I might say, with the aim of convincing a sceptic or of settling a doubt which may have arisen in my own mind, "I am quite sure that I remember the Duke of Omnium's motor-car, because it was a Rolls-Royce and had that distinctive bonnet." Only, in this type of case, it is precisely after this move has been gone through that one comes face to face with the question that is one way of launching oneself down the path taken by Hume and Russell; namely, in this instance, the question: But how do you know you remember it was a Rolls-Royce and had that distinctive bonnet? The situation one is in now is no different from the situation in which no doubt has arisen and there has been no call to elaborate upon one's initial recollection or to support it in any way; and yet one is able, without hesitation and with full confidence, to assert that one remembers. How, then, does one know this? Not because of any specific feature belonging to the particular recollection concerned: any such has now been ruled out as irrelevant. Is one not forced to conclude that it is because of some general characteristic belonging to recollections as such? If the attempts of Hume and Russell to describe it seemed to break down when pressed then it was our fault for pressing them too far. We feel that we know well enough the distinction they mean to refer to; and we believe that we are able to locate it in our own experience.

This belief, however, may be caused to appear in a different light by a consideration of some examples. Suppose, in the first place, that you are asked quite simply to imagine a Norman castle with a keep and a moat, and that you find yourself able to comply with this request. You will presumably draw upon your memories of castles you have visited, or heard described, or seen reconstructions of in antiquarian journals. Perhaps you will frame in your mind's eye a composite picture of a castle which will incorporate features drawn from many sources. But perhaps you will simply invoke an image of some actual castle, say Caernarvon Castle, which you are able to picture to yourself by calling it to mind as it is. The request will have been complied with irrespective of whether the castle you have before your mind is one you actually remember or not: whichever is the case you might describe what you are doing as 'imagining a castle.' The concept of imagining thus includes that of remembering. But obviously it was some different application of it from this that Hume and Russell had in mind.

Suppose, then, that the request had been that you should imagine a castle which was not one you actually remembered. What is required here is that your imagined castle should also be an imaginary one—a castle that is imagined in a further, additional sense over and above the one prescribed in the original example. Consider now some of the ways in which you might fail unwittingly to comply with this second request. For a start, you might not know what kind of thing a Norman castle is. Again, although you might know what a Norman castle is, proving this by your ability to recognise one when you see one or by your ability to distinguish between correct and incorrect descriptions of one, you might be unable to picture or draw or describe one to order. These are ways in which you might have failed also to comply with the request in the first example. But in the case of the second request there is a further possibility of failure: you might be picturing to yourself a castle which you believe to be a fictitious one, a product of your inventive genius, while all the time it is some actual castle which you have previously seen and are now, though unbeknown to yourself, recollecting. Maybe you discover the truth later when a friend shows you a picture of Caernarvon Castle and reminds you that you visited it long ago; you realize then with surprise that it was precisely this castle that you had had before your mind.

But although our second kind of imagining is something you might think you are doing when in fact you are not, what you cannot do is be exercising your imagination, in this sense of 'imagination,' and at the same time believe that you are remembering. The impossibility here is of a logical kind. For in so far as you believed you were remembering you would *pari passu* be believing yourself to be failing to comply with the request. It is immaterial whether the request is someone else's or your own; and it might, not inappropriately, be said to be your own whenever you spontaneously embark on a flight of fancy. According to Hume, it is precisely to safeguard us from falling perpetually into this impossible confusion that the Memory-Indicator exists: "A man may indulge his fancy in feigning any past scene of adventure; nor would there be any possibility of distinguishing this from a remembrance of a like kind were not the ideas of the imagination fainter and more obscure." To 'feign some past scene of adventure' is undoubtedly to produce an instance of the second of the two kinds of imagining we have distinguished. The idea that one could do this and at the same time think one was remembering were it not for the special character of the ideas involved seems to result, in part at least, from the misconstruction of a logical impossibility as a kind of psychological impossibility. Small wonder that the Memory-Indicator, the allegedly distinctive experience which is supposed to distinguish memory from imagination, should appear to be at once unmistakable and indescribable.

4. SCEPTICAL DOUBT ABOUT MEMORY

There is, however, another application for the concept of imagination in respect of which it *is* possible for a person to believe he is remembering and yet be imagining. This is the unconscious or involuntary kind of imagining which is spoken of in connexion with mistakes and illusions. In this sense of 'imagine' it could be said of a person that he did not really see a snake in the grass but only imagined he did, or that he did not really remember the church at Hyde Park Corner which he believed he remembered; it was only his imagination. But there can be no scope for a Memory-Indicator to prevent confusion between this kind of imagining and remembering, since it is only where confusion occurs, only where the distinction is not in fact made until after the event, that we can speak at all of something being imagined in this sense. We may on many occasions be quite confident that we are not confused; but it seems that no memory-belief can ever be *proof* against disaster of this kind.

"In the first place, everything constituting a memory-belief is happening *now*, not in that past time to which the belief is said to refer. It is not necessary to the existence of a memory-belief that the event remembered should have occurred, or even that the past should have existed at all. There is no logical impossibility in the hypothesis that the world sprang into being five minutes ago, exactly as it was, with a population that 'remembered' a wholly unreal past. There is no logically necessary connexion between events at different times; therefore nothing that is happening now or will happen in the future can disprove the hypothesis that the world began five minutes ago. Hence the occurrences which are *called* knowledge of the past are logically independent of the past; they are wholly analysable into present contents, which might, theoretically, be just what they are even if no past had existed" (Russell, *Analysis of Mind,* p. 159).

The disturbing thought that perhaps we remember, only without there ever having been anything to remember, just as we can be afraid when there is nothing to be afraid of, is a natural corollary of the idea that the essence of remembering is to be found in a private mental transaction. Though it is to be noticed that when he speaks of the logical possibility of a population that remembered an unreal past Russell feels obliged to enclose the word "remembered" in inverted commas, as if from a dim awareness that there is after all some logical impropriety committed by such a statement as "I remember the battle of Matapan though it did not take place." Russell goes on to repudiate the suggestion that the non-existence of the past should be entertained as a serious hypothesis,[1] and remarks elsewhere that although "no memory is indubitable . . . our confidence as regards memory in general is such that we cannot entertain the hypothesis of the past being wholly an illusion." [2] Here he leaves the matter, having taken up a position that is curiously reminiscent of Hume's attitude towards the existence of an external world. However, the suggestion that memory, conceived as a source of knowledge or information about the past, cannot be known to be trustworthy has provoked others into attempts to provide special philosophical proofs of its trustworthiness: which reminds one of a famous 'Proof of an External World.'

The philosophical proofs[3] of the trustworthiness of memory constitute an interesting appendage to the main body of the Empiricist Theory of Memory, though the fact that they have invariably been proffered without due regard to the logical peculiarities of the doubt they are intended to allay may foster the illusion that there was here

---

[1] *Analysis of Mind,* p. 160.

[2] *Inquiry into Meaning and Truth,* pp. 156–57.

[3] See, for example, the articles by R. F. Harrod (*Mind,* 1942) and E. J. Furlong (*Mind,* 1946), and especially the latter's recently published essay, *A Study in Memory.*

some quite self-contained philosophical problem awaiting solution. But in fact this sceptical doubt about the trustworthiness of memory is a doubt whose settlement is possible only when the motives behind it have been unearthed and when the distorting metaphysical picture of remembering upon which it is nourished has been removed. In this it resembles the Cartesian doubt about the Arch-deceiver, and also the classical doubt about the validity of induction. There are several points at which these doubts run parallel to one another. First, the sense of disconnexion between our experiences of recollecting and the alleged objects of our recollections is like the sense of a hiatus between the "internal" world of our sensations and the "external" world of perception. It is, indeed, an exacerbated variant of the same complaint; for while the experience of recollecting is a directly accessible part of my or your private mental life, its alleged object in the public, material universe is not directly accessible; and furthermore, while the experience belongs to the present, the object has been engulfed by the past. A comparable gulf is felt to exist between inductive conclusions and the premises on which they are based, the unfulfilled ideal of direct access having an analogue here in the unfulfilled ideal of deductive certainty; and here, too, the complaint may be aggravated by a temporal disparity, in this case between present and future. Secondly, the lack of any rules to aid us in judging from the quality of our "memory-experiences" precisely what degree of credence, if any, is to be placed in our various recollections may be compared with our lack of rules for deciding how many peeps, looks or glances shall suffice on any particular occasion for one to be sure that there is *e.g.* a butterfly on the rosebush. Compare too the cases where to our discomfort we are unable to decide or would rather withhold a decision as to the number of instances which shall suffice to render a generalization probable. Thirdly, there is the initially apparent analogy between the sceptic's doubt about memory in general and our ordinary doubts about specific recollections, which makes the question the sceptic asks seem like a *factual* question; and this may be compared with the corresponding effect of the apparent similarity between Descartes' question about the existence of the Arch-deceiver and questions about the existence of ordinary deceivers, or between the question: What is it that justifies any induction whatever? and questions raised in specific contexts about the relative weight of the evidence offered in support of this or that conclusion or the merits of this or that particular method of scientific procedure.

As soon as one considers the kind of steps that might actually be taken, in some situation in everyday life where the truth of the matter is not immediately obvious, to decide, and decide beyond all doubt, about the trustworthiness of a remembrance, part at least of the logical peculiarity of the sceptic's doubt and also of the conception allied to it of what it means to remember should become apparent: for one is in this way forced to recognize what the essential criteria for speaking of a remembrance really are.

Suppose that Smith claims to remember having seen H.M.S. *Nelson* at Dover some time last year, but we are not prepared to take his word for it. Our first step towards establishing the truth or falsity of his claim will be to find out, perhaps by looking up the newspaper reports or other relevant documents, or by asking other people for corroboration, or by inferring from the present state of naval affairs what must have happened previously, whether or not that particular ship was at that particular place at the time mentioned. If it was, this in itself might be enough to enable us to decide to our satisfaction that Smith's recollection was genuine. There is the possibility that it was merely by coincidence that the ship happened to be there; but assuming Smith's recollection to have been reasonably full and precise, the tallying of details would suffice to rule this out. There is the further possibility that when Smith told us his story he may not have been calling the past to mind but, say, reading out notes which he had previously written on his cuff, or passing on to us information he was receiving over a wireless receiver concealed upon his person. We should have to rule out the possibility of trickery of this nature; but we know quite well how to do so. Even then there would remain the possibility that he was employing, not his memory, but some form of clairvoyance. However, I think that all we should need to know, in order to be content to rule out this last possibility, is whether or not Smith had actually been in Dover at the stipulated time and so in a position to have seen the ship he claims to remember seeing. Provided it is established that Smith has had the opportunity of observing, of finding out or learning—the opportunity of doing whatever it may have been necessary for him on some occasion to do in order to be now in a position to remember, then we should not only be satisfied with his claim to remember, but should have no compunction, owing to the extreme rarity of clairvoyance, in correcting him if he should say that he knows what he knows clairvoyantly. In such a case we should insist that he actually remembers, although he may not himself think so. In short, then, the questions which, if satisfactorily answered, enable us to decide with finality whether or not a person remembers are subsumable under the following two headings: (1) Did what he claims to remember actually happen? and (2) Is his past history such as to have put him in the position now to remember it?

Not that an example of this kind, however detailed the account it might give of the tests whereby the veracity of recollections is established, may be supposed to be efficacious by itself in allaying the sceptic's doubt. For it is abundantly clear that his is a doubt that cannot be allayed however much we multiply our tests and however stringently we apply them; and an essential part of any answer to him will consist in pointing this out. His doubt is like that of the man who still professes that we do not really know there are biscuits in the box, although we have seen them, heard them rattle, smelt them, touched them, tasted them, and applied to them every conceivable laboratory test, finding our expectations exactly confirmed at every juncture: we have no idea what it would be like to know in his sense, and can only challenge him to tell us. However, there seems to be a belief current among those who have given thought to this matter that the sceptical doubter is obliged to take over the offensive at this juncture and to provide an *ad hoc* demonstration that our ordinary tests are in any case inadequate. The argument attributed to him is that all our proofs that we have on any occasion remembered must at some point and in some degree involve the use of the memory on the part of someone or other: hence we cannot ever validate a claim to remember without falling into a *petitio principii*, and so we have after all no way of showing conclusively and beyond doubt that our memories give us information about the past. In Russell's version the argument runs as follows: "Since memories are not indubitable we seek various ways of reinforcing them. We make contemporary records, or we seek confirmation from other witnesses, or we look for reasons tending to show that what we recollect was to be expected. In such ways we can increase the likelihood of any given recollection being correct, but we cannot free ourselves from dependence on memory in general. This is obvious as regards the testimony of other witnesses. As regards contemporary records they are seldom *strictly* contemporary, and if they are, it cannot subsequently be known except through the memory of the person making the record. Suppose you remember on November 8th that last night you saw a very bright meteor, and you find on your desk a note in your handwriting saying: 'at 20 hr. 30 min. G.M.T. on November 7th, I saw a bright meteor in the constellation Hercules. Note made at 20 hr. 33 min. G.M.T.' You may remember making the note; if so, the memory of the meteor and of the note confirm each other. But if you are discarding memory as a source of knowledge, you will not know how the note got there. It may have been made by a forger, or by yourself as a practical joke" (*Inquiry into Meaning and Truth,* p. 157).

Now if it be true that in showing any given recollection to be correct we cannot "free ourselves from dependence on memory in general," we shall need to inquire what can be the foundation for the distinction which we certainly draw in ordinary life between those recollections which can only be supported by further recollections and those which are supported by something better. To take an example: if I claim to remember putting some money into a box and certain other people saw me do it and later the box is destroyed by fire, then, supposing my recollection to be called in question, there may be no better means open to me of supporting my claim than to bring forward these other people to bear me out by saying that they also remember my putting the money in the box. But suppose that the box is not destroyed. Then I can if necessary fetch it and display its contents. How can it be said in this latter case that my recollection is only supported by other recollections in the way it was in the former case? For the box and the money are there to be seen. Where does the need for further recollecting come in? If it is merely a question of our being on our guard against practical jokes and the like, then have we not other and far superior means of doing this than by the use of our memories—*e.g.* combination locks, electrical fences and burglar alarms?

Broad and Furlong hasten to Russell's rescue at this point: "When I claim to remember a certain event, I may test my judgment by inferring what events would be likely to follow such an event as I claim to be remembering. If I find that I can remember and perceive these consequences, my memory judgment will be supported by inference. If I can remember and perceive events which are incompatible with these, my memory judgment will be made improbable. But even when I test the memory judgment by present perception and not by memory, I presuppose the general validity of my memory judgments. For I start by inferring that I shall be likely to perceive so-and-so if the event which I claim to remember really happened. And, if the chain of inference be of any length, my guarantee for the conclusion is my memory that the earlier stages of the argument satisfied me" (*Mind and its Place in Nature,* p. 234). According to Furlong, the sceptic can buttress his argument with the claim that "inductive sciences rest on evidence supplied in the long run by memory," and even an anti-sceptic has to admit that "such a simple belief as . . . that the expanse at which I am looking is green . . . presupposes that I know what greenness is; and for such a piece of information I am indebted to memory" (*A Study in Memory,* pp. 11, 16).

Cases are imaginable where it might be asserted, and cases where it might be denied, that a person in drawing an inference has had to rely upon his memory: a man may embark upon a complex chain of inference and, without writing down the initial premises or any of the intermediate steps, successfully reach a conclusion which he might, owing to forgetfulness, have been precluded from drawing; but he could have saved relying upon his memory by setting forth the whole argument in writing. It is from this kind of contrast that the assertion and the denial alike take their sense. To commit one-self to either where no such contrast is in point is to pull the concept of remembering out of shape, so that communication is blocked by its deformity. Broad's contention about the dependence of inference on memory, therefore, if it is not to be dismissed as an obviously false generalization, must be regarded as involving an eccentric use of the word 'memory.' In either case the charge of the *petitio principii* falls to the ground. Furlong's plight is similar. A scientist is imaginable who in propounding some novel theory, not of course before the Royal Society, may have been content to rely for his evidence upon memory: his case would be distinguishable from others where dependence on memory is eliminated. Again, a distinction is to be made between judgments about colour which rest on memory and those which do not. When asked which of two fabrics is Pea Green and which is Apple Green I may succeed in remembering; but if I happen to carry a colour-chart I shall not even try. That both are *green* I can neither remember nor forget. The supposition that all scientific conclusions and all judgments about colour rest on memory, if it is not simply false, involves the use of the word 'memory' in an esoteric and dubious sense.

5. MEMORY AS A MODE OF ACQUAINTANCE WITH THE PAST

(a) The "Transcendental Deduction"

The absence, in the eyes of the protagonist of the Empiricist Theory of Memory, of any logical connexion between our experiences of recollecting and the past objects or occurrences to which they purport to refer obliges him, after he has either ignored or answered the sceptical doubter, to postulate a connexion of an *ontological* kind. It is, in fact, as a part of the mechanism of this connexion that the Memory-Indicator, be it of whatever sort, has its fundamental *raison d'être*. Its existence was not, as it were, disclosed in the psychological laboratory but rather deduced in Kantian fashion as one of the things which alone makes remembering possible.

When a person, to use Hume's example, feigns some past scene of adventure, the scene which passes before his mind's eye conveys to him no knowledge of the past. When by contrast he recalls such a scene it is, one is inclined to say, the actual past which is presented to him and which he is aware of. But how can this be possible? The past has ceased to exist, so apparently he cannot now be aware of it directly, but only through the mediation of the images he now has: they alone can be the contents of the present situation. The problem is to understand how he can get from these present images to past events. In the case of the images in which imaginary adventures are depicted no such step is taken, and one may be inclined to suggest that this is because the images in this case have been more or less deliberately fabricated, built to the owner's specification. It is in the nature of memory-images, on the other hand, to be unalterable replicas of the past, offshoots of past sensations perhaps, which well-up of their own accord and cannot be tampered with. But how do we *know* that our memory-images are representative of the past? We cannot resurrect the past bodily and compare it with our images.[4] The fact that our memory-images are genuine representatives of the past must somehow be conveyed to us, and conveyed by the images themselves: to use a phrase of Bergson's, the representation they provide is one which "bears the marks of its origin." Broad explains the matter as follows: "the objective constituents of memory situations are not in fact past and . . . they do not even seem to be past. But they do seem to have (and there is no reason to doubt that they actually do have) a certain peculiar characteristic which is not manifested by most images or most sensa. Let us call this 'familiarity.' Now we are so constituted that, when we are subjects of a cognitive situation whose objective constituent manifests the characteristic of familiarity, we inevitably apply the concept of pastness; and, if we make an explicit judgment, it takes the form: 'There *was* an event which *had* such and such empirical characteristics.' Familiarity is an empirical characteristic and pastness is a categorial characteristic; but the former 'means' the latter to such beings as we are, and this 'meaning' is primitive and unacquired. . . ." (*Mind and its Place in Nature*, p. 266).

We need not be deceived by Broad's allusion to Familiarity as an *empirical* characteristic into supposing that his belief in its existence rests upon the result of a psychological investigation. On the Empiricist interpretation of what recollecting involves, its presence, or the presence of something like it, is a sheer metaphysical necessity. It is an indispensable part of the machinery by which is conveyed to us our knowledge of the past. Our images constitute the main part of the mechanism, for they are the primary purveyors of information: but in the absence of Familiarity they would never be taken for such; moreover, their information is useless until it is properly interpreted, and it is the function of Familiarity to do this interpreting. In short, Familiarity is in the first place a signal, and in the second place an adaptor, converting what would otherwise be simply an awareness of

[4] Cf. *Analysis of Mind*, pp. 158–59.

something present into an awareness of something past. Without it the two related problems of our knowledge of the past and of the meaning of the past would be insoluble.

One may be inclined at this point to ask how, within the terms of the Empiricist Theory of Memory, an account is to be given of the sort of recollecting in which images are obviously not involved. I might go to a certain drawer and open it in order to retrieve an object I placed there some time ago, and I might while doing this have no image before my mind; or I might be conversing about a disconnected topic and having images related to this disconnected topic.

(b) The Two Kinds of Memory

The Empiricist remains unimpressed by such feats; for associated with his theory is a segregation from one another of two contrasting kinds of memory, one of which is sometimes designated "true memory" and monopolizes attention, while the other tends to be dismissed as philosophically uninteresting and unproblematic.

Anyone pausing to scrutinize the various accounts of this dichotomy cannot but be struck by their perfunctoriness. Russell's discussion of it, for instance, is of the flimsiest kind, and he is content to refer his readers to Bergson as an authority.[5] But while Bergson's account (in *Matter and Memory*) is certainly lengthier and more involved than any other, it is so patently full of misconceptions and so ingenuously pressed into the service of a preconceived metaphysical dualism that one stands amazed at Russell's confidence in it. A recent advocate of the dichotomy is A. D. Woozley in his *Theory of Knowledge*—a book which, since it purports to be written for beginners, may fairly be expected to make the ground of the division plain to the uninitiated.

There is on the one hand (Woozley begins p. 36) such a thing as remembering how to ride a bicycle, to hold a rifle, to swim: this "need not involve any act of thinking." Also there is remembering how to do Pythagoras' Theorem, which does involve an act of thought; similarly, there is remembering the dates of the Kings of England. But there is one "quite different use" of the words 'memory' and 'remember'—"the sense in which I remember meeting Jones at Newhaven last Tuesday . . . or reading *Macbeth* for the first time when I was in bed with mumps at the age of thirteen or fourteen." The contrast is said by Woozley to be that between remembering a soliloquy from *Macbeth* in the sense of being able to recite it, and remembering a particular declamation of this soliloquy. "Remembering in the latter sense is not necessary to remembering in the former sense, although

[5] *Analysis of Mind*, p. 166.

sometimes it may be a help (and sometimes not). . . . The important point, however, is that remembering in the sense in which I can remember a particular recitation of the soliloquy is extraneous to remembering the soliloquy. We are concerned here only with the first, the sense in which remembering is a cognitive act of the mind which occurs *now* and has for its object an event or series of events belonging to the past. . . . We may contrast this sense of 'memory' with others, and we may, as I shall for our purposes, ignore the other senses. . . ."

That is the substance of Woozley's exposition. Notice first how the words 'extraneous to' suggest a fundamental gulf: this is just what Woozley wants. Yet all they mean, as far as the information Woozley gives us goes, is that the one thing can be done without the other. Thus, to adapt Woozley's example, I might have remembered meeting Jones at Newhaven, but not that it was on Tuesday; or I might have remembered meeting him on Tuesday, though not that the meeting took place at Newhaven: these two recollections would then have qualified for the title 'extraneous to one another.' Notice next how the expression 'cognitive act of the mind' is slipped in, as if it had some explanatory force. The adjective 'cognitive' and the verb 'cognize' may have a vague sort of sense to us by analogy with 'recognize' and from our recollections of a traditional psychological classification. But in what way is the one sort of remembering cognitive while the other is not? What would Woozley give, if we pressed him, as examples of other cognitive acts? One can only conjecture, but the likely things would be seeing, hearing, touching, etc.—any ways of becoming aware of something, of finding out what is there, of getting to know what we did not know before. The suggestion may be, then, that the essential difference between the two kinds of remembering is that in the one case we find out something, whereas in the other case we do not. To which suggestion one might wish to reply that in neither case could it be appropriate to say that we do this. Recalling an event to mind is not a way of discovering, of obtaining new knowledge.[6]

But let us go back to Woozley's contrast between remembering a soliloquy from *Macbeth* and remembering reading the soliloquy for the first time; for we are not yet clear about the criteria by which we may distinguish in practice between the two kinds of memory whose operation is held to be so different in theory. What are the observable differences which, presumably, form the basis of the theory? Obviously the intended contrast cannot be, although some of Woozley's remarks suggest that it is, that between the dispositional and the non-dispositional senses of remembering, since this distinction may be applied to each of Woozley's examples equally. We might be tempted to think that the contrast must be that between recollecting one's own private experiences—sensations, emotions, etc.—and recollecting other things. But on applying this to Woozley's example of remembering meeting Jones at Newhaven we may wonder whether we have made the 'cognitive' category too narrow. For surely this was not counted as a cognitive act only to the extent that it involved the subject's recollection of his own reactions to the meeting, events quite private to himself? If, on the other hand, we try to include in the 'cognitive' category the remembrance of any events whatever, we are likely to find that we are making this category wider than Woozley intended. For instance, although I did not see the last Boat Race I can remember a great deal about it from the reports of other people. But it is not likely that Woozley would allow that in these recollections I am performing 'cognitive acts directed towards' the Boat Race: this sort of remembering, he would presumably say, is not so very different from remembering the dates of the Kings of England. However he would, it seems, allow that I am performing cognitive acts in the case of my recollections of the Rugby match at Twickenham, at which I was actually present. Now it looks as if the difference between these two cases lies solely in the manner in which I obtained my information. Why should this difference be thought important?

There is, of course, one way in which I can recall the Rugby match that is not open to me in the case of the Boat Race, and that is by picturing to myself parts of it as I saw them; and it seems likely that it is recollections in which visual imagery occurs that Woozley has mainly in mind when he segregates one sort of remembering from all others as being cognitive. Yet if this is the case, one wonders why he does not say so plainly.

But even now we are only at the beginning of our difficulties. For instance, suppose I recall the Rugby match by describing it verbally without the aid of images. Would I still be performing a cognitive act? If not, why not? If so, then what about my verbal recollections of the Boat Race? Could we not say that here too there is a cognitive act, only perhaps one which has for its object not the Boat Race itself, but the occasion on which my informant told me about it? This seems queer, for I might easily have forgotten about this occasion while still remembering about the race, or I might have had a whole host of informants on different occasions. Besides, if it be allowed that there is a cognitive act here, it must surely be allowed that there is one in the case of remembering the dates of the Kings of England. But this Woozley denied.

One's suspicion that this distinction between two kinds of memory is to be viewed rather as an effect of the Empiricist Theory of Memory than as a possible cause of it is turned into a certainty by Broad who, in the introductory paragraph to the chapter on Memory in *Mind and its Place in Nature,* writes as follows: "It seems plain that there is one and only one kind of memory which can plausibly be regarded as closely analogous to perception; and this is the memory of particular events, places, persons, or things. Let us call this 'Perceptual Memory.' My main object in this chapter is to discuss perceptual memory, to compare it with perception, and to consider some of the epistemological problems to which it gives rise." A group of four other kinds of memory is accorded brief mention later under the heading 'Non-Perceptual Memory,' but these are said not really to deserve the name of memory since "in themselves they are modes of behaviour, and not modes of cognition." Broad, then, has offered us two criteria for distinguishing the philosophically interesting kind of memory from other kinds: (a) it bears a close analogy to perception, and (b) its objects are particular events, places, persons, or things. Why, one wonders, should these two criteria be thought to operate in conjunction with one another?—unless as a result of the crude mistake of supposing that, whereas it is roughly true that the list 'particular event, place, person, or thing' exhausts the range of what we can visualize, of what we can have an image of, it is also true that, conversely, the only way we can recall these things is by having images.

(c) The Perception Analogy

Broad's choice of the title 'Perceptual Memory' is significant, for the analogy with perception has dominated the Empiricist Theory of Memory. The model that is initially adopted is of the mind gazing into the past and picking out features of the landscape there; looking back across an expanse of time, analogously with the way we see across an intervening physical space. The expressions 'cognition' and 'cognitive relation' then suggest themselves as an appropriate terminology: just as in sense-perception it is said that we are put into a cognitive relation with the present state of the physical world, so in memory there is an inclination to say that we are put into a cognitive relation with the past. But exactly how does this relationship with the past come to be established? It is with the raising of this question that the more sophisticated puzzles and controversies belonging to the philosophy of perception begin to exert their influence. Discussion may centre on the possibility or impossibility of a 'naive realism' with regard to memory analogous to what has been called Naive Realism in perception, and to the question: Are we in some cases *directly* aware of the past? an affirmative answer is occasionally suggested.[7] But it is more natural for a kind of representational theory or memory-datum theory of remembering to be developed, in which images are made to stand to past events or objects in a relation somewhat analogous to the relation in which sense-data have been held to stand towards present material objects. The question which Russell asks, arising out of the representational theory of memory: How do we know that our images are representative of the past, since we cannot resurrect the past bodily and compare it with our images? has its counterpart within the representational theory of perception: "How shall the mind, when it perceives nothing but its own ideas, know that they agree with things themselves?" (Locke, *Essay*, Book IV, Chap. IV, § 3); though in neither case is the question construed as a *reductio ad absurdum* of the theory. It is, of course, found necessary for what are called "memory experiences" or "memory situations" to be divided like sense experiences, into those that are veridical and those that are delusive; George IV [8] being made to do for the philosophy of memory what the bent stick in water has been thought to do for the philosophy of perception. But illusions and delusions notwithstanding, our images or memory-data are regarded, like sense-data, as the self-sufficient sources of a primitive kind of information; to be confronted with one is to be confronted with an unmistakable item of fundamental knowledge. This identification of knowledge itself with a kind of quasi-perceptual awareness, called by Russell at one time 'acquaintance,' [9] is also an essential part of the theory. It is assumed that to know something is, in all ultimate cases at least, to be actively engaged upon a process of inspection. In one's recollections one is inspecting the past by proxy, and in this way having knowledge of it.

To point out that I cannot, for example, recall a certain visit which I made to London, unless I did in fact make that visit, is to call attention to something that is obvious and seemingly trivial. Putting the point in the terminology of the Empiricist Theory of Memory one might say that memory-knowledge, the knowledge one has in recollecting, is necessarily a knowledge of something one has also known at some time before. With perceptual knowledge this is not necessarily the case. But to a person in whose mind "perceptual knowledge of

[7] E.g., Stout, *Studies in Philosophy and Psychology*, Essay VIII; Price, *Aristotelian Society Suppl.*, 1936, pp. 24–25; and Woozley, *Theory of Knowledge*, pp. 52–55.

[8] Broad, *Mind and its Place in Nature*, p. 231, and Russell, *Human Knowledge, its Scope and Limits*, p. 230.

[9] On page 75 of *The Problems of Philosophy* it is said that "all our knowledge, both knowledge of things and knowledge of truths, rests upon acquaintance as its foundation"; and on page 76 memory is instanced as one kind of knowledge by acquaintance.

the present" and "memory-knowledge of the past" have been thoroughly assimilated there will seem to be but one important difference between them, namely the one marked by the words "present" and "past" respectively—the difference in the temporal status of what is known. It is this that monopolizes his attention and diverts it from the paradox to which his way of thinking about memory gives rise. For if one's attention is firmly focused on the fact that whatever I am supposed to have memory-knowledge of now is necessarily something I have had knowledge of before, a question one is inclined to ask is: Why, if a person once knows something, should he not know it for always? Or suppose one were to ask: Under what conditions, in what kind of circumstances, might a person have to come to know again something he once knew before? An obvious reply would be: When he has forgotten what he originally knew; when he has ceased to remember it. The paradox of the Empiricist Theory of Memory is this: if recollecting is what the theory makes it out to be, then it is a feat the accomplishment of which is neither necessary nor even possible except for someone who has actually forgotten what he is supposed by the theory to be remembering. In the very name Familiarity, which they find it natural to use for the distinguishing characteristic of memory-images, Russell and Broad give their whole game away. We are dwellers in the present, the present of to-day; but yesterday's present in becoming past is alleged to have turned into a kind of recluse, so that images are henceforth needed to effect an introduction between us and it. The images bring the past before us. But the introduction is attended by an aroma of familiarity. It is as if we knew already what was in store for us: we knew and knew intimately all that the images were to bring, even before they brought it. Their bringing it was, in fact, a work of supererogation, for between old friends introductions are superfluous.

One must evidently relinquish any idea that our images in recollecting can be transmitters of information or independent vehicles of knowledge. If this idea be abandoned, then need ceases to be felt for a specific experience which should function as an Indicator, distinguishing those images which do happen to be informers, in recollecting, from those in fancy which happen not to be. For there now appears to be no significant difference between the rôle of images in recollection and their rôle in fancy. In either case, any image that may come before the mind will owe its existence to some knowledge which is possessed by the knower independently of the image; and it will be this knowledge which makes it possible for the image to be created at all, just as it might equally make possible a pictorial representation on paper or a verbal description, each of these being alternative manifestations of the same knowledge. In an earlier example it was supposed that a person be requested simply to imagine or picture to himself a Norman castle, and this situation was compared with another situation in which a person is requested to recall to mind and visualize a specified existent castle. The ability to comply with either request is contingent upon some knowledge which the subject may or may not possess. In the first case he cannot comply with the request unless he has knowledge, and intentionally utilizes his knowledge, of the kind of appearance a Norman castle presents: he must know, and know to this extent, what kind of thing the expression "Norman castle" refers to. In the second case he cannot comply with the request unless, in addition to this, he has knowledge of whatever castle is specified and unless he intends his image to represent the appearance of this particular castle and no other. This more determinate kind of knowledge is not a prerequisite for compliance with the first request, though if any such should happen to be possessed it would very likely be utilized. It might, if possessed, be utilized again, though in a different way, in the variant case where the request to imagine a castle is supplemented by the injunction that the imagined castle should also be an imaginary one; for here the subject may have to make considerable conscious effort to secure that his visualized castle should represent for him something *other than* the existent castle whose appearance he is familiar with.

If in the three situations outlined in this example we separate what is done from the context in which it is done and proceed to strip the image of the knowledge and the intention that go with it, what are we left with? In the first stage of stripping, the image of the recollected castle is bereft of its specific reference. This castle ceases to be a recollected castle and becomes completely anonymous. The deliberately fabricated castle cannot any longer be regarded as a deliberate fabrication. All distinction between the three performances is lost. In the final stage, the image cannot even be regarded as an image of a castle; it has been reduced to a meaningless concatenation of shapes and colours. One cannot, as Hume thought, contemplate an idea of the memory and an idea of the imagination and, *feigning ignorance of their origins,* begin to distinguish them afresh by means of a difference in their respective qualities.

WILLIAM EARLE

Memory

~~~~~~

Memory, as a phenomenon, would seem to be especially suited to a purely descriptive analysis. It is not some foreign datum or motion imposed upon us, but rather something we ourselves enact, and enact frequently. We have an abundance of examples, and so it might seem that nothing remains but to turn our attention upon a few clear cases, and say right out what we find. If we are not concerned with discovering hypothetical physiological explanations, but simply with phenomenological description, the problem might seem to be solved as soon as it is posed. But if we turn to the philosophical and psychological literature, expecting to find unanimous agreement upon the matter, we will be disappointed. There is no agreement, and, after two thousand years of discussion, the phenomenological facts themselves have become radically obscured. The problematic character of the facts is acutely experienced when we ourselves try to return to the pure phenomenon to check one or another of its purported descriptions.

Memory, of course, is not a trivial or isolated act, and therefore truth or falsity in descriptions of memory will have consequences for large reaches of our philosophical theory. Memory at least purports to give us our only direct knowledge of the past. And our only indirect knowledge of the past, through inference, must credit some memories somewhere. If then our knowledge of the past is vitiated, what remains of our knowledge of the present, or our expectations for the future? But if memory lives up to its pretensions of acquainting us with the past, then what sort of world is it where an existent mind

From William Earle, "Memory," *The Review of Metaphysics,* X, No. 1 (1956). Reprinted by permission of the author and the editor of *The Review of Metaphysics.*

now can become directly acquainted with what is no more existent, but passed away? What, in other words, are the ontological presuppositions of the act of memory?

We shall ask the following questions about memory: (1) what is memory as a phenomenon, what is its structure as it presents itself to our reflective attention? (2) can its phenomenological claim to acquaint us with the past be credited? (3) what are the ontological consequences of the phenomenon? It is clear, I think, that we must first arrive at some clarity about the phenomenon of memory before we can further investigate its claims, physiological causes, or ontological presuppositions, for it must be about this phenomenon and not some other that any further reasoning must be. Further, we can not rule upon what the phenomenon *must be;* we can only look. Having looked, we may then search for the conditions, presuppositions, or validation of what we see. And since it is the phenomenal character of memory which has become problematic, we shall turn our attention first to it.

A. THE COPY THEORY

There would be little purpose in surveying all the theories which have ever been suggested, but let us focus our attention upon one principal class of theories, one which certainly is most wide-spread, most directly opposed to common-sense, and, in my opinion, opposed to the truth as well. This is the famous copy theory of memory, and for a good account of it we turn to William James.[1] In principle, the theory is remarkably simple. Memory is the feeling or belief that a certain complex image, formed in my imagination, resembles the past. The complex image in which I believe has three factors: the *event imaged,* its *reference to the past,* and its reference to *my past.* It is not sufficient simply to form an image; the event must also be located in its past context, and further it must be thought to be in my own past. Such, I believe, are the basic elements of any copy theory. James adds that the idea of the past itself comes from conceptual extrapolation from the past I directly intuit in the specious present. But whatever the detail, the copy theory will be examined here only insofar as it describes memory as an indirect knowledge of the real past, mediated by images. I believe there are three things wrong with the theory, namely each of its distinctive features.

In the first place, when I recall a past event, there is, I believe, no sense in which I can be said to form an *image, copy,* or *representation* of anything. The objection at this point is not to the somewhat sim-

[1] *The Principles of Psychology* (New York, 1890), I, Chap. XVI.

plified "picture" theory involved, which is subject to qualifications on other grounds, but rather to the logical paradoxes involved in phenomenological copying. This particular species of theory in effect describes what memory is by first taking its proper place within the mind in order to become aware of some past event, and then slipping outside the mind altogether in order to look at the real past event and affirm that the remembered event is indeed a copy of the real past event! Surely this is neither what memory presents itself to be, nor can it be the truth about memory from any but a very confused alternation of standpoints.

It is certainly not the structure of memory as we enact it. For if what I remember *presents itself to me* as a copy of the past event, then indeed, still within memory, I must have both that past event itself and my copy of it present to my mind, in order to affirm that my memory image is a copy. But in that case, of course, I already have the past event itself present, in person, and what on earth would be the utility of forming a copy of it? Further, the presence of that past event itself would be the genuine act of memory, and not the copying of it. What I remember, then, cannot appear to me, the rememberer, as a copy of the past, but must appear as the past event itself.

Now it is possible of course to become aware of one thing copying, representing, or imaging another; but such cases are only possible where both the copy and the original are present, as when I see a picture and its model, and also see that the one copies the other. But this is not memory.

There is another sense in which I may only have an image of the past, and not the past itself before my remembering mind. Here I remember something which I *assume* is a copy of the past itself. I simply "take" it to be a copy, make it into a copy, or endow it with this role. However, this can not be the phenomenological character of memory either. For memory now becomes even more complicated and ridiculous than before. Here memory consists in the complex of forming an image of the past, and then deliberately forming a second image of the past, or conceiving that there is such an image, again comparing the two, and finding either agreement or disagreement. In the case before, we compared an image with the real past itself. Now we compare the image with a past constructed to resemble it, a second past which itself can be but one further image of the genuine past, and the whole weary round begins again. In short, if the image is to *appear* in any form whatsover as an image or representation, both it and what it copies must appear; but that implies that eventually the past itself and not any image of it must appear to the remembering mind. If memory does not seem to itself to grasp images or copies of things, then such can not be the phenomenon.

Let us suppose then that it is *not* the phenomenon, but rather a mixture of the phenomenon of memory plus the objective, external truth about it. Unknown to memory itself, the past which we seem to recall is *in fact* nothing but a copy of the real past. But now for *whose* mind can such a theory be even *meaningful?* If to ours, then we must have at least the idea of a past which is not remembered, but only conceived in independence of all memory. We must then have at least the idea of the genuine concrete past against which we compare any remembered image of it. And now what about this idea of the genuine past? Is it one *more* copy of the real past, or does it at last confront us with the past itself? If the first, we have an infinite regress; if the second, we have simply another name for memory, and the point is granted that somehow we have a direct acquaintance with the past itself and not merely with its copies.

Thus, as far as I can see, there is no way of fixing up the copy theory which makes any sense at all. It is neither phenomenologically correct, nor is it a possible theory about the truth of memory. It isn't true at all. And the logical absurdities which follow are not accidental, I believe, to some particular formulations; they follow from the roots of the conception, from the view, in other words, that memory gives us only indirect or mediated knowledge of the past, and not that past itself.

Now if we turn to the second feature of all copy theories, we encounter some further distressing results. The copy theory says that we are faced with a number of images or copies, some of which we "refer" to the past, and others of which we do not. All the images are of the same genus, essentially products of the imagination, perhaps "traces" left by what we hope was previous experience. No matter; as rememberers we can not know which are traces and which not. But we do have the problem of which we shall refer to our past, and which not. But the only criteria which the copy theorists can employ to differentiate a memory image from a pure work of the imagination must be some internal present characteristics of the image itself. And so most frequently the criterion employed is that of "vivacity"; the image which we are to refer to the past must be of less vivacity than a present perception, so as not to become confused with it, but of greater vivacity than something purely imagined. And so we are faced with the problem of measuring the relative strengths of images in order to know which image is to be called "memory." But this is of course absurd. First of all, it is obvious that many times our imaginations are stronger than our memories, and that we rightly show no inclination whatsoever to regard as memory itself a present strong imagination, which may be a good deal stronger than any memories. Nor do we have any inclination to take rather weak memories as imaginations on grounds of weakness alone. I submit that strength and weakness of image have and should have little or nothing to do with which "images" we are to regard as memories and which imaginations. Secondly, what *reason* should we have for regarding a *degree of vivacity* as a sign of memory in the first place? Degree of vivacity is on a continuous scale, whereas the *significance* of memory makes it radically distinct from imagination; they belong to absolutely different genera, the one being a recapture of what once was, and the other being something constructed in the present. Now this radical difference of internal significance has no logical or other relation to "degree of vivacity." In short, when we "refer an image" to the past, we must have some *logical motivation* for our act, or it will appear even to us as the most arbitrary attribution in the world. We are not at liberty to remember whatever we like, or rather, to treat as a memory any image we like. The first aspect of the copy theory separates what we remember from the genuine past, relating them only by possible resemblance. This second feature ends by making memory an arbitrary act of positing or referring some images to the past. The image itself is not already past, or we should have to remember it by still another image; it is present then, and merely referred to the past. Our question is what in the present image can cue or motivate such a reference?

Suppose I perform an experiment. I form an image, say that of myself walking about among the craters of the Moon. And now I simply "refer" this image to my own past, and accordingly I should find myself "remembering" it. But somehow or other I do not find myself remembering any such thing, and it remains what it is, nothing but an imagination. The stronger I exert my powers of imagination and of reference the more I feel myself slipping into hallucination. *That* cannot be what memory is. The dilemma may be stated thus: either memory is identical with the act of "referring," in which case we have explained nothing, or the two are distinct, in which case the act of referring becomes arbitrary.

The third feature of the copy theory touches on a matter essential to any description of memory, but unfortunately, as it occurs in the context of this theory, it becomes perverted. James says we refer the image to *our* past. "It must be dated in *my* past. In other words, I must think that I directly experienced its occurrence. It must have that 'warmth and intimacy' which were so often spoken of in the chapter on the Self, as characterizing all experiences 'appropriated' by the thinker as his own." [2] Now this is true enough, so long as we forget that the "appropriation" of an experience as mine is itself for

² *The Principles of Psychology*, p. 650.

James and for anyone else holding the copy theory nothing but a present attribution or feeling and therefore represents no genuine acquaintance with my genuinely past self. "I must *think* that I directly experienced its occurrence." But what makes me think that *I* experienced some imaged events and not others? "Warmth and intimacy." Forgetting warmth, let us look at intimacy, for what we remember *is* more intimately connected with our past than what we imagine, since it indeed *was* a part of our past. What is intimate is mine; and I must recognize that what I remember was indeed my experience once. But it is quite insufficient to assimilate our recognition of our past with a present feeling of intimacy with the imagined event. Thus the entire insight is transformed by the supposition that I need only *think* now that the event was mine, whereas memory claims to *recognize* that it was mine. Again, the alteration is from a theory of memory which credits it, to one which seeks to describe it purely "psychologically" as a series of present images, all of which is but a "complex representation" of what may or may not have been the truth.

In a word, the copy theory must find the remembering mind enclosed within a gallery of present images, embarrassed by its task of choosing which are to be regarded as memories, and frustrated by the very *significance* of regarding them as memories. To make the rickety theory work, we must be both within and without our minds at the same time, we must both credit and discredit our only access to the past, and we must be endowed with faculties for measuring quantities of strength, vivacity, warmth and intimacy, which have, as interpreted, no particular significance anyway.

Now the philosophical motivations for the copy model are not far to seek. What is it but an elaborate device to quiet an epistemological fear: the notorious fallibility of memory? And indeed if memory is in principle fallible, then we might have to construct some sort of representational theory, to put the real past at one remove from direct knowledge. The copy theory can account for some sort of error, but it is questionable whether it can account for anything else. Error, or what seems to be such, shall certainly have to find its explanation; but it would seem to be dubious procedure to become so impressed with error, that we introduce it as a permanent possibility within any unique mode of awareness. If any unique access to an object is declared fallible in principle, wherewith shall we correct it?

To make memory in principle fallible, and therefore dependent upon external inferences for validation, seems to solve one problem; but of course it merely conceals it under another name. For how are we to validate the very rules of inference by which we are to check memory, if all memory is fallible? If memory in principle is fallible, then every memory can be wrong; and the past becomes a perfectly gratuitous assumption. Not only is it a gratuitous assumption, but ultimately a meaningless one. For if our only knowledge of the past is mediated, or constructed from present materials, by what magic does the mind arrange, rearrange, or interpret ever present data and acts, to make them copies, traces, or representations of that which never appears in person? Is it not like some attempt to construct sound out of colors?

There is need therefore for returning to the phenomenon of memory itself, first suspending our epistemological dreads and ontological suppositions, to see whether memory as it presents itself to reflective consciousness is not what common sense supposes it to be, a direct vision of the genuine past, and veridical to the extent that it is clear. We shall then see whether such a description of memory is not perfectly capable of taking care of the erroneous cases as well, and further, whether it may not have important implications for ontology.

B. MEMORY AS DIRECT AWARENESS OF THE PAST

1. The first thing to be decided about memory is precisely *what* it is that is remembered. At first glance it might seem that what I remember is simple past events, the building burning yesterday. And indeed, this is where our explicit attention usually focuses, upon the thing or event remembered. But it is equally clear that in fact I am not simply related to a past burning building, but rather to my past *experience* of the burning building, since if I did not experience it in the past, I certainly could not now remember it, that is, remember myself experiencing it. It is emphatically true, that when I remember the past event, my explicit, thematic attention is on the *past event,* and not upon myself; but reflection discloses that in fact I am also implicitly aware that the event was an object for a past act of experience. However, since that act of experience itself was intentionally directed upon its object, the burning building, it becomes relatively invisible or transparent, leaving me now simply with the explicit event itself. That what I now remember, the event, is not an event taken simply but an *event as experienced,* is not itself a hypothesis but a present phenomenological fact.

And, of course, I do not exclusively remember sense experiences, but also any past object so long as it was the object of some mode of consciousness; thus I can remember reasoning about mathematical objects, entertaining ideal entities, etc. Hence I can remember any object whatsoever, so long as that object was the object of some past act of consciousness.

Thus the total fact remembered now is a past act of consciousness directed to its own object, wherein the *object* is explicit and thematic since the past act of consciousness was itself directed to it intentionally. Or, in other words, I now remember (myself looking at) a burning building. Now this is obviously a *reflexive* conscious act, for insofar as I am now aware of a past awareness of an object, that past object has become accessible to me only through my present awareness of a past awareness, an awareness of an awareness. If consciousness were not capable of this reflexivity, memory would be impossible. It should be noticed that the reflexivity in question is not that of one act of consciousness folded back over another simultaneous or present act of consciousness, but a present act of consciousness reflexive upon a *genuinely past* act of consciousness, and through that reflex, upon a genuinely past object. It should also be noted that in this view, nothing copies anything else. I am now directly aware not of a copy of the past experience with its object, but of that past experience itself. And even if we extend the analysis to that past experience, it is not the awareness of a copy of its object, but of its object itself. This latter problem carries us into the vexed problems of neo-realism, critical realism, idealism, etc., and a further discussion is not strictly necessary for our present purposes.[3] For in the present case we are not concerned with the so-called past *physical* object, but solely with its past appearance. A physical thing is not related to its sensory appearances in the same way in which those sensory appearances are related to our memory of them. For in the first case we may suppose there to be no homogeneity of categories between cause and effect, but in the second this is impossible, since we are only trying to recall a past experience as it was at the time, and not its physical causes. It is this content of a past act of awareness which I now try to recover through memory. Our first observation then is that memory is a reflexive act of awareness wherein a present act of awareness has as its direct and unmediated object a past awareness of some object.

2. The second observation concerns the *content* of memory. If we turn to the intrinsic character of what it is we are remembering, it is clear, I think, that it does not and can not contain within itself the predicate "past." Now it *is* past, of course; but it is only past relative to my present act of remembering it; and what could *it* have known of me now? And so what I recall is myself in the past seeing a burning building, but the content, myself seeing a burning building, is in its own present and not at all past with respect to itself. Hence nothing remembered can carry the predicate "past" stamped on its face for

[3] For a fuller analysis see the author's *Objectivity* (New York, 1955).

easy identification, neither the past experience nor its past object. They are in their own present.

If we should suppose, for a moment, that the event recalled had as one of its internal properties the fact that it was past, we should find ourselves in the ludicrous position of remembering an event which is past with respect to itself, an event whose very passage was retrospective, which lived for the sole purpose of being remembered, an event which was, precisely while it was occurring, something which had already occurred. If then the content recalled is in its own present, and I who am recalling am in my own present, where does the past come in? How do I ever become aware that it is indeed a past event I am now recalling? It is a mistake, I believe, to look for some intrinsic character in the *object experienced* which will suggest to us that it is past, either its vivacity, its coherence or incoherence with present perceptions, or some other internal part of it such as its inclusion of a calendar page. None of such criteria could conceivably result in memory of that object, or distinguish it from anything imagined. That object is *remembered* solely by virtue of the fact that *I experienced it before;* and therefore we must look to the character of the reflexive act of consciousness which brings it forth again. When I am aware that I experienced it before, I then remember it. Otherwise I simply entertain it as an imaginative object.

The essence of memory then is located in the relationship between two acts of *consciousness,* my present and my past; and, descriptively, what more can be said but that I now am simply aware that I was aware of something before? Since, according to our first observation, our thematic attention is on the *object* of the past experience, and since according to our second observation, this object itself contains nothing of the past in it, we should now say that our awareness of the pastness of our *experience* of that object is "lateral" or "implicit." Hence the more we turn our attention upon the objective content remembered, the less certain we are that we are remembering and not imagining, since the same object might be given imaginatively. But the more we become aware of the fact that we did actually experience that object, the more certain we are that we are remembering.

Our awareness of the past then focuses itself *between two acts of consciousness,* the present recollecting act, and the past recollected act; and while our attention directs itself to the object of that past experience, we have a lateral awareness that it is an object *once experienced.* The conjunction of past and present occurs then within reflexive mind, and is a genuine conjunction of the actual past of consciousness with the actual present of consciousness, and has nothing to do with images, copies, or representations of anything.

3. The third and most important aspect of memory is one which was noted by James, although I think incorrectly interpreted. It is that when I remember, I invariably remember *myself* having had an experience. Thus, part of the original and immediate deliverance of memory is that some particular event happened to *me*. Obviously, I do not remember *another's* experiences or an experience that happened to nobody. But what interpretation should this receive? And here it should be borne in mind, first, that when I genuinely remember, I do not *infer* that the past event happened to me, but rather *recognize* it as mine. And secondly, the me to which it happened in the past, is itself not wholly a past me, but also precisely *me* now, identical with the I that is now remembering, for it is the I now which claims the past experience as its own. Now these simple facts are, I think, rather remarkable. I have the same assurance of them as I have that *I* am now *remembering*. But what does it mean for me now to recognize some past experience as *mine*? Again, the direct deliverance of memory itself makes a claim which I believe can not be denied, nor explained away no matter how complex our hypotheses. And that claim is that on one level, *I am numerically identical now and then,* that there is only one myself which once had some experiences I now recall as mine. The inescapable fact is that they could not be recognized as *mine now* unless I am the same now and then. Otherwise, they would have belonged to another. It is always the I *now* which says that the past experience *belongs* to it, not that it once belonged to it: The "mine" therefore is the name of the relation which unites past with present.

If the I is identical now and then, it is, of course, atemporal; time has made no bite into it, nor differentiated it into passing events. The I is of course related to passing events, or time itself would be an illusion. And it is related to them by its *acts* of consciousness, which are temporal acts, unrepeatable, and separated in time. My present *act* of remembering is not identical with my past *act* of experiencing; but the *I* which then experienced and now recalls must be one and the same, or its past acts would not be "its" now.

One further point. We should be careful not to think of the identity of the self as some sort of *endurance,* as though there were a tube of selfness stretching back through a duration, one end of which looks at the other and notices that they are *similar.* Similarity presupposes numerical diversity; and what that past similar self experienced would not be mine now, but rather an act of a merely similar self. When I remember some experience as mine, I am not in the least peering down a corridor of the past, noticing various myselves stationed along the way wearing more or less similar clothes. Rather the beginning and end of the tube must be made to coincide, which means of course that there is no tube but instead sheer identity. The self then in its core is atemporal, while its various acts are enacted in time. Time differentiates only the acts, not the self which acts.

Of course, any description involving the word "eternity" has a good chance of being taken for a "speculative hypothesis." But our common inner conviction of the eternity of the self is hardly of this order. The conviction of the eternity of the self is found in children, savages, and sophisticated alike; it can hardly have the status of a theological or metaphysical hypothesis designed to account for rare and subtle matters of whose very existence we have no certain belief anyway. And since such a conviction is not a hypothesis, it can not be argued away, and remains in spite of all theoretical interpretations or refutations; a more likely source, then, is simply that it is uncovered by our own instinctive explorations of consciousness. We have tried to show how there is the possibility of a lateral awareness of our own eternity simply in the phenomenological exploration of the act of memory.

4. Let us now try to gather together all these remarks and see if they form a coherent description of the phenomenon. Our first observation is that memory is reflexive, and that the reflex is within *consciousness,* not the objective world. It depends upon a consciousness of consciousness. The second observation was to the effect that there was a genuine factual difference between the past and present acts of consciousness, and that memory was simply the presence of a past act of consciousness to a present act of consciousness, along with the awareness of their factual temporal difference. The third finds that there is an intrinsic binding together of past and present in the identity of the self which both experienced that past event and now recollects it. Has not then the third aspect of the total phenomenon unified the whole into an intelligible scheme? The past event has gone and is no more; but now I have the power of calling it forth, or putting it in my presence. But that presence to me now of what is no more is rendered possible by the self which was identically present at both times. There is a genuine gap between the past and the present acts, but to say this is not to say the last word. If it were, how could we recall it? The gap must be bridged by the self which presided over both occasions, the same and identical self. The entire affair occurs within mind, but there it is a *genuine event.* The past object can not act *physically* upon a present one; it has gone forever. But it can stand in the *presence* of ourselves now. The presence of the past to the present through memory is thus an actual event, occurring within the whole of Being; but it is not a *physical* event. It is an enacted relationship, where one leg of the relation stands in the present while the other stands in the past—in the past itself, and not in some present copy of

it. Thus, memory supplies us with one of the most curious phenomena in the world: the past and non-existent appearing in person to the present and actual. Nothing like it is to be found in the physical world, and from what has been said, no purely physical or physiological mechanism can account for it. For we must either attribute to such a mechanism powers identical to those of the mind, which is of no explanatory help, or we leave them physical, which means located in their own space and time. But the phenomenon to be accounted for spans the gap; how can a mechanism which is itself located purely in the present, render present the real past?

Such then, I believe, is the phenomenon of memory. And this is all that I have to say positively about it. But there are some objections which may be considered which give us pause when we wish to accept the phenomenon of memory as it presents itself.

C. TWO OBJECTIONS

1. The first is epistemological. If memory is a direct vision upon the past itself and not the awareness of an imaginative copy of the past, how then is error possible? And yet we all know the difficulty in some cases of knowing whether one's memory is correct or not. It is the fallibility of memory which has led many thinkers to suppose that we are in principle at one remove from the real past, that we know it solely through the mediation of present images which pretend to copy the past, but which may not live up to their pretentions. About this objection or epistemological worry a few things should be said. In the first place the *choice of example* is crucial. If we want to know the structure of memory, we should choose as our example the *very clearest case* we can find, the freshest recollection of the most immediate past, and not the most obscure case. This should go without saying, but is frequently violated in theory. If I wish to know what desire is, I should not choose some obscure mental act whose character is so indeterminate or indeterminately grasped that I do not know even whether it *is* an instance of desire and not perhaps emotion, thought, or perception. If we are interested in differentiating the essential structural peculiarities of things, we must select the simplest and clearest cases possible. If I am illustrating a geometrical theorem, I must draw a figure which is unmistakably a circle, and not an oval or square, or smudge of no particular outline. From vague and indeterminate instances, nothing can follow of any theoretical interest, except indeed that now we no longer know what we are talking about. Hence our examination should begin with the clearest and most unmistakable instances of memory, and not with dim, vague, fleeting phenom-

ena whose character is too unstable to favor *any* theoretical inter- pretation. Having before us the clear cases, we must then indicate *precisely how* it may lose its outlines so as to become confused with something else. An ellipse is not a circle, but after having defined their differences, we can indicate how an ellipse with centers imper- ceptibly close may be *taken* for a circle. Now in the present case, mem- ory is most frequently confused with imagination, so that "erroneous memory" is in fact simply imagination, accompanied by the judgment that what is imagined is indeed a past event being remembered. Let us then compare the clearest cases of imagination with the clearest cases of memory. I now deliberately feign having been in the next room a moment ago. I compare it with my clear memory of having been at this typewriter. Now I can not, in all honesty, declare that these two acts intrinsically resemble one another in the least, or that their differentiation rests upon external evidence. They should have to be very confused indeed to be mistaken for one another; whereas the clearer they are, the more clearly they seem to be acts of a radically different order. When I *deliberately* feign an event and attribute it to my past, I know precisely what I am doing, namely what I have just said. The imaginative surrogate for memory is my own construction, an act of my constructive will forming and holding together volun- tarily an "image," which I then assert by another act of will to be in my past. In the case of memory, I am aware of the past event and of the fact that it is in *my past.* Now an immediate awareness of a past event as in my past, is not at all the same as an awareness of an event combined with a *judgment* that it is in my past. Of this I can assure myself by deliberately judging events to be past, or feigning that they are past, or trying to believe they are past and comparing such an act with immediate memory. In the case of memory, I have the past event itself given through a lateral awareness that it was an event in my past; in the case of judgment or feigned memory, I have no such lateral awareness, but rather the lateral awareness of a deliberate act of judg- ment.

In these clear cases then there is no doubt whatsoever as to which is memory and which imagination. Memory declares itself to be mem- ory by its own intrinsic character of being precisely an immediate awareness of the past, and imagination declares itself to be such by the accompanying awareness that indeed its bogus, memory-like ap- pearance is the product of our own will. If the clear cases are indubi- table, we must conclude that memory, to the degree that it is clear, is immediate and indubitable, and that it not only is not mistaken for imagination but cannot be, so long as it remains clear. The *structure* of memory then is to be an immediate vision upon the past; this is an eidetic truth about it. It now follows that any *given instance* will participate in this indubitability to the degree that it *is* an instance of memory, and, that the instance *of itself* can exhibit the essential properties which qualify it as memory. Hence any act to the degree that it is clearly memory will be to that degree an indubitable awareness of the past.

But, as we remarked above, not every act of the mind is an indubitable instance of memory. In fact, there are no acts of the mind which cannot lose their outlines and share in the essential character of some other act, or at least seem to do so when our attention on them becomes distracted, weak, or faltering. And so when the direct lateral awareness of an event being in my past weakens, or conversely, when my awareness of my own voluntary role in the production of imaginative images weakens or passes unnoticed, then I am no longer sure whether I am remembering or imagining. Hence, the data supplied for our problem by cases drawn from the reports of children or of psychotics are of a most questionable relevance. To unclear, dreamy, unfocussed, or disintegrating minds, nothing whatsover need be clear. What follows then of any significance for minds which are not so distracted? If there is some mind which is too distracted to see that one equals one, does this truth then become in principle dubitable, and all the intuitive insights of reason questionable? Must we then conclude that we really *do not know* when we see that one equals one and when we do not? Or that we are actually reasoning about *images* or *copies* of the mathematical truth, and not about that truth itself? Or, to take a more relevant example, if someone should adduce a rational error in a very complicated proof, does that invalidate reason when it works on something simple?

If then we do not know in certain cases whether a given act is memory or imagination, the explanation may be that the acts themselves are too dim and vague to be clearly classified. But most usually, the error is not so simple. Most usually, I genuinely remember something, but add to it certain imaginative contents. There remains a core of genuine memory but dressed up with imaginative additions. But the explanation of this is not difficult. The mind is of course enormously and systematically complex. The act of memory becomes itself the subject of another act of memory, and because the mind is invariably active, soon the original core is overladen with additions from later perceptions, later memories, and later imaginations, all of which are again subject to intermodifications and further complexities. No wonder that we can hardly have much confidence about our memories of a week ago, unless the event was so novel or interesting that it emerges out of the matrix with especial clarity. And it is this mish-mash which worries us when memory is said to be indubitable. But it is certainly not such complex and compounded products that should supply us with examples, but the clearest cases possible such as our memory of a moment ago.

In *certain cases* then, it may be difficult if not impossible to distinguish memory from imagination, that is to say, to decide on internal evidence whether a given act is memory or imagination. But what would be the *sense* of trying to distinguish if memory were nothing but imagination which happened externally to agree with the past? In that case, *in principle,* there woud be no utility in *trying* to distinguish, in *trying* to remember, since we would be exercising exactly the same faculty.

The second matter to be noticed in this connection is that the copy theory makes the relation between its "image" and the genuine past purely coincidental. That is, it is accidental to the image whether the past resembles it or not, and no inspection of that image can reveal its correspondence. Our own theory makes the past itself *internal* to the act of remembering, given along with the event itself which is past. Now clearly our sole acquaintance with the past must come through memory. Hence if we relocate ourselves back into our true position, that of minds whose exclusive access to the past is through memory, it turns out that according to the copy theory we are in a rather foolish box. For the past according to the copy theory is always given *external* to the act of memory, and therefore, since we are not external to our own minds, we have in principle *no* access either to the past itself, or even to the meaning of "past."

It is clear what has happened. The copy theory has intruded into its description of the essence of memory, a theory of a method of verification, so that memory becomes a compound of both itself and a method for verifying it. This is absurd in its own right, and futile in the long run, since the method of verifying memory by indirect means also presupposes precisely that validity of memory which is deemed questionable. The end result is that according to the copy theory there need be no past whatsoever, for all memories might be false copies; hence the very past itself becomes a gratuitous assumption, bolstered up by a series of elaborate arguments about the coherence of experience supposed to result from the assumption of a past. Phenomenologically however the past is no assumption, but rather a datum given directly in some clear cases to the mind.

2. The second objection to the notion that we can directly inspect the past is hard to specify but nonetheless effective in controlling our beliefs. Memory has two aspects; it is a *cognitive* act claiming to acquaint us with the past, and therefore it must defend such a claim against epistemological objections; but also, since it is an *act*, it is something which occurs in the universe, something which must, there-

fore, defend itself against *ontological* objections which maintain that such an event *can not* occur. What, after all, does the phenomenological description of memory ask us to believe? Nothing less than that the mind here and now can establish actual relations to a past which is no more, or, that what has passed away forever can be called up and stand in the actual presence of an existing mind now. It maintains therefore that the remembering consciousness can somehow span one of the most fundamental diremptions in our experience, that between the past and present, or between what is no more and what is. Finally it takes seriously the eternity of the self, finding it not only a phenomenological *datum,* but precisely that mode of being which might conceivably make possible the union of past and present in memory. Now all of this is a good deal to believe, and surely one level of our common sense must cry out in protest that *this* sort of thing is simply impossible! And so once again we find ourselves with a *philosophic* problem: our own common sense would like to believe that its memory is a direct acquaintance with the past, but it also finds precisely this order of event quite incredible. In this paper, I have defended common sense in its first conviction, but I shall now oppose common sense in its fundamental ontological convictions. It goes without saying that common sense of itself is no touchstone for theoretical truth. At the same time, it has a long and intimate acquaintance with its own non-theoretical activities. We find accordingly that our immediate or naive views of memory, our pre-theoretical interpretation of memory, is quite stable, whereas our *theory* of what the whole thing is about is apt to shift with every shift in prevailing views of the nature of the universe. The *theories* of common sense then, being little but echoes of dominant theories, have little claim upon our attention, whereas its pre-theoretical interpretation of its own immediate life, where it has some practice and interest, is more likely to be of interest. Let us try, then, to render explicit the character of the ontology which forces our disbelief in the immediate deliverance of memory, and see whether it itself is at all credible.

There are, I think, two basic premises of such an ontology, one having to do with time, and the other with causality. The first is an insistence upon the absolute finality of temporal distinctions. Within any specified coordinate scheme, past is past, and present is present; what exists is actual now, and the past has simply disappeared. This premise stated more abstractly identifies *being* with *present being.* All that is, in any sense, must be existent now. But the past does not exist now, and therefore it has no being whatever; and, having no being, how can I inspect it? It does exist for inspection. Therefore I am not inspecting it, but rather a present image of it.

The second premise has to do with causality. One of our convictions is that each thing is situated where it is and when it is. Things are dispersed in the media of time and space, each in its own pocket. If one thing is to affect another, its influence must travel through the medium, until it touches the thing to be affected. So long as two things remain separated in space or time, they must be indifferent to one another, neither acting upon nor knowing one another. In a word, no action at a distance. How then can the remembering mind pretend to jump across the gap of time and cognize directly something which lies in its past? What it cognizes therefore does not lie in its past, but is, again, a present image. Such then are some ontological reasons for insisting that what I now cognize in memory is nothing but a present image. The phenomenological description presents us on the contrary with a most paradoxical situation, where the act of remembering is enacted now, by a *present* mind, but the terminus or object of the act is in the genuine *past*. How then can the relationship between present act and past object be thought? It is a relation with one leg in the present and the other in the past; where or when is *it*?

Now both of these presuppositions should be well examined. The subject can not be discussed here with the thoroughness it demands, but enough can be said, I hope, to indicate that there are very solid reasons for rejecting both. The first premise reduces itself to a one-dimensional ontology. If indeed being is confined to the present instant, then memory is incredible. Similarly, if nothing is but the eternal, there could be no memory. Memory becomes incredible if being is reduced to *any* single dimension. The solution lies then in conceiving dimensions in being, such that neither the present nor the eternal by itself is an exhaustive interpretation of being. We have then no intention of declaring that the past is the present, nor that the past is not at all, nor that the past is eternal. All such assertions can be nothing but radical confusions of language and thought. What is the past? What mode of being does it have? Let us look again.

The past does not exist now. It is simply a flat contradiction in terms to imagine the past as now existing, for then indeed it is not past. The past as past is never present, and it is futile to try to imagine it as having some shadow or ghostly existence hovering around the same place it once occupied in full right. That would be precisely to deny the pastness of the past, which itself is a phenomenological datum. How would such a belief differ from the rank superstition which would like to believe that the dead, insofar as they are dead, are still living but simply invisible (or perhaps just *barely* visible to the believer), watching us, and ready to intervene for or against us? Souls may or may not be immortal, but they surely are not immortal in this fashion. Nor does the past still linger in the present, with its own subtle matter, and its own mode of efficacy. We can not then collapse the distinction between past and present; they are different, and never shall they be simultaneous.

Nor can we say that the past is not at all. As past, it is the subject of true propositions, and precisely what would such propositions be *about* if their subject matter had fallen back into pure nothingness? Propositions about the past are certainly not propositions about other propositions in the present, nor about our ideas of what the past might be like, but precisely about the past. If then they are true, their subject matter must have its own determinate mode of being and character. The past must be what true propositions assert it to be; the past therefore has its own distinctive and determinate mode of being.

Is the past then eternal? No, *as past,* it certainly is not simply an eternal fact. For the event which is now in our past, was once present; it *became past.* It was not eternally past, or it never would have happened in the first place. To be sure, it has its fixed and immutable *order* in the series of events; but such an order simply dates it in the series and does not determine whether the event is occurring or not. It simply determines that the event is before another event in our present and after other events in its past. Thus the past can not be assimilated without remainder into an eternal serial order. We say, "Caesar *crossed* the Rubicon"; Caesar's contemporaries said, "Caesar *crosses* the Rubicon." The past therefore, insofar, as it is past, is not an eternal fact.

The past is not nothing at all, nor is it existent now in the present, nor is it laid up in eternity. All such notions rest upon a conviction that Being has no modes, that it is literally reducible to one of its own specifications. And so then, what mode of being *does* the past have? But is there any authentic puzzle here? There is only bewilderment in conceiving the past if we try to reduce it to something it is not. The past quite simply is past, and that is the end of it. It once was and now it is no longer, hence it is not present. It is what once was, a determinate something, hence it is not nothing; it once was but now is gone, hence at least that fact about it is not eternal. Precisely what further question then are we asking about the past which is not answered by its very name? Or has this term also suddenly become meaningless? We must, as Descartes remarked, stop asking questions when we already have something so clear that any further "explanations" would only obscure the object. The problem then is not *what* the past is; that is known as clearly as anything can be known. The problem is in *extending the notion of being* to include the past. And that problem is not solved by further analysis of the past, but by extensions in imagination and reason to render them adequate to what undoubtedly is.

If this is what the past is, how is it related to the present? It is, as we have been arguing, distinguished from the present. But is its distinction final? If so, how can we, in our present, inspect it? Is not the inspection itself a bond between them? If temporal *distinctions* are final, then again memory becomes incredible. But of course, as Hegel argues at length, distinctions are never final. Items that are distinguished are also united, not in the same sense in which they are distinguished but in a higher sense. A distinction is a separation of what is not separated prior to the distinction. Distinction distinguishes within a whole, and the very *sense* of distinction implies the connectedness of what is being distinguished. Or, put otherwise, the sense of a distinction can never be to sunder the distinguished aspects into unrelated universes. Thus the past is past and present is present, and on this level, neither is ever simultaneous with the other. On the other hand, *what is it* that is being so differentiated? Within what whole are these moments distinct? That whole or unity can not be characterized by terms appropriate to the level where the distinctions are found; that unity therefore is itself neither exclusively in the past nor in the present. Nor is it unrelated to past and present, since it is precisely the whole of such moments. The traditional name for such a unity is of course "eternity."

The example of hearing a melody is used so frequently I hesitate to use it once again; but it is clear and decisive. The notes, we recall, are not heard atomically and wholly separated from one another. Individual notes are not a melody. Nor are they heard simultaneously, which also is not a melody but a chord. They are heard both together and separated; not in the same sense, which would be contradictory, but in their serial order, such that all are heard at once, yet preserving their order. Their serial order is a distinction within the whole, and that whole is not itself a member of that series. Now hearing the whole melody is itself an event within a larger whole. But we are not here talking about the event of *hearing* the melody, which is a psychological act, but the heard *melody* itself, and that melody is a whole of the same order as that which presides over all moments of time.

But external events do not remember themselves. *We* remember our former acts of *consciousness*. What is relevant to memory then is the eternal being of consciousness, since memory is an act of consciousness. And the eternal dimension of consciousness, which is identical now and then, and which is consciously so identical, we have called the eternal ego or self. In short, while all events strung out in time participate in eternal being, they do not all do so consciously; when it is done so consciously, and on the level of intuitive perception and not hypothetical inference, we arrive at the possibility of memory with its collateral consciousness of the eternity of the self. The notion of eternity then is essential not only for any adequate description of objective temporal events, but also for any adequate description of the subjective act of remembering. And it is not such as to cancel temporal distinctions, but rather preserves them in a higher unity.

The second premise of "common sense" metaphysics, whose influence lends an air of extreme paradox to memory, is a conviction about causality. Our notions of causality are derived for the most part from science, or what was science, until recently when notions of statistical constants assumed the role. No action at a distance, whether that distance be in time or space. If anything *was*, it can only act now by its influence being transmitted or enduring up into the present. And thus we feel that "brain traces" are the causes of memory; there must be present modifications of the physical matter of the brain to account for anything now occurring in the mind.

Now whatever the role of the brain is, and we do not wish wholly to forget it, we should also be clear about the categorial question. Let causation be what it is, it is certain that the mind is not related to the objects of its consciousness by *any causal relation* whatsoever. The relation between the conscious subject and its object is that of *presence* and not physical influence, touching, or any mode of causation whatsoever. When I recall the past, that past event as past can not be *acting* on my mind since indeed it is passed away, which means precisely that it has lost all power of acting. Nor is my consciousness acting upon it. How indeed can I alter in any way a past event insofar as it is past? In short, that past event is not modified in its own intrinsic character by my becoming aware of it, nor is it acting upon my present consciousness through any effort or influence of its own. It stands in my presence, and presence is not a physical relation. This is true of course not only for memory but for *any* cognitive act. Even in present perception, the external physical stimulus does not act upon my *consciousness*, but only upon my sensorium. I must become aware of its influence by my own free conscious act, by which I pose it as object. Hence the worry about causation is a monstrous *ignoratio elenchi*. The conscious subject is in *no* case, let alone memory, touched, moved, or physically acted upon by any physical influence, whether it is actually perceiving such a physically existent thing or not. The problem then should be relocated from the sphere of seeking for some peculiar mode of causation by which the past actually acts now on present mind, into that of the phenomenological investigation of presence itself. And this of course will introduce other and unique categories. For the moment, we can only conclude that an ontology which finds the direct presence of the past to a mind in the present impossible rests upon assumptions which themselves need reexamination. Ontology can at best render possible the phenomenological datum; it can not serve to discredit or nullify data by declaring on *a priori* grounds what data are *possible,* or in general what is and what is not possible within the whole of being. Our argument, it should be repeated, is not directed against ontology; it is directed only against those ontologies which have forgotten memory.

E. J. FURLONG

Memory

I

"In mature years, and in a sound state of mind, every man," wrote Thomas Reid, "feels that he must believe what he distinctly remembers." [1] This piece of psychology no one would dispute: as Reid went on to say, the evidence of memory is considered sufficient to take a man's life. But there is less agreement about a question which Reid's remark raises, namely, what right have we to believe what we distinctly remember? Reid himself said that the belief was "unaccountable": it just occurs. And many philosophers have found themselves driven to agree with him; deriving what comfort they can from the hopeful reflection that there must be some limits to scepticism. Others, indeed, have regarded the unaccountability as nothing to be ashamed of, declaring roundly that we do know many things about the past, even though we may not know how we know them. A few writers, however, have taken the dangerous line of attempting to support our belief in memory by argument; dangerous—because it is so difficult to support memory without appealing to memory. The fallacy of *petitio principii*, like a sword of Damocles, menaces any such attempt.

Here the plain man's attitude to memory is instructive. He is apt to regard the question, "What right have you to trust your memory?" with some impatience. But he is impatient, not as some have thought, because he regards the question as unanswerable and therefore trivial,

From E. J. Furlong, "Memory," *Mind,* LVII, No. 225 (1948). Reprinted by permission of the author and the editor of *Mind.* Professor Furlong gives a more complete account of his views on memory in his book *A Study of Memory* (Camden, N.J.: Thomas Nelson & Sons, 1951).

[1] *Essays on the Intellectual Powers of Man,* III, 1.

but because he thinks the answer is obvious. He trusts his memory because he has so often found it trustworthy. Thus he remembers locking the hall-door last night and finding it locked this morning. He remembers shaving two hours ago, and his face is still smooth to the touch. He remembers sending a cheque to the income-tax people last week and receiving a receipt for it this morning.

But his reasoning, in this form at least, is only too easy to puncture. He trusts his memory because he *remembers* that it has been so often trustworthy. This will hardly do. And, more subtly, how does he know that smooth faces are shaven, or that receipts often follow cheques, or that doors don't lock themselves? Such beliefs rest on evidence which only memory can supply.

The other extreme, wholesale distrust of memory, is also, of course, apt to beg the question. For it appeals to the cases in which memory has let us down; and these can only be known through memory.[2]

Is there then nothing in the plain man's argument, or can it be so modified as to escape the charge of *petitio principii?* The main aim of this paper is to try to show that this can be done. It will be argued that there does exist good evidence for our belief in the information supplied by memory; and moreover, that the strength of our belief is largely, if not entirely, accounted for, and proportioned to, that evidence.

Closely connected with the question what right we have to trust our memories is another, about which there is also little agreement, namely, what exactly happens when we remember some past occurrence? Some hold that we are acquainted with a 'memory-image' which, they say, we refer to the past. Others will have no truck with images, and declare that when we remember we are directly apprehending the past occurrence; what we remember is admittedly not present, but that, they contend, does not prevent it being presented. In this paper an attempt is made to answer this question also. It will be argued that while there is a strong case against the view that we do apprehend the past occurrence, the memory-image theory, as usually stated, is also inadequate. The true account, it will be maintained, is that not merely our sense-experience, but our whole state of mind on the past occasion is reproduced, though with certain important differences, mainly concerned with what we believe on the two occasions.

The argument which I shall employ to validate memory consists in taking its trustworthiness as a hypothesis and showing that this hypothesis is verified by experience. A view of this kind has been ad-

---

[2] Cf. H. H. Price, "Memory-Knowledge," *Aristotelian Society Supplementary Volume XV*, where this argument is developed.

vanced in a recent article by Mr. R. F. Harrod (*Mind*, Vol. LI) to whose reasoning the present paper is much indebted. The arguments I shall use to support the view differ, however, in some respects from his.

There is another theory which, like Mr. Harrod's, attempts to show that our belief in memory can be justified. This is the well-known view of Stout, which has gained considerable support. According to this theory a memory-belief has an 'intrinsic' probability; it carries its evidence, as it were, on its face. To quote a typical passage (Stout, *Studies*, p. 176), "If I ask myself how and why I am justified in asserting, on the evidence of memory, that I have had this or that experience, I find only one answer, and this seems sufficient—my actual present would not be such as it is if it had not behind it a certain actual past. Hence I maintain that in relying on memory we are relying on immediate present experience. We can have one leg in the past only because the other has a foothold in the present." The evidence for a memory-judgement, like that for such a judgement as that $2 + 2 = 4$ is contained within itself "in such a way that it cannot be extracted and asserted by itself in a distinct proposition."

But, is it not clear that this theory, like that of the plain man, begs the question? For how are we to know that our "present experience would not be such as it is if it had not behind it a certain actual past?" The answer can only be that memory tells us so.

Yet, in such a phrase as "We can have one leg in the past only because the other has a foothold in the present," Stout is drawing our attention to an important point. Prof. Harvey has well-expressed it when he remarks that "the kind of knowledge that passes for such without question [viz. knowledge of 'present sense-contents' and 'timeless conceptual truths'] presupposes, and is indeed intimately fused with, the kind of knowledge they (i.e., many philosophers, e.g. Plato, Descartes, Kant, Mill and the modern empiricists) tend to disparage, viz. retro-cognition." [3] To put the point concretely. If I am to know that this expanse (at which I am now looking) is green, I must know, for one thing, what greenness is. I must know this without any shadow of doubt. Or, in other words, I must have what we might call an 'infallible grasp' of the concept greenness. And *per contra*, any shakiness in my grasp of this concept will affect my cognition of the proposition "This expanse is green." Considerations of the same kind apply to my judgement that $7 + 5 = 12$; or indeed to any judgement. Now, although a concept is a 'timeless' entity our grasp of any given concept presupposes the occurrence of certain past mental acts, e.g.,

[3] J. W. Harvey, "Knowledge of the Past," *Aristotelian Society Proceedings*, Vol. XLI.

comparison and abstraction; and the firmness of this grasp depends on our ability to retain the result of these acts over a period of time, i.e. it depends on the reliability of memory. In short, if I cannot trust my memory then I cannot know that this is green or that $7 + 5 = 12$; indeed, I have no ground for believing that I even understand these propositions correctly.

Some people will no doubt be inclined to say to all this, "what nonsense! Of course I know that this is green. That is the kind of fact from which we must start." But to them there is open the reply, "what you mean is that *you* are certain this is green; but how do you know that it is certain?" And they may be invited to reflect on the reaction of someone who has dwelt in a greenless region for twenty years, when confronted with a sample of the colour; or to consider the various shades of confidence through which one passes when learning to recognise some unfamiliar quality like, say, magenta-ness.

This then is the important point which Stout's view emphasises, although as an attempt to validate memory his theory has not helped us. A word may be said here about Reid's view. Though, as we have seen, he declared our belief in memory to be 'unaccountable,' he did, in fact, offer a basis for the belief. Memory, he held, is part of our original constitution which we owe to a benevolent Creator; it cannot therefore be inherently deceptive.

But this argument too is circular; for in whatever way we come to be assured of God's existence, whether by philosophical argument, historical revelation, or religious experience, we cannot avoid some appeal to memory.

The following illustration will depict the theories we have been considering. A juryman, let us say, is forming an opinion on an accused person. He might say, "I believe this man is guilty—though how or why I believe it, I cannot say." This corresponds to Reid's view. Or he might say, "I believe this man is guilty—for I can see his guilt in his face." This gives us Stout's view. But, of course, he is much more likely to resist such travesties of justice, and to say "I believe the prisoner is guilty; and I have good reason for my belief, viz. the evidence that has been brought against him." This corresponds to the type of theory which this paper will defend.

Lest this illustration may seem to place the third view in too favourable a light, I hasten to add that it also exhibits the grave danger to which the view is exposed. For the evidence which justifies the juryman's belief will be *remembered* evidence, or, at least, evidence that presupposes the validity of memory; e.g. a witness may have stated "This is the man who knocked me down." But, when it is our belief in memory that is at stake, remembered evidence may not be admissible.

It might be objected at this stage that we are overlooking an obvious, or at any rate plausible answer to our question. Why not accept what we might call the Direct Awareness Theory—the view that when we remember we are directly apprehending the past object? Why not, as Prof. Harvey has urged, take memory at its face value as a *sui generis* way of knowing, or indeed of experiencing, the past. It would perhaps seem odd to say that we can experience what doesn't now exist, but perhaps past events do exist; or perhaps objects can be 'prolonged in time.'

The objection is reasonable, and discussion of it can hardly be postponed. We must therefore examine this theory in some detail. We shall find that it draws our attention to some important aspects of memory. I shall make one preliminary remark. There is an interesting parallel here between memory and our belief in other minds. Many people have considered our belief in the existence of other minds to be so strong that no argument (from e.g. analogy) could explain it; and, besides, in Cook Wilson's well-known phrase, "we don't want inferred friends." They have therefore been moved to conclude that we must, in some way or other, be directly aware of other minds. But as Prof. Price has argued, a strong case can be made against such a position: first, by pointing out that such an awareness is extremely hard to credit; and secondly, by removing the motive for asserting it. The latter may be done by showing that the usual argument by analogy can be replaced by another argument which is quite sufficient to justify the strength of our belief in other minds. (Cf. H. H. Price, "Our Evidence for the Existence of Other Minds," *Philosophy*, 1938). We, in the same way, may find that there is serious objection to the view that we can be directly aware of the past, and that the urge to postulate such awareness can be satisfied by showing that there is sufficiently good evidence available to justify the strength of our belief in memory.

With this preliminary let us now examine the Direct Awareness Theory. The theory has been advanced in a weaker and a stronger form. The weaker form asserts that *sometimes* when we remember we are directly aware of the past, but at other times, perhaps more often, what we are aware of is only an image, about which we believe or take-for-granted certain propositions. The stronger form asserts that in *all* remembering there is acquaintance with the past. If the weaker form were true, then there ought to be some perceptible difference between those rememberings which are direct awarenesses and those which are not. But introspection does not, I think, reveal any such difference. At 2 p.m. to-day I can, for example, remember eating my lunch; I can also remember this event at 3 p.m. and at 5 p.m. But the differences between these acts consist only of a distinctness, etc., in my imagery, and a firmness in my belief. I can conceive of no difference in 'kind' between them.

In connexion with the stronger form of the theory, two features of memory, which must be taken account of by any view, emerge. One operates against the theory; the other seems to operate for it. The following example will serve to illustrate both. Suppose that we examine some common object, e.g. our neighbour's garden-gate. We notice various things about it—its colour, shape, material, the nature of its latch. Later on, when we remember the gate, we find that we can recount several of these details. But we cannot, I suggest, recount more than those we actually noticed at the time. If, for example, we are asked how many vertical bars the gate contained, we are unable to say. Now this inability raises a difficulty for the Direct Awareness Theory. If, when we remember, we really are acquainted with the past situation, it is hard to understand why we should not be able to read off the required number of bars, as we could do on the original occasion.

It might be replied, in answer to this objection, that although we are, in memory, aware of the gate, we are aware of it dimly, as one might see an object blurredly through imperfect glass or stirring water, and that this accounts for our inability to tell the number of bars. But this suggestion will hardly do; for, according to it, the object should be homogeneously blurred; whereas what we find is that we can recount quite definitely certain of the gate's features, viz. those that we noticed, but that the others are either just missing or else vague and incomplete.

This objection to the Direct Awareness Theory may perhaps be strengthened by the consideration that our memories err not merely by being omissive: they sometimes apparently make mistakes of commission also. Prof. Broad, for example, has urged that the positive discrepancies between a situation as remembered and as it actually occurred are very grave; and, more serious than this, that we may sometimes remember a situation which did not, in fact, take place at all. In a case of this latter kind, we cannot be apprehending a past situation, for there is no such past situation to apprehend. And yet there seems no intrinsic mark by which we could distinguish such illusory remembering from the genuine kind.

I do not think, however, that too much emphasis should be placed on this extension of the objection. My reasons are, first, that it seems to me slightly suspicious that appeal is so frequently made to one particular alleged example of illusory memory, viz. the case of George IV and the battle of Waterloo; and secondly, that the cases which spring to mind from one's own experience can generally, on closer scrutiny, be explained away in one manner or another, e.g. as due to erroneous inference or forgetfulness.

The fact which seems to favour the Direct Awareness Theory derives from the 'negative memory situation.' To return to our neighbour's gate. If someone were to suggest that perhaps it had *three* vertical bars, we might repudiate this number, declaring, "No, the number certainly wasn't *three*." We might similarly refuse to accept twenty. Thus we do seem to know what the number was *not*. Now how do we know this? It would seem that we must have some kind of direct access to the actual past: we must, when we remember, be re-experiencing it in some way. Again, there is the tantalising experience of attempting to remember some elusive name. "No, it's not Smith; nor Tackaberry, nor. . . ." How do we know these things which the name is not, unless we, in some way, know what it is? And lastly, there is the less striking, yet important fact that when we inspect some memory-image, say, an image of a familiar room, we are aware of its imperfections. We are aware that it is omissive, schematic, and sketchy. But how do we recognise these defects unless we are, in some way, aware of the real thing?

Nevertheless, plausible though this suggestion may seem, there may be a simpler explanation of the negative memory-situation. Take first the example of remembering a name. "No, it's not Smith," we said. But if we inspect our state of mind closely we will find that there is more to it than this mere denial: there is also a premise, albeit suppressed. "It's not Smith, *because it is an unusual name*." Again, "it's not Thackeray, because (*sotto voce*) it is a short name." Or we may say, "It's a name like Tighe." "I think it begins with a T"; and so on. Thus, although we fail (temporarily) to recall the name itself, we can recall certain things about it; and these assist us in rejecting the wrong candidates. These features which we remember are not, of course, our only clue. There is also the well-known 'click' of conviction when the right name presents itself. "Taft! yes that's the name." And the other names' failure to click is a further reason for rejecting them. This click does not, however, require us to postulate any awareness, subconscious or otherwise, of the correct name. It only means that we have, we believe, recalled the correct name. To show that such beliefs are reasonable is part of the main problem of this paper.

A similar analysis applies to the case of the gate. "The number of bars was not three." Why do we believe this? I think the answer is as follows. Suppose that in fact the gate has, say, nine bars. Now a gate having nine bars has a different 'look' from that of a gate having three bars. And what may well have happened is, that although we did not count the actual number of bars, we did notice the look of the gate; indeed, if we noticed nothing else in detail, we would be likely to have observed the look. Thus, when we are asked if the gate had three bars, we compare the look of a three-barred gate, which we can easily imagine, with the remembered look of our neighbour's gate. And so we may amplify our, "The number was not three" to "The number was not three; because it had a different look from that."

It might be asked, how do we remember so abstracted a thing as a look? Would this not be like Alice's seeing the grin of the Cheshire cat without its owner? The answer to this is that we remember the look, not *per impossibile* as a concrete image, but in the same way as we remember that Taft's name began with a T; i.e. we remember it in a proposition. We remember that the gate had such and such a look.

The third of our three examples can be explained on similar lines. We observe that our image of a familiar room is omissive, schematic, sketchy. The latter two qualities present no great difficulty. We can, I think, apprehend directly such form-qualities as sketchiness and schematicity; and there may perhaps be also a swift inference, "The room is not like this, or I would have remembered that it was." The omissiveness can be explained, as before, in terms of what we remember about the room: the image shows no window here, but we remember that there is one; the image has a blur where we remember that there is a door. Thus the image does, as Prof. Harvey observes, instigate us to remember; but it instigates us, not to re-experience the past situation, but to remember that it had such and such features. We may note here though we shall be dealing more fully with imagery later—that the image has a certain malleableness. It presents us with, say, a blur on the wall; but when we remember that in that position hangs a portrait of greatuncle James, the blur is gradually replaced by our relative's familiar features.

The upshot of our discussion of the Direct Awareness Theory is, therefore, that apart from any difficulties it may raise about time, there is one fact about memory which militates strongly against it, and none which really supports it.

It will be remembered that our comparison of memory-belief with our belief in the existence of other minds showed that it is not sufficient merely to criticise the logic of the Direct Awareness Theory; we must also satisfy the motive which has led people to hold it, i.e. we must show that our strong belief in memory can be justified on other grounds. This is the task we shall attempt in the next section. If this attempt should not succeed then we may be driven either to accept the Direct Awareness Theory despite its difficulties, or else to acquiesce in the Unaccountability Theory of Reid.

II

In this section we are to attempt to show that belief in memory, or memory-belief for short, is justifiable. I shall begin by considering Mr. Harrod's ingenious theory which, as already stated, is the pattern for the argument I intend to put forward. He argues somewhat as follows. Let us take the informativeness (i.e. the reliable informativeness) of memory as a hypothesis, and let us make predictions on the strength of this hypothesis. If these predictions are fulfilled, then we shall have so far verified the hypothesis. There is a difficulty about the predictions, for they must be *remembered;* but Mr. Harrod gets over this with the help of that much-abused but long-suffering conception, the 'specious present.' Thus, to quote his paper "I may (on the strength of memory) predict continuity (of existence) for the ordinary objects around me (e.g. tables and chairs) and the prediction may be fulfilled within one present totality . . . the success of the prediction within the specious present is therefore strong evidence of the informativeness of memory." Similarly we may predict 'death for the lightning flash,' and again, our prediction is fulfilled.

Such reasoning does, however, as Mr. Harrod sees, presuppose an inductive principle. For we predict stability for the tables etc., only because we believe (a) that tables have been stable in the past, and (b) that objects which have been stable in the past are likely to be stable in the future; (a) is our memory premise, (b) is a statement of a simple inductive principle. Now this inductive element might seem to raise a problem for Mr. Harrod; for it might be urged that whatever reason we have for accepting induction presupposes memory. But Mr. Harrod escapes this difficulty by taking the bold line of asserting that an inductive principle can be offered whose truth is evident *a priori.* His defence of this procedure rests on certain fundamental considerations on probability which we need not, for the present at any rate, examine.

Mr. Harrod ends his paper with a neat biological consideration. Someone might say, surely you don't suggest that the belief we all have in memory is produced by considerations so intricate as you have advanced. Mr. Harrod agrees. He well appreciates that the man-in-the-street, or the man-in-the-cave, might fail to understand, or at any rate to discover such arguments, resting as they do on nice questions of logic and probability. And for this very reason it is clearly a great practical advantage that man should have been endowed with a strong natural impulse to trust his memory. If he had refused to trust it, or if it had not occurred to him to trust it until he had been persuaded to do so by the doubtfully-irresistible force of logic, then *homo sapiens* would very likely be *homo extinctus.*

Before proceeding to comment on this argument there is a familiar and important distinction to which I must refer. The word 'memory' and its cognates apply to more than one type of act. Thus on the one hand I may say, I posted a letter in the pillar-box yesterday morning; and if I am asked my grounds for this assertion, I may reply that I remember doing so. Or, on the other hand, I may say, water freezes at 32° F.; and if I am asked why I believe this, I may reply that my memory thus informs me. (There are other usages of the term to which I shall later refer; in so far as they are relevant to the present problem I hope to show that they can be reduced to one or other of the above two types.) Let us now see how these two types differ, and what they have in common that leads us to call both of them memory.

In the former of these two cases what I remember is a certain event; and the fact that I do remember it determines me to believe a certain proposition, namely, that the event occurred. What the remembering of an event actually consists in is a question we shall deal with in detail later on; but we may briefly note here that this type of remembering includes a reference to a past experience of the rememberer, and that imagery plays a prominent part. In the second type, there is no past reference and little or no imagery; what happens is that a certain proposition presents itself to me in a characteristic manner, and I believe it.

Thus the two types differ in that the first contains a retrospection, a reference to a past experience; the second does not. In the first type there is imagery, in the second there is not.

Common to the two types, what leads us to call both memory, is the belief-factor and the manner in which it arises. In the first case I believe that a certain event occurred; in the second case I believe a scientific proposition. In neither case is the belief based on sense-experience: there is no pillar-box now within my range of vision; nor do I now observe water freezing. Again, the belief is not in either case based on record or on inference. I do not believe that I must have posted the letter yesterday because my diary says so, or because an answer to it has arrived to-day. Rather, what happens in both cases is that what I recall presents itself to my mind, independently of sensation or inference, with a certain spontaneity or involuntariness; and it is this chiefly which exacts my belief. When a belief arises in this way, then I am said to remember. *Per contra,* if this involuntary quality were to disappear, we would approach the region of imagination, of supposition and make-belief.

It is not easy to find suitable terms to apply to each of these two types. Stout uses 'personal memory' and 'impersonal memory,' but the adjectives are hardly appropriate. 'Propositional memory' would not do for the second, for the remembering of propositions plays a part in the remembering of events also. Nor would 'factual memory' do; for what we remember isn't always fact: pre-Copernican school-boys may have remembered that the sun went round the earth. And, of course, 'rote memory' would be unsatisfactory; for we are dealing not with the memory, parrot-like, of sentences, but with the remembering of what sentences mean. The least objectionable suggestion I can think of is that the first type, where a reference to past experience occurs, should be called 'retrospective memory,' or 'retrospection' for short, and the second type where no such reference occurs, should be called 'non-retrospective memory,' with appropriate cognates in each case. I shall therefore adopt this terminology. I shall also call the belief associated with memory a 'memory-belief,' and use the term 'memory-dictum' for a piece of information supplied by memory.

Having observed this distinction, I will now make the following two comments on Mr. Harrod's argument.

(1) Although his paper begins with an example illustrating retrospection, the argument he develops to validate memory is primarily, if not solely, applicable to non-retrospective memory. "Only if memory is informative," he writes, "should I have grounds for predicting continuity for the chairs and tables and death for the lightning flash." Here it is a matter of remembering the propositions that chairs are stable and flashes short-lived; it is not a matter of remembering that chair A, chair B, etc., were stable objects, nor of running over in one's mind a bevy of lightning flashes, all short-lived.

Now it *may* be possible to deduce the trustworthiness of retrospection from that of non-retrospective memory; or alternatively, to design examples, analogous to those Mr. Harrod has constructed, in order to validate retrospection. But until one or other of these things is done, we have still some way to go before we can fairly be said to have put memory on its feet.

(2) Mr. Harrod's argument requires that his inductive principle should be conceded as an *a priori* truth. Now this daring demand is certain to be resisted by more than one type of opponent, and it would be better tactics, if it were possible, to offer an argument which justified our memory-beliefs without appealing to induction.

Can this be done? I think it can. Perhaps the following suggestion will help us to deal with non-retrospective memory, after which we may be in a position to tackle retrospection. The inductive ingredient entered through his appeal to the behaviour of tables, chairs, etc. Now, if we could construct an argument of a similar kind but from which the tables, chairs, etc., were eliminated, it might give us what we need. Do we, then, possess any information, for which non-retrospective memory could be held responsible, and which does not introduce induction? I think we do. The old distinction, however inaccurate it may be, between induction and deduction, offers us a clue. Perhaps our mathematical and logical information may give us what we need.

Let us see how the argument would run. We need not resort to any advanced mathematical or logical theorems. Quite elementary information such as we all carry round with us in our heads, may do. I refer to such simple propositions as that $9 + 8 = 17$, that there are eight half-crowns in a pound, that if all crows are black, some black things are crows. Consider the first of these. Suppose that we are asked, what is $9 + 8$? The answer 17 springs to our minds. We have probably no recollection of having ever learnt this. It is an example of a non-retrospective memory-dictum. We decide to test its validity. We take any 9 objects; we add them to any 8 others; we count the total. And lo, the number *is* 17. We repeat the experiment: what is 9×3? We answer 27. And again, the answer is 27. Here, then, we seem to have two pieces of evidence for the trustworthiness of non-retrospective memory. We may continue the process, and all the time, assuming that we get no unfavourable results, we are verifying the hypothesis that non-retrospective memory-information is reliable; or in other words, we are showing that it is reasonable to believe what memory tells us.

Two objections might be urged against this argument. One of these has little force, but the other is more serious. It might be objected that the process of testing the memory-information is bound to take time, so that here is an inlet for memory. But this objection can be answered by recalling the elementary nature of the experiments we have chosen. It is not a question of verifying some marathon theorem; our simple sums can be performed and tested within that short span of time that goes by the name of the specious present.

The more serious objection is that the argument does not really avoid an appeal to memory; for, to take our $9 + 8$ example, we are here relying on memory not only for the value of this sum, but also for the very meaning of the symbols employed, the 9, +, 8, =, 17. Thus the trustworthiness of memory enters, not once but twice, and this, it might be said, destroys the force of our argument.

Can this objection be met? I think it can. What we need is to state our argument in rather ampler terms. Let us re-state our $9 + 8 = 17$ example as follows. If non-retrospective memory is trustworthy, then, when what we believe (on the strength of memory) to be 9 objects are combined with what we believe to be 8 objects by the process we believe to be addition, the resulting number of objects should be what we believe to be 17. But this is what we do find to be the case; the number does turn out to be what we believe to be 17. We have here good evidence for the hypothesis that memory is trustworthy. This evidence is, I think, of considerable strength; for the 9 + 8 might, for all we knew, have added up to anything, and yet the one answer we were prompted to offer turned out to be correct.

Now suppose we perform another such test, and it also proves successful, what will be the position? We cannot simply carry forward the probability created by the first test, for we could do so only by memory. But when the second test has succeeded, it by itself raises some presumption that memory is in general a reliable informant (there is an appeal to induction here which I will consider in dealing with retrospection); and one of the pieces of information supplied by memory is that a previous successful test did take place. This information can now be used as further supporting evidence. By this cumulative process we can justify that high degree of confidence with which we believe such propositions as that 7 + 5 = 12, that Paris is in France, that the colour of grass is green, and that the battle of Hastings occurred in 1066.

There are a few remarks to be made about this attempt to validate memory.

(1) The method we have adopted is similar to the way in which we would test the trustworthiness of some new acquaintance: we consider his statements and examine whether they are true or not. It is thus that we form an opinion on the reliability of a witness in court, or of a weather expert. Moreover, the successful outcome of our experiments does show that it is reasonable to accept non-retrospective memory-information. Indeed, we have here an example of what we mean by a reasonable belief. To make this clear, suppose that the proposition 'the earth is round' is proposed to me as a hypothesis; and suppose that I perform all the relevant tests I can think of, and that the hypothesis emerges from them unscathed. If I were then to declare, "No, I still remain sceptical," or "I still believe that the earth is flat," my attitude would be considered *un*reasonable. *Per contra,* if I do accept the hypothesis, then I have embraced a reasonable belief.

(2) We may throw further light on the testing process we have employed by considering the case of a situation which conflicted with our hypothesis. Suppose that we set out as before to test our belief that 9 + 8 = 17; but that when we combine the 9 and the 8 we find the result to be not 17, but 18. What would our reaction, or reactions be? I think we would entertain something like the following series of suggestions, arranged in an order of decreasing plausibility: (a) I must have counted up the total wrongly. Let me see. No, it *does* seem to be 18. (b) Perhaps I miscounted the 9 or the 8. No. (c) There must be something queer about these objects. No, they seem quite ordinary.

(d) Well, perhaps 9 + 8 *isn't* 17; it looks as if my memory isn't what it was. I'll have to put less trust in it in future.

Such an illustration, though rather fanciful, is not entirely so. Lapses of memory do, we believe, occur—especially with advancing age. And the illustration brings out, in reverse as it were, the way in which our trust in memory, however instinctive it may be, is not fixed and unalterable, but is influenced by the evidence of experience. This thesis may be supported by the following important consideration, which is sometimes overlooked. It is usual when discussing memory, and so far we have followed the practice, to talk of the validity of memory (in general), the trustworthiness of memory (in general), and so on. But this, though convenient, has the disadvantage of obscuring the fact that our actual subject-matter is the particular memories of particular people, Peter, James and John. And one reason why this is a disadvantage is that it may cause us to overlook the admitted differences between individual memories, or between one man's memory at different times. But now, why is it that we have a greater trust in Peter's memory than in John's, or that our trust in James's memory may vary from time to time? The answer is again, experience. Thus what we have is not a fixed, neutral belief in Memory, but a variable, sensitive trust in the retentive power of this man or that, at one period of his life or another.

(3) This brings me to my last remark on the present argument. Mr. Harrod, we saw, holds that while evidence for our belief in memory does exist, the apprehending of this evidence could not account for the firmness with which the belief is held, except perhaps in the case of those few logicians who would follow and assent to his reasoning. He agrees therefore with Reid, and others, that there is a natural propensity to entertain this belief; and he points to the biological usefulness of such a propensity. Now, Prof. Price, who as we noted earlier in this paper, defends our belief in other minds by a type of argument similar to that used by Mr. Harrod to support our belief in memory, gives a different turn to the reasoning on one point. What he argues, if I understand him rightly, is that not only does strong evidence for our belief in other minds exist, but in fact it is that evidence which is mainly responsible for producing our belief. In other words, Prof. Price is denying that our belief in other minds is entirely natural or unaccountable. And he argues his case by pointing to the vast amount of evidence there is for the belief; and how it is continually knocking against our minds, even though we may seldom place it at the focus of our attention, or sum it up into a single explicit argument.

Now if the type of very simple experiment we have suggested to validate memory, as opposed to the more complex kind used by Mr. Harrod, is successful, then Prof. Price's version of the biological consideration fits memory admirably. Here also we move in an atmosphere highly favourable to the production and growth of a strong belief. We are continually doing experiments of the '9 + 8 = 17' type, and it is reasonable to think that even if we do not consciously sum up all this mass of evidence, it does influence our minds. In somewhat the same way, a country-dweller learns to tell the weather from the sky and wind, even though he has never heard of the magic word induction; it is in a similar manner that a man's literary style may be subconsciously formed; and thus indeed it is that we learn to perceive the external world.

We need not, however, feel too strongly about this point. Some natural propensity to trust our memories there may be. But we will not need to concede that there is not a large mass of easily apprehended evidence to nourish the propensity.

We may add here that the very simplicity of the considerations by which we have validated non-retrospective memory has perhaps led to these considerations being overlooked. The remarkable thing is not that we have the ability to reproduce information at will, though perhaps that is striking enough: but that such information is generally valid. It is on this fact that our vindication of non-retrospective memory is based. And although I cannot claim to feel no anxiety lest the present theory may not also prove open to the charge of *petitio principii,* I believe that any theory must take account of this simple fact which I have stressed.

For convenience I am going to call Mr. Harrod's view the Verification Theory, and the view advanced in this paper the Modified Verification Theory. Let us, by way of summary, state what the latter theory asserts.

The Modified Verification Theory, being confronted with the fact that we do believe, with varying degrees of conviction, the information afforded by non-retrospective memory, asserts two propositions. (a) Good evidence for this belief does exist, and an argument can be constructed to show that there does; (b) this evidence accounts, partly or entirely, for the existence and strength of the belief.

Of these two propositions the first is the main contention of the theory; it could afford to relinquish the second, if compelled to do so.

Having dealt with non-retrospective memory, let us now consider retrospection. Can it be shown that there is good reason for the belief which we all accord to the information supplied by this source? To take a simple example: we think we have shown that if we remember that 9 + 8 is 17, then 9 + 8 probably is 17; but can we show that if we remember learning yesterday that $9 + 8$ is 17, then we probably did learn this yesterday?

We saw when validating non-retrospective memory that the evidence for its trustworthiness lies ready to hand, and is simple enough for anyone to comprehend. Perhaps the same thing is true of retrospection. Let us consider how the plain man would justify his belief in a particular retrospection if that belief were questioned. Suppose, then, that he is asked "Did you switch off the hall-light last night?" and that he replies "Yes, I'm sure I did." To the query "How do you know you did?" he answers, "I remember distinctly doing so." If we then asked him "What right have you to regard this memory as good evidence for your belief that you switched off the light?" he might reply, with some impatience, "Well the light *is* off, and lights don't switch themselves off; therefore, since nobody else could have entered the hall, it is highly probable that I did switch off the light, as I remember doing." And he might add, "If you would like another example of the kind of consideration that leads me to trust my memory, I also remember posting a letter to Uncle John last Saturday, and here is a letter thanking me for it."

In both these examples there is, to put it roughly, a combination of non-retrospective memory, induction and retrospection; and we might reasonably hope that if we could eliminate the non-retrospective and inductive elements we should obtain samples of good evidence for the validity of retrospection. To take the first example: suppose the man were asked "How do you know that lights don't switch themselves off?" he might reply, "Well, they have never done so in the past; and that seems a good reason for believing that they didn't do so this time." The first proposition in this reply is clearly a non-retrospective memory-dictum; the second expresses belief in a simple principle of induction. We might express this example formally in the following way. (a) If later behaviour is likely to resemble earlier behaviour; and (b) if the non-retrospective memory-dictum that lights have not switched themselves off in the past is correct; and (c) if my retrospective memory-dictum that I did switch off the light is correct; then (d) it is likely that the light is switched off. But (e) I find that it *is* switched off; therefore (f) the complex hypothesis (a) (b) (c) has been verified in this case.

It follows that if we could eliminate hypotheses (a) and (b) we would have verified hypothesis (c); that is, we would have gained some evidence for the truth of the hypothesis that the information supplied by retrospection is trustworthy.

Now can we eliminate (a) and (b)? Of these, (b) seems to present no difficulty; for we have shown that non-retrospective memory is a reliable informant; whence it follows that lights have probably not switched themselves off in the past.

We are left therefore with (a), the inductive hypothesis, on our hands. This is not quite so easy to dispose of. However, let us begin by asking, suppose that we could establish the trustworthiness of retrospection only by assuming the validity of induction, would our proof be any the worse for that? We may imagine that in such circumstances a generous critic might say, "Well, of course, your proof would be a finer one if it didn't assume induction; but you'll be in good company in making the assumption; few sciences can avoid including it in their first premises. And indeed some logicians would grant you that the truth of the assumption can be seen *a priori*. There is, however, one proviso I must make. You must show that in making this assumption you are not thereby assuming what you wish to prove, viz. the trustworthiness of retrospection."

If this is not an over-optimistic estimate of the position in which we shall find ourselves if we cannot dispose of hypothesis (a), then our immediate task is to consider the proviso our critic has entered. Let us therefore consider how memory and induction are connected in the present theory. We shall find that there are three points of connexion, but that none of these implies assuming the validity of retrospection. These I shall state briefly.

(1) The belief we all have in induction has been, if not created, at any rate fostered by our observation of particular past uniformities, e.g. cold-in-the-head often following sitting-in-a-draught, disappearance of hunger generally following consumption of food, etc. This is not, of course, to say (as Mill did) that these past uniformities are evidence for our belief in induction. Nevertheless, if someone were to suggest to us that our beliefs in these past uniformities are quite baseless, then our faith in induction would be gravely shaken. And there was nothing to exclude such a suggestion, so long as the reliability of non-retrospective memory was in question. But since we have shown that this type of memory is reliable, this form of scepticism is barred. To put the point succinctly. We have not established the validity of induction by proving the reliability of non-retrospective memory. What we have done is to remove a possible cause of doubting its validity.

It is clear that there is no question here of begging the question by assuming the validity of retrospection.

(2) Our argument to establish the validity of non-retrospective memory is really an inductive one. For what we did was to take various non-retrospective memory-dicta, and having shown that they were credible, to conclude that non-retrospective memory is in general a reliable informant. Thus our belief in such memory as a witness trustworthy not only now but also in the future and the past pre-

supposes the validity of induction. Similar considerations would, of course, apply to retrospection, and, indeed, perhaps to all our faculties. But it is clear that this relation between memory and induction does not leave us open to a charge of *petitio principii*. The induction occurs *after* we have done our 'experiment,' not during it; and its role is similar to that which it performs in any inductive science.

(3) When we were showing the reliability of non-retrospective memory-dicta we appealed in our experiments to scientific propositions like '$9 + 8 = 17$'; but we have now assumed that such *dicta* as that 'lights have not switched themselves off in the past' are also reliable. Such an analogical extension of memory's region of validity is also inductive, but clearly it does not require us to assume anything about retrospection.

This discussion of the relation between memory and induction in the present theory has shown two things: first, induction permeates the arguments we have offered; we cannot avoid assuming its validity. But, secondly, by making this assumption we are not implicitly taking for granted the validity of retrospection. Thus we have complied with the proviso entered by our critic.

We may now revert to our main argument. We had a threefold hypothesis (a) (b) (c) on our hands, of which one part (b) had been disposed of. We have now found that we cannot eliminate the inductive constituent (a). What the argument therefore entitles us to conclude is, that assuming the validity of induction, which so many sciences have to assume, we have in our 'light-switch' example some evidence for the trustworthiness of retrospection. But now, as in the case of non-retrospective memory we can easily multiply such arguments; we can pass from switched-off lights to turned-off taps and bolted doors. There is no end to the evidence. And in this way we may show that the confidence we all place in retrospection is highly reasonable; in other words, that the information supplied by retrospection is trustworthy.

Here we may briefly adapt to the present type of memory-information some remarks we made about non-retrospective memory.

(1) The way in which we have tested the trustworthiness of retrospection is the standard method of testing the trustworthiness of some new acquaintance. It is the way in which we should test the reports of a news correspondent or the promises of a plumber.

(2) We may consider our reactions in some hypothetical case where retrospection seemed to be misleading. Suppose that we were to remember distinctly turning off the light last night, and yet when we come down in the morning it is switched on. We might entertain the following series of explanations: (a) Someone else must have turned it on. (b) There must be something queer about the switch. (c) I mustn't

have turned it off; my memory has been playing me tricks; I shall be more wary about its information in future.

Such a case illustrates features of retrospection analogous to those we noticed in the case of non-retrospective memory. Thus it shows what great confidence we usually place in retrospection. It reminds us that it may be a misleading abstraction to talk about the trust-worthiness of retrospection in general: the memory of one man may be much more reliable than that of another. It suggests that the belief we have in retrospection is not unrelated to the evidence that exists for the belief; and that it derives its strength, not by virtue of being an unreasoned natural impulse, but through an implicit consciousness of such simple arguments as we have used to show its reasonableness.

(3) It must be admitted that here, as in the case of non-retrospective memory, not all the information supplied can be tested by the method we have described. Information about switched-off lights and other events with suitably observable consequences can certainly be tested; but many restrospective memory-dicta are not of this nature. Suppose that I remember learning Milton's sonnet "On His Blindness" yester-day; how am I to test whether I did learn it or not? Hardly by the fact that I know it now, for that would be perhaps equally compatible with my having learnt it last week or last year. We could multiply such examples and many would be even less tractable than the one we have given. There are two courses open to us here: first, to at-tach those non-testable retrospections, if possible, to testable ones; e.g. I may remember putting my *Milton* on a certain shelf after I had learnt the poem. Secondly, to argue by analogy from the testable to the non-testable types. It is noteworthy that these difficult cases may even be the exceptions that prove the rule. For would not our belief in some testable *dictum* such as, that we switched off the light, normally be stronger, other things being equal, than our belief in some non-testable dictum such as, that we whistled six bars of "Annie Laurie" while walking along some lonely lane? And if the latter type of belief is sometimes stronger than it should be, may this not be an example of our non-rational tendency to place too much reliance on analogy?

This concludes the application of the Modified Verification Theory to retrospection. And as in the case of non-retrospective memory we may state in two propositions what the theory asserts.

The Modified Verification Theory, in order to account for the fact that we do believe, with varying degrees of conviction, the information afforded by retrospection, asserts two propositions: (a) there *is* good evidence for this belief, and it can be discovered, not by postulating an 'immediate knowledge' of the past, but by a certain method of verification. (b) This evidence accounts, partly or entirely, for the ex-istence and strength of the belief.

It will be readily seen that it is the trustworthiness of memory this theory claims to have established; it does not claim to prove that memory is ever infallible. The arguments it employs lean too heavily on appeals to induction and verification for it to claim so much as that. And this accords with fact, for do we not often have to confess with Miranda,

> 'Tis far off,
> And rather like a dream than an assurance
> That my remembrance warrants?

On the other hand, we may fairly claim to have shown that when the evidence for some of our memory-beliefs is fully marshalled—and in doing this we can often appeal not only to the witness of one man's memory but to the confirming evidence afforded by the memories of a group of men—then we have reasons of so great a cogency as to justify the very high degree of confidence with which such beliefs are often accepted. Thus, if we have not proved that any memory-information is knowledge in the strict sense, we have shown that some of it is very likely to be true. And such a strong assurance is perhaps all that fallible beings can reasonably expect.

The further question arises, but there is not space to discuss it here, if memory enters in some form into all our judgements, can there be any knowledge at all in the strict sense?

III

Having concluded our attempt to show that it is reasonable to trust our memories, we may now turn to our other main problem—to describe what happens when we remember. "When we remember" is, of course, ambiguous, for it might refer either to retrospective or to non-retrospective memory. We must deal with both of these. I shall begin with retrospection, since it, with its explicit reference to a past context, offers a more "full-blooded" type of remembering than does non-retrospective memory; and we may find that the latter can be treated as a limiting case of the former.

Let us begin by considering a simple case of retrospection. Suppose that at 4 p.m. as I sit at this table in the College Library I hear the sound of the door opposite me opening. I look up and perceive my friend Dr. X in the doorway; i.e. I see a familiar shape, and I believe or take-for-granted certain propositions such as—that is Dr. X and not his double; that is a human body and not a hallucination; if I were at the doorway I could have certain X-ish experiences of touch and resistance. And my state of mind will, so far, be the same whether it *is* Dr. X or some one of the illusory alternatives. Of course, if the figure were suddenly to vanish into thin air, my state of mind would alter considerably; but, for simplicity, let us suppose that I just perceive Dr. X, i.e. I believe or take-for-granted certain propositions; I need not enquire whether I am perceiving correctly, i.e. whether these propositions are true or not.

What happened then at 4 p.m. was that, first, I saw something, and then I had a state of mind in which the taking-for-granted of certain propositions was the main constituent. (There were probably also certain feeling elements and subconscious sensations, pleasure, fatigue and so on, but we may neglect these.) I shall add a further instalment to my illustration in a moment, but first, let us examine what happens when I remember, say, two hours later, the events just described.

Let us try to get all the details clear. First, there will be a belief element: I believe that I perceived Dr. X two hours ago in the Library context. Secondly, I am aware that I am not now perceiving Dr. X; i.e. I am aware that I am not seeing an X-like shape, nor taking-for-granted any such proposition as that if I moved in a suitable way I could have certain X-ish experiences of touch and resistance.

These two elements, however, are not the whole story. They might occur on the strength of a diary entry to the effect that I perceived Dr. X at 4 p.m. to-day. There is also an 'imaginal' element to be considered. A proper account of the nature and function of this element is the key to a satisfactory theory of memory-consciousness. We must therefore examine it in some detail. Some would say that this element is a 'memory-image,' and that when we remember we are aware of such images. This view, though not entirely mistaken, fails as we shall see, to take account of all the facts. And it has the tactical disadvantage that since it stands openly, if not unashamedly, for a representative theory of memory, it has provoked an extreme reaction from those to whom representative theories are anathema. They have been inclined to assert "I most certainly am not aware of a mere image when I remember; therefore I must be aware of the past event itself." Now, we saw, in section I, that it is highly unlikely that in memory we are aware of the past event. What we might reasonably aim at giving, therefore, is an account which will preserve the truth in the image-theory, and yet will not annoy the non-representationist unnecessarily.

What, then, *does* happen when I remember perceiving Dr. X at the Library door? When I inspect my state of mind, what I find can, I think, be fairly expressed by saying that I have a state of mind, like the state I remember, in some respects, though unlike it in others. I am doing something like perceiving Dr. X; but I am not actually perceiving him, for I do not believe he is there. I might say that I am 'entertaining' or 'contemplating' the state of mind I remember without being actually *in* it. Or, I might say that I am 'imaging' it. Perhaps the phrase 'I image my previous act of perceiving' will give us what we want.

This, however, is still but a phrase. We must try to develop and justify its implications. Perhaps the following analogy may help us. We know what it is to place ourselves 'imaginatively' in the position of someone else, e.g. of a person who believes, say, that the end of the world is due in a fortnight, even though we ourselves do not share that belief. We can understand how such a person may feel, though we don't experience his feelings. How exactly do we do this? What we do, I think, is to entertain the proposition he believes and to consider what would follow from it if it were true. Since then we are entertaining the same proposition as he is, our state of mind does, so far, resemble or 'image' his, though of course ours differs from his in that he believes the proposition, whereas we don't.

Now when we remember, we do something very like this. We might say that we place ourselves (or perhaps *are placed*) imaginatively in our own position in the past context. In that past context (as described in my illustration) there was an act of seeing, and there were certain propositions believed (or taken-for-granted). And what I do when I remember it is to image the act of seeing and to entertain, without believing, the propositions. Thus I image the whole perceptual situation: I do not merely 'have a visual image.'

The analogy we used above, suggests a further point. We know that if we entertain for any length, or with great attention, such a proposition as that the end of the world is at hand, there comes a tendency, perhaps minute, to believe it. Now we can observe something similar in memory. If I concentrate on the past situation, and shake off the reminders of the present, then my state of mind will gradually approximate to one of perceiving; I am sliding back into the past, as we say; and it may need some jolt of sensation to bring me back to 'reality.' Of some people indeed we say that they live constantly in the past. Here we may also compare our state of mind when engrossed in a novel, or when watching a "gripping" film. Such considerations strengthen our contention that remembering and perceiving are not so diverse as might at first appear.

To sum up the argument so far: when I remember perceiving Dr. X in the doorway at 4 p.m. what happens is that (1) I believe that I did perceive him in that context, (2) I image the act of perceiving; i.e. (a) I image the act of seeing, and (b) I entertain the propositions I originally took-for-granted. But I do not now take their truth for granted; rather I take-for-granted that they are not true. For example, I do not now believe that if I moved towards the door I could touch

Dr. X, for he is not present (nor, perhaps, is the door); but I do entertain this proposition, and as we have seen, if I entertain it hospitably enough, a tendency to believe it may arise.

This account of memory-consciousness may claim the advantage that it goes some way towards satisfying the man, who says that when he remembers the past he is doing something more than being acquainted with a mere flickering schematic image. We offer him something more full-blooded than that, an imaging not only of the sensory element, but of his whole state of mind on the past occasion. We do not indeed give him *all* he wants; for he wishes to hold that he is actually acquainted with the past event. But we think that he ought not to want this, for there are serious objections to it.

The following illustration supports this account in a different way. I am, let us suppose, sitting at my desk in a familiar room. I close my eyes, stand up, feel my way to the door and grasp the handle. Now, suppose that I remember this simple series of actions. First, of course, I believe that I did perform them. But when I image what happened, I find that although my eyes were then closed, I am now "seeing" myself get up, walk across the room, and grasp the handle. My imaging is of a visual, not as we might expect, of a tactual nature. How are we to explain this? I think we can do so as follows. When I felt my way across the room I was not merely having sensations: I was also being prompted by them to perceive a number of familiar objects; that is, I was led to entertain and believe various propositions, such as "I am now touching the blue armchair." Now, when I remember the occurrence, then if our account is correct, I image, not merely the actual touch and motor sensations I experienced, but my whole state of mind. In the latter the perceiving of the room bulked largely, and since I do my perceiving mainly in terms of vision, I will image that past perceiving in a visual way; i.e. I will "see" myself performing the various actions. It may be added that if on the past occasion the tactual sensation had not merely been used as stimuli to perception, but had been given my particular attention, judgements being passed on them such as "This is hard and smooth," then, when I remembered the past occurrence, I probably would image these sensations.

One point in this account requires modification. I have asserted that when we remember, *we image,* and also that *we place ourselves* imaginatively in our own past position. This use of verbs in the active voice neglects the spontaneity or involuntariness of memory. Whenever we set ourselves to remember a past event, then we succeed in doing so only in so far as the act of imaging occurs with some degree of spontaneity. This element of spontaneity, as we observed earlier in this paper, is one factor determining the strength of our belief that the remembered event did occur; when it shrinks to zero, we have reached the border-line between memory and imagination. What we should say, therefore, is not that we place ourselves in our past position, but that we are placed in that position.

In studying the Dr. X illustration, we have confined ourselves so far to what happens when we remember an act of perceiving; and the latter is, of course, something more than sensing. It includes some entertaining and believing of propositions, i.e. it includes some thinking. Let us, however, consider now whether our account of remembering will apply to a more explicit act of thought. We may do this by taking a further instalment of our illustration. Suppose then, as I perceive Dr. X entering the room, the thought strikes me, "He will probably open all the windows." What happens when I remember this act of thinking? There is, as usual, the belief-element: I believe that I did think this. But again, the belief is not the whole story; for it might arise inferentially, on the strength of some record. May we say then, that here also I am somehow 'imaging' the past act of thinking? I think we may. First there is some sensory imaging, the room, Dr. X, etc. This gives context to my remembered act of thinking. Secondly, in remembering that act, I entertain the proposition "He will probably open all the windows"; but I do not now, as I did then, think that he will do so, for the good reason that he isn't there now to do it. Thus again I am placing myself, or rather being placed, imaginatively in my own position in the past situation; I do not believe that I am now in that situation, though I do believe it occurred.

A similar account would apply to remembered acts of hoping, inferring, etc. And about all such acts we may note, as we did about perceiving, that remembering may shade off into a state of mind in which we are almost re-living the past.

How do we perform these acts of entertaining propositions which figure so prominently in our account? To answer this, let us take an instance from our illustration. As I look up from my work, I see the familiar human shape, and I take-for-granted the proposition "This is Dr. X." Now to take this proposition for granted I must first entertain it; and since the process is extremely swift, the entertainment cannot be very elaborate. What probably happens is that fragments of a sentence half-come to my lips, or my ears, "Dr. X . . . there" and I take in what they mean. (The process is not unlike what happens when we read: our oscillating glance may take in only half-words, yet they are sufficient for us to grasp the meaning.) When I come to remember perceiving Dr. X, then I am again entertaining the proposition "This is Dr. X," but I am not now assenting to it. And I entertain it in much the same way as on the original occasion. Fragments of a sentence again half-come to my lips, and I take in what they mean. They need not, however, be the same fragments as on the original occasion, and they may come more faintly, but the process is much the same; and in both cases I entertain the proposition by imaging a sentence and taking in its meaning.

No special difficulty is raised for us therefore by the entertaining of propositions. I have not indeed attempted to show how we take in the meaning of a sentence; but this operation is not peculiar to memory; and we have enough on hand already.

We may now set down the main points in this account of what happens when we retrospect. When we retrospect some past event, then (a) we believe that that event did occur; (b) we image our state of mind on that past occasion. This imaging includes the imaging both of any acts of sensing, and of any acts of believing, hoping, wishing, etc., that occurred. The imaging of the acts of sensing consists in having experiences, like these acts in some respects, though unlike them in others; and this imaging helps to fix the context of what we remember. The imaging of the believing or hoping consists in imaging, however incompletely, and taking in the meaning of, the sentences which would express these mental attitudes, though we do not adopt these attitudes now. Finally, we must add that the imaging is largely involuntary, and the degree of involuntariness partly determines the strength of our belief that the remembered situation did occur.

According to this account then, the chief constituents of an act of retrospection are the holding of a belief and an act of imaging. There is no direct acquaintance with the past situation, as some have mistakenly maintained. We need not, however, fear the charge that this account leads to scepticism or agnosticism about the past; for we have seen that memory is a trustworthy informant.

We can now deal shortly with *non-retrospective* remembering. We have just seen that when we retrospect there is (a) a belief, and (b) an act of imaging. As the belief-factor tends to zero, we approach the limiting case of pure imagination. And as the ability to image the past situation diminishes, we approach the limiting case of non-retrospective memory. For the differentia of such memory is that its information presents itself to us as something demanding belief, although giving us no indication of when or where we originally acquired it.

Here is a convenient place to notice a point Prof. Broad has discussed. According to the present account of retrospection, what we do when we retrospect is to recall our own past acts of sensing and thinking. But Prof. Broad has remarked that "situations sometimes arise which it would be natural to describe as follows: 'I remember that man's face, though I do not remember seeing it before.' " [4] And

⁴ *The Mind and its Place in Nature*, p. 239.

a careful discussion of such situations leads him to conclude *inter alia* that there may be cases where there is no memory of our act of perceiving—we remember only the object perceived. It seems to me, however, that such cases should be assimilated to non-retrospective rather than to retrospective memory. Our state of mind in the situation instanced by Prof. Broad could, I think, be quite adequately expressed by the simple statement: "I *believe* I have seen that man's face before, though I don't remember doing so." Here, just as the proposition $9 + 8 = 17$ presents itself to us as something demanding belief, so "I have seen that man's face before" exacts my assent; not an unwilling assent, however, for I have come by experience to regard the spontaneity of such information as a mark of its reliability. This type of situation does not, therefore, require us to modify the view that in retrospection we are recalling our own past states of mind in imaged form.

A slightly different version of the point we have just been considering would be as follows. In our account of retrospection, we have confined ourselves to the remembering of events or situations. Now, we often speak of remembering *persons* and *things*. We say, "Yes, I remember old Mrs. Jones quite well." Can our account be adapted to such rememberings? I think it can. We must distinguish two cases. The first is where we say "I have a vivid memory of Mrs. Jones." The second is where we say "I can't picture her in my mind, but I think I would recognise her if I saw her." The analysis of the first case is quite simple. We are performing a certain act of imaging, and we are believing that we are imaging the visual appearance of Mrs. Jones. The second case makes reference to recognition, a full account of which I shall not attempt to give here. But, briefly, we may distinguish between an act of recognising and an ability to recognise. What we are claiming above is an ability to recognise Mrs. Jones, and this claim when analysed can be seen to be a statement of our belief that if we were confronted with Mrs. Jones we would then be prompted (by memory) to judge correctly who she is.

Before quitting the present topic, I shall consider briefly some traditional problems concerning 'memory-images.' It has been debated whether such images are present, past or future, whether they are public or private, and what their function is. If our account is correct in emphasising the *imaging* rather than the *image* these problems tend to lose their importance if not their point. But they cannot be overlooked completely. First, then, the question of date. When I at 6 p.m. remember an event that occurred at 4 p.m., I perform an act of imaging. That act is present—it occurs at 4 p.m.—though what I image is past. Still, it may be urged, you must distinguish in the imaging between act and object, just as in sensing between act and bers of the class. In this way we credit ourselves with having the required support for our inductive arguments.

When it comes, however, to the case of other minds, the fact of our being underprivileged appears, at first sight, very much more serious. For here it might seem not only that we were necessarily handicapped, given our actual situation, but that the handicap itself was necessary. To be privileged is to be the other person. Only he really knows when he thinks and feels. I do not and cannot because I am myself and not he. But is it even conceivable that I should be he? It is plainly a contradiction that I should both remain myself and be someone other than myself: yet this is exactly what here seems to be required. In the other cases which we have considered, the fact that one was underprivileged was the outcome of one's situation, the position that one happened to occupy in space and time; and it could be remedied, at least in theory, by the situation's being changed. But how could a change in my situation make me someone else? Unless I keep something of myself, that is, some characteristic which is peculiar to me, I have not just changed my situation, I am abolished altogether. But if I do keep something of myself, I have not attained the privileged position, I am not identified with the other person. Thus it seems that the thoughts and feelings of others are inaccessible to us, not merely because we happen to occupy the relatively unfavourable position that we do, but because we are respectively the persons that we are. The privileged position, in any given instance, which is that of being the person who has the thoughts and feelings in question, is one that only he could occupy. It would appear, therefore, that we are debarred from 'really knowing' one another's inner experiences in a more radical way than we are debarred from 'really knowing' events which are remote from us in space or time. For while we are underprivileged in these cases also, it is at least conceivable that we should not have been.

This reasoning is plausible but I do not think that it is sound. Admittedly, to say that an experience is not one's own but someone else's is to imply that one is not, and could not be, in the best possible position to know that it exists. But equally, to say of an event that it is remote in time or space is to imply that one is not, and could not be, in the best possible position to know that it exists: for the description of the event as occurring somewhere else, or as being future or past, already carries the implication that one is underprivileged. This does not follow from a mere description of the event, or even from a description of its place and date, so long as it contains no reference to the position of the speaker; and it is for this reason that it can be held to be contingent that the speaker's actual position is not the best possible. But equally, the implication that one is underprivileged is not sense-datum. The answer is clear: whatever data (presumably the present) is assigned to a sense-datum that I am now sensing, may also be attached to an image that I am now imaging.

We may deal in similar fashion with the question of privacy. Your act of imaging is one thing, mine is another; and it would be mere metaphor to talk of a public act of imaging shared by us both. But if someone again insists on picking out the 'objective constituent' of the act, then two remarks may be made. (1) Whatever degree of privacy sense-data possess, that of images is greater. When you hear a loud sound I can often hear one too; not so with images. (2) Our analysis of memory-consciousness has shown that we image not only acts of sensing, but also acts of thinking; and the latter imaging reduces ultimately to the entertaining of propositions by the imaging of words. This imaging of words is imaging of a sensory kind, whose privacy we have just considered. The propositions we entertain must indeed have some publicity; else communication would be even more difficult than it is. We need not, however, claim any greater degree of publicity for them than we accord to material objects like tables or chairs. These we commonly regard as public, despite the fact that no two people may ever see, touch or otherwise sense them in exactly the same way; and the same thing may apply to propositions, which must be couched in words that may never have exactly the same meaning for any two individuals.

The *function* of imaging in memory has already been considered more or less explicitly, and our findings may be collected here. (1) Imagery reproduces the past sensory context without which there is no retrospection. (2) It is an indispensable factor in remembering acts of thinking, hoping, etc.; if we do not image these, we do not remember them. (3) The involuntariness of the imagery is a factor in distinguishing between remembering and imagining. The greater the involuntariness, the stronger is our belief that what we are imaging occurred. (4) In so far as the imagery gives us sensory context, and images our past mental acts, it is informative; and in directing our minds to the remembered event, it renders us open to receive other information in the form of propositions remembered. Thus having imaged our breakfast table in a general way, we remember that there was a vase of daffodils in the centre, even though we do not image them.

How do we ever get the concept of pastness? So far I have said nothing about this question. Some would regard it as important; others might dismiss it as a pseudo-problem. Prof. Broad offers two answers, though confessing with characteristic frankness that neither satisfies him. I shall not go into deail here, but I think a solution can be found if we bear in mind, first, that pastness, no more than presentness or futurity, isn't a quality: a past event is merely one that has occurred; and secondly, that we can directly apprehend instances of having-occurredness, e.g. in the rat-tat-tat-tat of a door-knocker. On this basis we can build up the concept of pastness in general, and a theory of temporal vision on Berkeleian lines can be developed.

part two

CONCERNING
A PERSON'S KNOWLEDGE
OF OTHER MINDS

A. J. AYER

One's Knowledge of
Other Minds

Let use see how there comes to be a problem about one's knowledge of other minds. Consider the following propositions:

(1) When someone, other than myself, says that he is thinking about a philosophical problem, or that he has a headache, or that he has seen a ghost, what he is saying about himself is the same as what I should be saying about myself if I were to say that I was thinking about a philosophical problem, or that I had a headache, or that I had seen a ghost.

(2) When I say of someone other than myself that he is thinking about a philosophical problem, or that he has a headache, or that he has seen a ghost, what I am saying about him is the same as what I should be saying about myself if I were to say that I was thinking about a philosophical problem, or that I had a headache, or that I had seen a ghost.

(3) When I say that I am thinking about a philosophical problem, or that I have a headache, or that I have seen a ghost, my statement is not equivalent to any statement, or set of statements, however complicated, about my overt behaviour.

(4) I have direct knowledge of my own experiences.

(5) I cannot have direct knowledge of anyone else's experiences.

(6) Consequently, the only ground that I can have for believing that other people have experiences, and that some at least of their experiences are of the same character as my own, is that their overt be-

From A. J. Ayer, *Philosophical Essays*, (London: Macmillan and Company, Ltd., Toronto: The Macmillan Company of Canada, Ltd.; and New York: St Martin's Press, Inc., 1954), pp. 191–214. This essay was originally published in *Theoria*, XIX (1953). Reprinted by permission of the author, the publishers of *Philosophical Essays*, and the editor of *Theoria*.

haviour is similar to mine. I know that certain features of my own behaviour are associated with certain experiences, and when I observe
other people behaving in similar ways I am entitled to infer, by analogy, that they are having similar experiences.

There are philosophers who accept all these propositions, and to
them the question how one is to justify one's belief in the existence of
other minds presents no special difficulty. If they are concerned with
it at all, they are interested only in the choice of premises for the
argument from analogy. Thus they may maintain that the basis of the
argument is not so much that there is a physical resemblance between
other people's behaviour and one's own as that other people also use
language or that they behave purposefully. But none of this raises any
serious question of principle.

To many philosophers, however, this argument from analogy appears too weak for its purpose; some of them indeed, for reasons into
which we shall enter later on, maintain that it is altogether invalid,
or at least that it cannot be valid if the other propositions which I
have listed are true. But this leaves them rather at a loss to justify
their belief in the existence of minds other than their own. Some take
the view that the sixth proposition is incompatible with the fifth.
They hold that the argument from analogy can be valid only if it is
possible, at least in principle, for one person to have direct knowledge
of the experiences of another. Others, who will not allow this to be
possible, try to resolve the difficulty by denying the second proposition
on my list. Their contention is that while the statements that one
makes about one's own experiences need not be equivalent to statements about one's overt behaviour, this does not apply *mutatis mutan-
dis* to the statements that one makes about the experiences of others;
to say of someone other than oneself that he is having such and such
an experience is, on this view, always to describe his actual, or potential, behaviour. But this asymmetry in the analysis of statements which
appear so very similar arouses objections on the score of common
sense. A way of removing it is to deny my third and fourth propositions, with the result that all statements about experiences, whether
one's own or anybody else's, are interpreted as statements about behaviour; and there are philosophers who take this heroic course.
Finally, there are those who, rejecting the sixth proposition but accepting the other five, find themselves inadequately defended against
solipsism. Let us try to see where the truth lies.

We may take as our starting-point the propositions that I can have
direct knowledge of my own experiences and that I cannot have direct
knowledge of anyone else's. What does it mean to say that I have
direct knowledge of my own experiences? Presumably the knowledge
claimed is knowledge that something or other is the case, that I have

a headache, or that I am thinking about a philosophical problem: and the point is that if the statement which expresses what I claim to know refers only to my present experience, I am in the best possible position to decide its truth. If I judge it to be true, it is on the basis of an experience which conclusively verifies it, inasmuch as it is the experience which the statement describes. Let it be granted that others besides myself can come to know that such a statement is true. Even so, their knowledge will not be direct. For it can be founded only upon experiences of their own, and however strongly these experiences favour the truth of the statement about my experience, they do not establish it conclusively. It remains at least conceivable that these experiences should occur and the statement in question be false. But no such possibility of error arises when an experience testifies only to itself. Thus the warrant for saying that I can have direct knowledge of my own experiences but not of anybody else's is just that my experiences are exclusively my own. The reason why I cannot directly know the experiences of another person is simply that I cannot have them.

But is it true that I cannot? There is a good and familiar sense in which two different people may be said to perceive the same object, hear the same sound, feel the same feeling, and from this it follows that they do have the same experiences. But, it will be answered, even though they may perceive the same objects or hear the same sounds, they do not sense the same sense-data: the sense-data which they respectively sense may be qualitatively similar but they cannot be numerically the same. And if it be asked why they cannot, the answer is that sense-data are made private by definition; they are characterized in such a way that the statement that one person has another's sense-data describes no possible situation. Similarly, if one person is afraid and another shares his feeling, it will still be said that there are two feelings of fear and not one. To say that the feeling is shared is to say that the two feelings are qualitatively similar and that they have the same ostensible object: it is not to say that they are numerically identical. But how are they differentiated? It is not to be supposed that one can number people's feelings as one can number the things that they may carry in their pockets. The answer is that we are to say that there are two feelings and not one, just because there are two persons. It is made a convention that any feeling that one has is an experience which is private to oneself. And so it becomes a necessary truth that one person cannot have, and therefore cannot strictly know, the experiences of another.

In this sense, then, to wish that one directly knew the thoughts and feelings of others is to demand a logical impossibility. It is not surprising, therefore, nor should it be a matter for dissatisfaction, that the wish cannot be gratified. The situation, however, is normally not so simple as this. In the end one may be in the ridiculous position of deploring a necessary truth; but at the outset the complaint that one does not know what others are thinking or feeling may very well have its source in empirical fact. It may in fact be the case that other people baffle or deceive me. I have some evidence to show what they are really like, but it is not sufficient for me. Even though they tell me, with every appearance of honesty, what is going on in their minds, I may still doubt whether they are telling me the truth. How can I ever be sure, in such a case, that I am not mistaken? A question of this sort frequently expresses a felt anxiety.

But how is this anxiety to be allayed? If someone finds himself in this position, what can be required to reassure him? Perhaps only that he should get to know other people better, and this he may achieve; it is at all events a practical problem. Perhaps he needs something out of the ordinary, like telepathy, which he may not in fact be able to achieve. But even if he were to achieve it he would be doing no more than add to his current methods of communication. What is strange about telepathy is that a message is transmitted, apparently without the employment of any physical means. But to be informed of another's feeling telepathically is not to share it; and even if it were to share it, there would be exactly the same grounds here as in the case of any other shared feelings for saying that there were two feelings and not one. There is the experience of the person who makes the communication and the experience of the person who receives it. These experiences are necessarily different, since they are the experiences of different persons, and this remains true no matter how the communication is made. In this respect telepathy is no better than the telephone.

The reason why telepathy is apt to be appealed to in this context is that it is regarded as a possible means of bridging the gap between one person and another. But if the gap is empirical in character, if it is a question of practical ignorance or misunderstanding, then there are surer ways of bridging it than by telepathy. And if the gap is logical, nothing can bridge it. It is suggested that in order really to know what another person is thinking or feeling, I have literally to share his experiences; and then it turns out that to share his experiences, in the sense required, is to have his experiences, and that in order to have his experiences I have to be that person, so that what is demanded of me is that I become another person while remaining myself, which is a contradiction. The contradiction is masked when the requirement is put in the form of my needing to know another person's experiences in the way that I know my own. For this may not seem too much to expect, until it is realized that the way in which I am supposed to know my own experiences is by actually having them, and that the reason why I cannot in this way know the experiences of others is that my literally having their experiences has been made a logical impossibility.

Just as the factual complaint that other people are opaque is carried to the point where the knowledge sought is made logically unobtainable, so there is a tendency to try to overcome this logical impossibility by making it only factual. No doubt telepathy is not enough, but if I were co-conscious with another person, then perhaps I should really know his experiences in the way that I know my own: I should really then succeed in being two persons at once. Now there is no reason why we should not describe certain paranormal phenomena by speaking of co-consciousness: and if someone who complains that other minds are closed to him is complaining only that he does not have such unusual experiences, his problem is still practical; he may hope to find some means of acquiring them. But even in an instance of co-consciousness it may still be argued that the gulf between persons remains. For either there is only one person involved, in which case all that is in question is his knowledge of himself, or there are two or more, and in that case there are as many sets of experiences as there are people. Each person has his own experiences, and no one can have those of any other person. The gap is not bridged, and never can be bridged, because, for someone who argues in this way, nothing is ever going to count as one person's having the experiences of another.

It is the crossing and recrossing of the line between the empirical and the logical that makes this a text-book problem in the theory of knowledge. The undoubted fact that one sometimes does not know what other people are thinking and feeling gives rise to the suspicion that one never really does know; the next step is to pass from saying that one never does in fact know what goes on in another person's mind to saying that one never can know, and interpreting this statement in such a way that it is necessarily true. But this appears to concede too much to scepticism, and so a move is made in the reverse direction. It is suggested that even if we never do in fact know what goes on in the minds of others, there might be circumstances in which we should. The assertion of our ignorance is thus reconstrued as empirical but, like an alien without a valid passport, it is constantly liable to deportation. As soon as an attempt is made to treat it seriously as an empirical statement, it tends to change back into a necessary truth. At this point it is tempting to lose one's patience with the problem. It is simply, one may say, a matter of what one chooses to understand by knowledge. If in order to know what another person is thinking or feeling I have literally to share his experiences, and if at the same time nothing is going to count as my literally sharing his experiences, then plainly nothing is going to count as my knowing, really knowing, what he thinks or feels. But the moral of this is just that if we interpret 'knowing' in so strict a fashion we deprive ourselves of the right to use it in this context. All that one has to do to defeat the sceptic is to give up the stipulation that in order to know what goes on in another's mind one must literally share his experiences; or, if the stipulation is to be retained, we must interpret it in such a way that it is at least theoretically capable of being met; one must allow it to be possible that experiences should, in the relevant sense, be common to different persons. In either case the question whether we can know what goes on in the minds of others becomes, what it ought to be, a question of empirical fact.

But this solution of the problem is too simple. The philosopher who raises doubts about our knowledge of other minds is not primarily concerned with questions of linguistic usage. He may readily admit that there is a sense in which different people can be said to share the same experiences: he may admit even that, as words are ordinarily used, it is perfectly legitimate to speak of a person's knowing what goes on in someone else's mind. Nevertheless he will insist that there must still remain a sense in which it is necessarily true that experiences are private, and necessarily true also that one cannot know the thoughts and feelings of others in the way that one knows one's own. Consequently, he will maintain, the statements that one makes about the experiences of others stand in need of justification in a way in which the statements that one makes about one's own experiences do not. The fact, if it be a fact, that it is socially correct in certain circumstances to speak of knowing such statements to be true is beside the point. The question at issue is what such claims to knowledge can be worth.

Even so, it may be said, the sceptic's difficulties are illusory. Let us allow it to be necessarily true that I cannot know the experiences of others in the way that I know my own. It by no means follows that I cannot have good reasons to believe in their existence. Such reasons will indeed be supplied to me by experiences of my own, just as the reasons which someone else may have for believing in the existence of my experiences must ultimately be supplied to him by experiences of his own. But they may be good reasons none the less. Even if knowledge is defined so strictly that one can never rightly claim to know what others think or feel, it will still be true that we can attain to states of highly probable opinion. It may well be thought perverse to insist on speaking of highly probable opinion in cases where attention to ordinary usage should lead us to speak of knowledge; but this is not a point of any great importance. What is important is that many of the statements which one makes about the experiences of others are fully justifiable on the basis of one's own.

But once again this manner of disposing of the problem is too simple. We are still left with the question how these statements can be justified and how the insistence that they shall be justifiable conditions their interpretation. There is here an instructive parallel to be drawn with the case of statements about the past. Thus, just as it is necessarily true that I cannot have the experiences of another person, so is it necessarily true that I cannot now experience a past event. Accordingly, if I am asked what reason I have to believe in the truth of any statement which refers to the past, the best answer that I can make is to produce a record, whether in the form of memory or some other. And with this most people would be satisfied. Even though no form of record be infallible, when different records agree they are willing to rely upon them. But philosophers are not so easily satisfied. They point out that it is logically possible that all the records should be false and, what is more, that it is logically impossible to test them, since that would require returning to the past. Then some attempt to elude the logical necessity by claiming that in remembering an event we actually return to the past, a view which they express less crudely by saying that memory is, or may be, a form of direct knowledge, that when an event is remembered it may be literally re-experienced. And others argue that since our reasons for believing a proposition about the past always come down to our having some experiences in the present, or expecting to have some experiences in the future, propositions about the past are really propositions about the present or the future in disguise. But both are mistaken. Propositions about the past are not about the present or future: they are about the past. And if an event is past in the sense which is here in question, its occurrence is logically independent of any present experience, even if the present experience is a memory of it and the memory is veridical. In the same way my knowing, or believing, that some other person is having an experience of a certain sort is not my having his experience; and in saying, on the basis of certain evidence, that he is having this experience, I am not merely giving a redescription of the evidence.

But if my statement is not just a redescription of the evidence, then one is inclined to say that it must be an inference from it. And this brings back the question whether, and how, the inference is justified. To which, as we have seen, the usual answer is that it is justified by an argument from analogy. But here we come upon the difficulty that the argument, at least as it is commonly presented, is not like any ordinary argument of this type. In the ordinary way, an argument from analogy is a substitute for direct observation. Suppose that the symptoms of two diseases are similar in certain respects and that I have discovered that one of the diseases is caused by a microbe of a certain sort: I may infer by analogy that the other disease also is caused by a microbe which I have not so far observed, and I may then set about trying to detect it. Had I already detected it, I should not need the argument from analogy to establish its existence. But what is the direct observation for which the argument from analogy is a substitute in the case of other minds? There is nothing describable as detecting the thoughts and feelings of another apart from adding to the premises of the argument, that is, collecting further information about his behaviour. And it is for this reason that many philosophers hold that the argument from analogy is invalid in this case. Yet surely part at least of my reason for ascribing thoughts and feelings and sensations to others is that I have them myself. Suppose that someone tells me that he has had a tooth extracted without an anaesthetic, and I express my sympathy, and suppose that I am then asked, 'How do you know that it hurt him?' I might reasonably reply, 'Well, I know that it would hurt me. I have been to the dentist and know how painful it is to have a tooth stopped without an anaesthetic, let alone taken out. And he has the same sort of nervous system as I have. I infer, therefore, that in these conditions he felt considerable pain, just as I should myself.'

Now here I do argue by analogy and up to a point the argument proceeds like any other. By analogy with what I have observed of other people and what I have learned about myself, I infer that someone with the relevant sort of nervous system, when operated on in such and such conditions, will show signs of pain, signs that I may well be able to detect if I watch him closely enough. But then I want to go further and argue from the existence of these signs to the existence of his actual feeling of pain, which *ex hypothesi,* since it is not my feeling, I cannot detect. And at this point some philosophers will object. 'You want to infer from the shadows on the blind to the existence of the people inside the room; but the parallel does not hold. For there is nothing which corresponds in this case to going into the room and meeting the people. It is rather as if you were to look for the invisible fairy that you supposed to animate your watch. You are succumbing to the myth of the ghost in the machine.' [1] Nevertheless I maintain that my feeling pain when the dentist operates on me does supply me with a reason for believing that my friend feels pain when the dentist operates on him; and that when I say that my friend feels pain, I do not mean merely that he shows signs of pain. I mean to ascribe to him a feeling of the same sort as I have myself. But what, it may be asked, are we to understand by this?

This question takes us back to the first of the propositions which I began by listing, 'When someone other than myself says that he has a headache, what he is saying about himself is the same as what I

---

[1] Cf. John Wisdom, *Other Minds, passim,* and Gilbert Ryle, *The Concept of Mind.*

should be saying about myself if I were to say that I had a headache.'
A shorter and more familiar form of this proposition is: "When someone other than myself says 'I have a headache' what he means is the
same as what I mean when I say 'I have a headache.' " But when it is
put in this way, there is clearly a sense in which the proposition is
false. For when he says 'I have a headache' he means that he has a
headache, and when I say 'I have a headache' I mean that I have a
headache, and since we are two different persons our meanings are not
the same. There is, however, a sense in which they are the same. For
if he is using the English language correctly, he uses the words 'I have
a headache' to state that he has a headache and not, for example, to
state that he has a toothache or that he has seen a ghost; and I too, if
I am using the English language correctly, use the words 'I have a
headache' to state that I have a headache, and not that I have a toothache or that I have seen a ghost. Rules can be given for the correct use
in English of expressions like 'I have a headache,' and these rules are
intersubjective in the sense that not only I but anyone can follow
them. Thus the reason for saying that what my friend means when he
says that he has a headache is the same as what I mean when I say
that I have a headache is that our use of the expression 'I have a
headache' conforms to the same rules.

The next question to consider is whether, when I say of him that
he has a headache, what I am saying about him is the same as what I
say about myself when I say that I have a headache. And here again
the answer is that it is the same in so far as the use of the expression
'he has a headache' is governed by the same rules as the use of the expression 'I have a headache.' There are, indeed, peculiarities about
the use of personal pronouns, especially in the first person, which make
these two expressions function somewhat discrepantly; but there is
still a sense in which they may properly be said to conform to the same
rules. Thus, the statement that he has a headache is not entailed by
'he says he has a headache,' or by 'he groans and clutches his head,'
or by any combination of such statements, any more than the statement that I have a headache is entailed by any statements about what
I say, or about my overt behaviour, or by any combination of such
statements. And just as my saying that I have a headache and my behaving in certain ways is good evidence in favour of my having a headache, and none the less good because I myself do not require it, so his
saying that he has a headache and his behaving in certain ways is good
evidence in favour of his having a headache, and none the less good
because he does not require it. But the evidence, though good, is not
conclusive. It does not constitute the meaning of the statement whose
truth it supports. What it means to say of any person, whether myself
or any other, that he has a headache is that he has a headache, that his

head is hurting him, that he feels pain in his head. It does not mean that he says he has a headache, or that he gives any outward signs of pain. But his saying that he has a headache, or his showing signs of pain, may be the best evidence that those who are not the person in question ever in fact have for concluding that he really is in pain.

But now some philosopher may say: 'Is it really good evidence? Prove to me that it is good evidence.' To which one might answer, 'He is a truthful sort of person, and people do commonly tell the truth in these circumstances unless they have special reason not to, and he seems to have no motive for lying to us in this instance'; or 'When people behave in this sort of way they generally do have headaches.' 'But how do you know that they do?' 'Well, I do for one, and So-and-so says that he has a headache when he behaves in this way, and he usually tells the truth.' 'But how do you know that he is truthful?' And then I give the evidence. 'But perhaps he is truthful about the things that you can test, but not about his own thoughts or feelings. How do you know that this is not so? Can one ever really know anything about the thoughts and feelings of another?'

This threatens to bring us back to the point from which we started. Let us see if we cannot now find a way of escaping from the circle. It would seem that this is one of the cases in which the denial that knowledge is attainable has its source in the fact that those to whom it is denied are regarded as being in some way underprivileged. We cannot really know what happened in the past because we cannot go back and look. The best evidence that we can now obtain is not the best conceivable; this follows simply from the fact that we are not contemporary with the events in question. So, if really knowing is to be equated with having the best evidence conceivable, it becomes, as I have said, a necessary fact that one cannot really know the truth of any statement about the past. In the same way, we cannot really know what is going on in some other part of space. This seems a smaller deprivation than the other because of the possibility of visiting the place in question. If we cannot visit it, it is for a practical and not a logical reason. Even so, it takes time for us to travel, and by the time we get to the distant place the event will be past. Our evidence for its occurrence will not be so good as it could be, as it might have been if we had been at the right place when the event was still present. But it is impossible, logically impossible, that, being where we are, we should also be somewhere else. Once more we are necessarily underprivileged, given our actual situation. It is not necessary that we should be in this situation, but it is necessary that if we are in this situation, then we are not also in some other which is incompatible with it. One might have lived at a different time, though it is arguable that this is not to be admitted without qualification. To say of someone living now that he might have lived many million years ago provokes at least the query whether he could, in that case, still be the same person: on the other hand, it appears to make quite good sense to say that one might be a few years older or younger than one is. And clearly one might at any given moment be in a different place from that in which one happens then to be. A statement which misdescribes a person's spatial position is false but not self-contradictory. But if the best possible evidence for the truth of a statement is to be obtained only by those who are in a spatio-temporal situation which happens not to be ours, it does follow necessarily that we cannot obtain it. And if it is, by definition, only the privileged, the eyewitnesses, who can really know the fact in question, then, given that we are not among them, it is necessarily true that we can never really know it.

It does not follow, however, that we are reduced to scepticism. So long as we hold it to be theoretically conceivable that we should be in the privileged situation, the fact that we are not is not regarded as condemning us to utter ignorance. We are not inclined to say that the evidence we can obtain is good for nothing at all just because it is not, and in the circumstances cannot be, the best possible. Thus, when it is a question of knowing about events which are remote from us in space, we are quite ready to accept inductive arguments. For, in such cases, the handicap from which we suffer, though logically insuperable, is easily overcome in our imagination. It seems to us that we might very well be privileged, even though we are not; that in some straightforward sense we could be there among the eyewitnesses, rather than here where we are, in fact. And this assumption that direct evidence is theoretically accessible to us is all that we require to make us content with indirect evidence, provided, of course, that this is good of its kind. When the handicap is due to our position in time, it does indeed appear more serious. We find it less easy to conceive of ourselves as occupying a different position in time than as occupying a different position in space; and this difficulty, as I have remarked, increases as the time envisaged is more remote. The doubt arises whether events occurring at a distant time are even theoretically accessible to us, whether there is any sense in saying that we might have been in the best possible position to observe them; and this in its turn throws doubt upon the validity of the evidence that we are in fact in a position to obtain, however good of its kind it may appear to be. Nevertheless this doubt does not, as a rule, take serious hold even upon philosophers. The fact that some at least of the events which are now remote from us in time have been, or will be, offered to our observation secures their admission into the category of those that are theoretically accessible, and the warrant is then extended to the other mem-

contained in any mere description of an experience, or even in a description of the person whose experience it is, so long as no reference is made to the identity of the speaker. The use of pronouns like 'he' and 'they' and 'you' shows that the speaker is not himself the person whose experiences are in question, and consequently that he is not in the most favourable position to know about them, just as the use of tenses or of words like 'miles away' shows that the speaker's spatio-temporal position is not privileged. But the implied, or explicit, reference to the situation, or identity, of the speaker is logically irrelevant to the facts which he describes. When these demonstratives are replaced by descriptions it becomes an open question whether the speaker is, or is not, in the best possible position to verify his statement. Suppose that the statement does in fact refer to the experience of some other person. Even so, what is stated is just that someone who answers to a given description is having such and such an experience, and from this it does not follow, with regard to any person who is not actually identified as one who does not answer to the description or is not having the experience, that he is not the person in question. It does not follow, therefore, that the description is not satisfied by the speaker himself. Once it is stated that an experience is the experience of someone other than myself, the possibility of its also being my experience is indeed ruled out. But so long as the statement contains no explicit or implicit reference to me, it can be no part of its descriptive content that I am relatively ill-equipped to verify it. In a sense, therefore, there are no such things as statements about other minds. There are many statements which do in fact refer to the experiences of persons other than the speaker. But they do not themselves state that this is so. Considered only with respect to its descriptive content, no statement says anything about the point of view from which it is made.

What is asserted, then, by a statement which in fact refers to the experience of someone other than myself is that the experience in question is the experience of someone who satisfies a certain description: a description which, as a matter of fact, I do not satisfy. And then the question arises whether it is logically conceivable that I should satisfy it. But the difficulty here is that there are no fixed rules for determining what properties are essential to a person's being the person that he is. My answer to the question whether it is conceivable that I should satisfy some description which I actually do not, or that I should be in some other situation than that in which I am, will depend upon what properties I choose, for the occasion, to regard as constitutive of myself. Ordinarily one does not regard one's spatial position as constitutive of oneself, and so can readily conceive that, apart from casual obstacles, one might at any given moment be in a different place from that in which one is. Neither does one regard as constitutive the property of living at the precise time at which one does. On the other hand, the property of living at about that time does tend to be regarded as constitutive of the person: and this is the explanation of the fact, which we have already noticed, that while one can easily imagine oneself to be a year or two older or younger than one is, the picture of oneself as living many million years ago has about it an air of contradiction. But it is contradictory only if one chooses to make it so. It is logically, although not causally, possible that having the character I have, nothing else being regarded as essential, I should have lived in the ice age. It is logically possible even that I should under this condition have had my actual memories, though of course they would in that case all have been delusive. In general, it would appear that one can imaginatively deprive a person of any particular property that he possesses without falling into contradiction, but that as this procedure is continued there comes a point where he ceases to be the same person. But the determination of this point, that is, the decision to regard a certain set of properties as being indispensable, is very largely arbitrary. So long as some are kept constant, all the others can be varied, and with the choice of a new set of constants the ones that were previously held constant can be varied in their turn.

Let us now see what bearing this has upon our present problem. The analogy between two persons is never perfect: this follows simply from the fact that they are two different persons. Neither can one suppose it to be perfect; for to suppose it perfect would be to merge the two persons into one. At the same time, it may be very extensive, and it can always be conceived as being more extensive than it is. Now when one ascribes some inner experience, some thought or feeling, to another, the rational ground for this ascription consists in one's knowing him to possess some further properties. The assumption is that there is a uniform connection between the possession of these properties and the undergoing of an experience of the sort in question. I infer that my friend is in pain, because of the condition of his tooth, because of his nervous system, because of his wincing, and so forth; and the connection of these properties with a feeling of pain is one that I can, in principle, test, one that I may in fact have tested in my own experience. But, it may be objected, the connection may not hold good in his case. How can you tell? But if it does not hold good in his case, this must be because of some other property that he possesses, the addition of which creates a counter-example to the rule. It would not hold good, for instance, if the additional property were that of his having been hypnotized to feel no pain. But with regard to any further property that he possesses it is conceivable at least that I should test the rule so as to find out whether the addition of this property does make a difference. Sometimes I can carry out the test directly by myself acquiring the properties concerned. Of course there are many properties that I cannot acquire. If I happen, for example, to have been born on a Thursday, I cannot directly test the hypothesis that people who were born on a Wednesday do not in these circumstances feel pain. But I have no reason to suppose that this is a relevant factor, and good indirect evidence that it is not. And, if our agument is correct, there will be no properties that I am in principle debarred from testing, however many there may be that I cannot test in fact. But even if my friend has no properties which make him an exception to the rule about feeling pain, may he not still be an exception just as being the person that he is? And in that case how can the rest of us ever know whether or not he really does feel pain? But the answer to this is that nothing is described by his being the person that he is except the possession of certain properties. If, *per impossibile,* we could test for all the properties that he possesses, and found that they did not produce a counter-example to our general hypothesis about the conditions in which pain is felt, our knowledge would be in this respect as good as his: there would be nothing further left for us to discover.

To sum up, it is necessarily true that, being the person that I am, I am not also someone else. It is necessarily true that I could not conceivably satisfy all the descriptions that some other person satisfies and still remain a distinct person. And if this is made the requirement for my really knowing what he thinks or feels, then it is necessarily true that this is something that I can never really know. On the other hand, with regard to any given property, which I may or may not myself in fact possess, there seems to be no logical reason why I should not test the degree of its connection with some other properties: and what I am asserting when I ascribe an experience to some other person is just that the property of having it is co-instantiated with certain others. The inference is not from my experience as such to his experience as such, but from the fact that certain properties have been found to be conjoined in various contexts to the conclusion that in a further context the conjunction will still hold. This is a normal type of inductive argument; and I cannot see that it is in any degree invalidated by the fact that, however far one is able to extend the positive analogy, it always remains within the compass of one's own experience.

C. H. WHITELEY

Behaviourism

To say of somebody that he is in a given state of mind is, as a rule, to attribute to him characteristics of two different kinds. On the one hand, it is to say something about his actual or potential behaviour, behaviour being something which can be observed by other people just as well as by himself. On the other hand, it is to say something about feelings, sensations, thoughts, etc., which he is aware of, but nobody else can be aware of—in one word, his "experiences." Thus we may say that mental concepts comprise factors of two kinds, an inner or private and an outer or public. One can feel angry and behave angrily, feel drowsy and behave drowsily, feel anxious and behave anxiously, feel gratified and behave in a gratified manner, and so on. In these examples, both factors in the concept are integral to it, in the way in which both being covered with fur and having a propensity to mew are integral to the concept "cat." Cases in which a man feels drowsy but behaves alertly, or feels fresh but behaves drowsily (like cases of cats which don't mew or have no tails) can occur, but are anomalous. In such cases we should be reluctant to use the word "drowsy" without qualification. Similarly, a man may behave sympathetically without feeling sympathetic, or feel sympathetic without behaving sympathetically; but these cases are anomalous, and we cannot apply the words "sympathy" and "sympathetic" to them in a quite straightforward way.

Many philosophers of the past have treated mental concepts as though only their inner components were essential, the behavioural factors being merely accessories, attached to the concepts because a certain sort of behaviour normally accompanies the sort of experience

From C. H. Whiteley, "Behaviourism," *Mind*, XX, No. 278 (1961). Reprinted by permission of the author and the editor of *Mind*.

which primarily constitutes the state of mind. This is an error, which not only misrepresents linguistic usage, but misrepresents the character of mental life as we perceive and understand it. My concern is with the complementary error, that of supposing that mental concepts can be construed as essentially behavioural, the private components being either ignored or regarded as dispensable accessories; so that a man's being drowsy consists in his behaving in a certain way, and the way he feels is irrelevant in determining whether he is drowsy or not. This is what I shall mean by Behaviourism. I shall maintain that this view also misrepresents both linguistic usage and the acquaintance we have with the operations of our minds.

Behaviourism seems to me to draw most of its plausibility from a single argument, which I shall now consider. The argument goes like this: Since experiences are private, it is impossible for one man to know what experiences another man is having. Therefore, if being in a given state of mind involves having certain kinds of experience, one man can never know that another man is in a given state of mind. If mental-concept words referred to inner experiences, we could not learn their meanings, and we could never know whether we were applying them correctly or incorrectly. But it is clear that we often do know that other men are angry, drowsy, anxious, and so on. Since all that we can know of other men is their behaviour, it is to their behaviour that words of this type must refer.

It must first be observed that this argument splits into two, which have different conclusions. They are sometimes made more plausible by not distinguishing between them. "Smith cannot know what Jones is feeling" may mean that there is no process of observing and thinking whereby Smith may come to have a confident belief as to what Jones is feeling; or it may mean that any such process of observing and thinking fails to come up to the standard required for calling it "knowledge." The former argument is psychological; it is concerned with what we actually believe. The latter argument is epistemological; it is concerned with what we have a right to believe. The two arguments lead to different conclusions. The psychological argument leads to the conclusion that we do not really have firm beliefs about one another's experiences, and therefore such beliefs cannot play a part in the formation of our mental concepts. Thus a behaviouristic analysis must be given of the concepts everybody actually employs. This is sometimes called Analytical Behaviourism. The epistemological argument leads to the conclusion that though we may have such beliefs, and they may play a part in the mental concepts we actually employ, yet these beliefs ought not to be taken seriously, and in rigorous thinking we should do well to replace our existing hybrid concepts by purely behavioural ones. This is sometimes called Methodological Behaviourism, since it advocates the adoption of behavioural concepts for scientific purposes. The two arguments coalesce only on the assumption that the mental processes by which concepts come to be formed always conform to high standards of logical propriety. This assumption is not plausible. It is especially important to notice that the epistemological argument is quite irrelevant to the analysis of common-sense concepts. "The Greeks could not have *known* (i.e. had adequate reason to believe) that there were creatures with men's heads and horses' bodies; therefore they must have meant something else by the word Centaur" is an obviously unsound argument. Thus it is incumbent on the analytical Behaviourist, not merely to show that there is no sound process of reasoning whereby men may have come to form firm beliefs about the experiences of other men, but that there is no such process of reasoning at all.

Now there is a traditional account of how these beliefs may have come about. I am supposed to have arrived at the conviction that other people have certain sorts of experiences by observing an analogy between my own behaviour and theirs. When I behave drowsily I also feel drowsy, when I behave irritably I also feel irritable. Therefore, I suppose, probably other people feel as I do when they behave as I do. This account is unconvincing. An individual who is in a certain state of mind gets a very different impression of his condition and behaviour from the impression he gets of other people who are in a similar state of mind. A man in a temper is aware of the offensive behaviour and impudent expression of the person who is annoying him, and of his own mounting excitement and tension; he is not aware, as outsiders are, of the way he changes colour and raises his voice. A drowsy man notices a muzziness of sensations, an intermittence of attention: he does not notice the slackness of his posture or his failure to reply to other people's remarks. He may indeed yawn; and this behaviour is physiologically similar to the yawning he observes in other people when they are drowsy. But it is not empirically similar; there is no resemblance between what I am aware of when I yawn and what I am aware of when you yawn in my presence (unless, what is unlikely, I do my yawning in front of a mirror). Thus the analogy between my own behaviour when in a given mental state, and that of other people when in a similar state, though it is genuine, is not obvious; and the more completely I am in the grip of a passion, the less likely I shall be to pay attention to it. It is not obtrusive enough to account for the firm beliefs about other people's experiences which we acquire at relatively early levels of intellectual development.

This analogical reasoning is, I fancy, the sole source of our opinions about the inner life of animals; and we may see from this how little it will tell us. What have we got in the case of human beings that we have not got in the case of horses and rabbits? The obvious answer is Language; and, as we shall see, it is the correct answer. Essentially, we know about other people's experiences because they tell us about them. We know that they feel drowsy as well as behaving drowsily because they say so. But this solution to our problem seems circular. For surely other people can tell us about their experiences only if we already understand the words they use to describe them. And how can we understand those words as applying to private state if those private states are unobservable to us, and cannot be shown to us as what the words refer to?

I think that if we look carefully at the way language is learned, and are not too much impressed by an over-simple notion of "ostensive definition," we can see how such words come to be understood, and how the connection is established between the inner and outer factors in our mental concepts.

Let us suppose that A and B are experienced users of a language and C is a learner who is in their company and hears them speak; and let us suppose that A and B from time to time use, say, the word "drowsy" both with reference to one another and with reference to C. Their criteria for using it of one another and of C will of course be purely behavioural. Now C, in the course of learning the language, will observe that A says of B "B is drowsy" whenever B behaves in certain characteristic ways. C will also observe that A says of him "You are drowsy" whenever he, C, has certain characteristic feelings. The connection between drowsy feelings and drowsy behaviour is established in C's mind by the fact that A uses the same word in connection with them both. I do not see how else it could be established. It would, of course, be possible for C to interpret "drowsy" as having two distinct and unconnected uses, one in which it refers to feelings like his own, and another in which it refers to behaviour like B's. It would also be possible for him to interpret it as referring to a complex phenomenon, part of which he notices in his own case, and part in B's case. Two things will dispose him to take the latter alternative, i.e. to connect the inner and outer features as parts of a whole. One is the analogy, already noticed, between his own behaviour when he feels drowsy and the behaviour of other people who are said to be drowsy, which enables him sometimes to apply the whole two-sided concept to himself. This analogy, though it is hardly obtrusive enough to serve as the sole foundation for our belief in other people's experiences, is obtrusive enough to be noticed to some extent under the guidance of language, and to help in the construction of one concept of drowsiness instead of two. The other relevant consideration is that A will sometimes say "I am drowsy" when he is not giving any evident signs of drowsiness. If this remark is to have sense, it must be taken as referring, not to A's overt behaviour, of which there is none, but to feelings, which A is aware of but C is not.

Thus the clue by which I learn about the inner states of others is the fact that the same words which people use on the occasion of certain outward behaviour of other people are also used by them on the occasion of certain inner experiences of my own, the criteria for their using these words being of course my behaviour. It is only by the use of language that men come to regard each other in anything but a behaviouristic fashion. I infer that animals, lacking the use of language, have only a behaviouristic understanding of one another. (One consequence of this is that animals cannot be moral agents.) The behaviourist wants to put us all on the animal level.

It would, of course, be possible for adult philosophers to adopt a purely behavioural definition of mental words, and to adhere consistently to this definition if they exercised sufficient care (which would be quite a lot). But it would not be possible for them to teach the words in these purely behavioural senses to their children or to other learners of their language. For any such learner would inevitably connect a word like "drowsy" when applied to himself with his own drowsiness as it appeared to himself, that is, mainly with his feelings. He would still, like the rest of us, have to be re-trained as an adult to replace his inner-and-outer concept by a purely outer one.

I turn now to consider the reasonableness of making this replacement. This involves examining the second, the epistemological, interpretation of the argument with which I am concerned. Let it be conceded that we do in fact entertain confident beliefs about one another's states of consciousness. It may still be argued that these beliefs lack the certainty and reliability required before we can allow them the name of "knowledge," or admit them as facts amongst the data of science. In particular, it may be argued, they do not reach the same standard of certainty and reliability as our beliefs about one another's bodily behaviour. Therefore, if we wish to achieve a genuinely scientific understanding of human nature, we must base this understanding on the established facts of human behaviour, and ignore whatever fancies we may indulge in about the inner experiences lying behind this behaviour. What men do can be observed; what they feel or imagine can only be guessed at. A scientific concept of the mind must therefore be framed entirely in terms of what men do, since only this can be known with the sureness and accuracy which scientific investigation requires.

This is a sceptical argument of a type very familiar in the theory of knowledge. How rash to believe that material objects continue to exist when we are not observing them, since we cannot possibly verify this belief! How reckless to assume that our memories correctly represent the past, for we can never go back into the past to make quite sure that we have remembered correctly! How naive to suppose that the laws of nature that held good in the past, which we have seen, will continue to hold good in the future, which we have not yet seen! How childish to believe in other people's experiences, when they are destined to remain for ever other people's, and not our own! Most philosophers are liable to occasional dizzy turns of this sort. The remedy against them is to remind ourselves that, although there are indeed logical risks in all these intellectual ventures, the risks are well worth taking, because by taking them we can get to know very much that we could not know otherwise; because by taking these classes of beliefs as on the whole reliable we can build up coherent bodies of truths which confirm one another, and fit in with truths learned in other ways. The belief that we can learn what people are experiencing from what they say and do is justified in the same manner as the rest.

But while the general complaint "I never really *know* what anybody else is feeling" does not deserve much attention, we must take seriously those arguments which are designed to show that our evidence for men's inner states is of a radically inferior character to our evidence for their outer behaviour. What is there to be said for this point of view?

If you are conducting a psychological experiment of which I am the subject, then there is, from your point of view, an important difference between assertions about my behaviour and assertions about my experiences. My behaviour you can observe directly; and you can take special and accurate note of those particular features of it which happen to interest you. But for information about my experiences you must rely on my testimony. You are therefore at the mercy of any negligence, dullness, mendacity or misdirection of attention of which I may be guilty. In this situation there is an important difference between the reliability of your beliefs about my behaviour and the reliability of your beliefs about my experiences. But this difference is confined to *your* knowledge of *your* experiments. It does not extend to the knowledge of psychologists in general about experiments in general. If you communicate your observations of my behaviour, and I communicate my introspective reports, to a third party, the difference which exists for you does not exist for him. For if he has to take my word for what I experienced in the course of the experiment, and allow for the possibility that I have mis-observed or mis-reported those experiences, he has likewise to take your word for what you saw of my behaviour, and allow for the possibility that you may have mis-observed or mis-reported it. (Let nobody suppose that setting a man up as a scientist to conduct experiments forthwith immunises him against all liability to negligence, obtuseness or mendacity.) If a man were to set out to construct a science purely on the basis of his own observations, taking as data only those facts which he had personally observed, accepting as laws only those generalisations which he had himself experimentally established, any psychology so constructed would have to be purely behaviouristic. But, of course, the enterprise is impossible. Scientific theories can be built up only by making use of the observations of many investigators. The data which any one scientist uses are, in overwhelming majority, reports of what other people have observed. We cannot do science without relying on the testimony of other men as to what they have seen—that is, as to their experiences. But if this is to be admitted, what reason is there for excluding testimony regarding experiences of other kinds?

There is a reason, and it is concerned with the possibility of confirmation. For, it may be argued, if I claim to see a movement or hear a sound, it is in principle possible for you to verify my claim by seeing what I see or hearing what I hear; whereas if I claim to have a pain, a mental image, or a wave of unexpressed emotion, you cannot verify my claim by feeling what I feel. Assertions of the former kind are therefore in a more secure position, because they can be verified by many observers, whereas assertions of the latter kind can be verified by one person only. Thus the former are suited, and the latter unsuited, for inclusion among the data of science, just because science rests on the collaboration and agreement of many observers.

There are here two different points. First, it is in general the case that if a man sees or hears or smells something, then any other person in his immediate neighbourhood (given normal sight, uninterrupted vision, *etc., etc.*) will see or hear or smell something very similar; while if a man feels a twinge or an itch, a feeling of elation or depression, it is not in general the case that any other person in his immediate neighbourhood will feel something very similar. This enables us to distinguish between cases in which a man is aware of something public, and cases in which he is aware of something private. When he is aware of something public, his account of that thing can be checked against the accounts of other people who have been aware of that same thing. Hence we may conceive the notion of resting our scientific generalisations entirely on the observation of public things, extruding the private from our consideration. This notion, however, is naive and short-sighted. For in order to carry it out we must first establish which of the objects of our awareness are public, and which are private. How can we do this? The data we are aware of do not carry any public or private character on their faces. There is nothing about an ache to tell you that it is private, nothing about a bang to tell you that it is public. Anybody who supposes there is had better consider how he distinguishes those sensations of heat which are awarenesses of a public rise in the room temperature from those which are awarenesses of a private feverish condition. It happens that vision is usually an awareness of public objects. But this is not obvious, nor is it true of everything that is seen. There are after-images and muscae volitantes and illusions and hallucinations, there are conditions like colour-blindness and diplopia, producing characteristics in my visual data which are not present in other people's. We have to *discover* which of these visible characteristics are public, which are private. There is only one way of finding this out, namely, by finding out what other people are aware of on particular occasions, by comparing different people's reports of what they are seeing, hearing, feeling. Thus, the very possibility of establishing a distinction between public and private depends on our having reliable information about the experiences of other people. The notion of a science which rests only on information about the public is therefore radically incoherent. A man who knows nothing about the experiences of other men can do no kind of science; for he lacks the means for distinguishing those features of his experience which are due to the nature of the external world from those which are due to the peculiarities of his own constitution or situation.

The second point is this. There are some respects in which nearly all human beings are affected in a fairly uniform way by similar stimuli, and other respects in which they are affected in widely different ways by similar stimuli. Visual experience is of the former type, emotional experience of the latter. This difference bears on the important principle of scientific method that experiments should be repeatable. I can test your claim to have perceived something in a given experimental situation by bringing about a similar situation and seeing whether I perceive something similar. But this test works only on the assumption that my perceptual experience will be similar to yours in a similar situation. Where people are differently affected by similar stimulation, experiments are not repeatable. Here we must use more complicated techniques, such as comparing the average responses of similar groups of people. This difference is, therefore, of some importance. But two points need to be made concerning it.

(1) It is a difference of degree, and not of kind. There is much similarity in what two people see who are looking at the same scene, but the difference does not amount to identity; visual acuity and direction of interest will always make a difference. This difference is methodologically important. Astronomers have to reckon with the "personal equation" which makes different observers record differently the insant at which a star is seen to pass a given point; thus the subjective and variable intrudes into the scientific record. The personal equation in the reports of, say, anthropologists must be of vastly greater

importance. Conversely, there is a good deal of uniformity even in emotional responses; what frightens one man fairly often frightens other men too.

(2) This contrast is not identical with the contrast between public and private. Smells are public, tastes private; i.e. when I smell gas you can smell it as well, but when I taste a chocolate, nobody can taste it but me. But people agree about as well in their sense of taste as in their sense of smell, and our knowledge of the one is as extensive and reliable as our knowledge of the other. Pain is private; but the things that cause it are pretty uniform. If you drop a hammer on my toe, it is very uncertain what my subsequent behaviour will be. But everybody knows that I shall feel pain. If anyone doubts my assertion that I do feel pain, we have here an eminently repeatable experiment; and I am prepared to repeat it by dropping a similar hammer on the doubter's toe as many times as may be necessary to produce conviction. That men feel pain when hammers are dropped on their toes is a generalisation concerning the private, concerning experience and not behaviour. But it is nevertheless an amply confirmed experimental generalisation. What makes feelings of depression or amusement difficult for the scientist to handle is not the fact that they are private; it is the fact that they do not follow uniformly on specific stimuli.

In sum: while there are some sorts of experience which are not only private but peculiar, so that their character is incapable of confirmation by other people, there are other sorts of experience which are sufficiently uniform for their character to be established in the same manner as the character of public objects is established, that is, by repetition of experiments and concurrence of testimonies. And unless we can establish such facts about other people's experiences, we can never distinguish in our own experience what is subjective, private or peculiar from what is objective, public or normal.

I have been maintaining that facts about the experiences of men can sometimes be well established, and may, indeed must, be included amongst the data of science. The attempt to study human psychology without taking any notice of what people tell us about their experiences obviously deprives psychologists of valuable information. Because this is so, some psychologists, who accept the arguments against the scientific respectability of statements about experiences, have tried to avail themselves of the information provided by such statements without admitting that by doing so they were abandoning Behaviourism. The device for reconciling Behaviourism with reliance on testimony is to admit what people say as part of the data of your psychology, but to call it "verbal behaviour." As a scientist, you are not allowed to know that one of your subjects felt dizzy, but you are allowed to know that he spoke the words "I feel dizzy." "Remarks about the experiences of subjects," says one writer, "must be transformed into verbal statements recorded by the observer." [1] This is clearly a subterfuge. If psychologist A reads a paper by psychologist B, he does not take that paper as a specimen of B's behaviour; he takes it as information about what B observed and thought. His datum is not "B wrote the following words," but "B observed the following phenomena." Likewise, when the subject of a psychological investigation tells you about his experiences, what he says is not taken as a specimen of verbal behaviour, but as communication of fact (it doesn't usually matter what particular words he used, or how rapidly he spoke or in what tone of voice, but only what he *asserted*). Of course, he may be mistaken; he may lie. What this means is that the subject of a psychological investigation shares to some degree the status of a fellow-experimenter. His co-operation has to be obtained; his good faith has to be either presumed or doubted. He does not merely behave; he gives true or false information about the matter under investigation.

Finally, I must refer to a different kind of reason for adopting a Behaviouristic standpoint. This reason is metaphysical. It may be supposed that conscious processes play no part, or a negligible part, in the causal explanation of behaviour, and therefore we need take no notice of them. Much of the argument of Ryle and Wittgenstein points in this direction. For this view, traditionally called Epiphenomenalism, there is a great deal to be said, and I shall not argue against it here. I shall only say that, even if Epiphenomenalism is true, it does not provide an adequate reason for adopting a Behaviourist methodology. For even if the determinants of behaviour are wholly material, and their effects or reflections in consciousness are causally negligible, yet these conscious concomitants often provide us with useful clues, or even the only clues available, to what the physical conditions actually are. A physician may be entirely concerned with his patient's stomach, and not at all with his "mind." But if for this reason he neglected to ask the patient what sort of pain he felt, and when and where he felt it, and to use this information in his diagnosis, he would be a fool. It is equally foolish to assume that introspective reports can tell us nothing illuminating about the physical conditions determining behaviour. What does follow from Epiphenomenalism— and from other less extreme views of the mind-body relation—is that we need not suppose that what goes on in an agent's consciousness gives him an adequate idea of the determinants of his behaviour. His introspective reports provide only part of the information on which the psychologist must build his explanations; and they may often be entirely irrelevant and misleading. With this conclusion I entirely

---

[1] M. Argyle, *The Scientific Study of Social Behaviour*, p. 55.

agree. In so far as Behaviourism means simply the view that the business of psychology is the study of *behaviour,* that is, of the total response of the organism to the influences to which it is subjected, and not the study of conscious processes in detachment from their physical concomitants, I have no quarrel with it.

H. H. PRICE

Our Evidence for the
Existence of
Other Minds

1. In ordinary life everyone assumes that he has a great deal of knowledge about other minds or persons. This assumption has naturally aroused the curiosity of philosophers; though perhaps they have not been as curious about it as they ought to have been, for they have devoted many volumes to our consciousness of the material world, but very few to our consciousness of one another. It was thought at one time that each of us derives his knowledge of other minds from the observation of other human organisms. I observe (it was said) that there are a number of bodies which resemble my own fairly closely in their shape, size, and manner of movement; I conclude by analogy that each of these bodies is animated by a mind more or less like myself. It was admitted that this argument was not demonstrative. At the best it would only provide evidence for the existence of other minds, not proof; and one's alleged knowledge of other minds would only be at the most well-grounded opinion. It was further admitted, by some philosophers, that our belief in the existence of other minds was probably not *reached* by an argument of this sort, indeed was not reached by an argument at all, but was an uncritical and unquestioning taking-for-granted, a mere piece of primitive credulity; but, it was claimed, the belief can only be justified by an argument of this sort.

This theory, which may be called the Analogical Theory, has come in for a good deal of criticism, and has now been generally abandoned. Perhaps it has sometimes been abandoned for the wrong reasons; for some of its critics (not all) seem to have overlooked the distinction between the genesis of a belief and its justification. However

From H. H. Price, "Our Evidence for the Existence of Other Minds," *Philosophy*, 13 (1938). Reprinted by permission of the author and the editor of *Philosophy*.

this may be, I shall not discuss the theory any further at present. My aim in this paper is to consider certain other theories which have been or might be suggested in its place, and to develop one of them at some length.

With the abandonment of the Analogical Theory a very different view, which I shall call the Intuitive Theory, came into favour. It was maintained that each of us has a direct and intuitive apprehension of other minds, just as he has of his own, or at least that he intuitively apprehends some other minds on some occasions, for instance in a conversation or a quarrel. It was said that there is social consciousness as well as self-consciouness, a direct awarenes of the "thou" as well as a direct awareness of the "me." I wish to emphasize that this consciousness was held to be a form of knowing, not merely belief (however well-grounded), still less taking-for-granted. And I think it would have been said to be knowing by acquaintance—extrospective acquaintance as we might call it—though doubtless this acquaintance would make possible a certain amount of "knowledge about," just as when I am acquainted with a noise I may know about the noise that it is shrill or louder than some previous noise.

This view might be worked out in several different ways. Do I have extrospective acquaintance with foreign selves, or only with foreign psychical events, from which foreign selves can somehow be inferred? Or would it be said that foreign selves, and my own self too, are only logical constructions out of extrospectible or introspectible data? Again, is my extrospective acquaintance confined to human minds, or does it extend to sub-human and super-human ones, if such there be? It is certain that some who held this kind of theory thought that it did extend to super-human minds at any rate; for they thought that religious experience, or at any rate one of the types of experience covered by that label, was an extrospective acquaintance with the Divine Mind. And I suppose that some might claim an extrospective acquaintance with what we may call ex-human minds, minds which once animated human bodies, but now animate them no longer (and perhaps with ex-animal minds, if there are any?).

We should also have to ask just what the special circumstances are which make this extrospective acquaintance possible. For clearly it does not occur in all circumstances. Otherwise we shall never be deceived by waxworks; we could tell at a glance whether the man we see lying by the roadside is unconscious, or dead, or only shamming; and we should know at once whether the words we hear are uttered by a gramophone or by an animate and conscious human organism.

I do not propose to pursue these questions any further. I only mention them to suggest that the theory requires a more detailed and thorough working out than it has yet received. But perhaps it is well to add that it derives no support whatever from the phenomena of telepathy. No doubt there is strong empirical evidence for the occurrence of telepathy. But the telepathic relation appears to be causal, not cognitive; it is more like infection than like knowledge. An event E_1 in mind No. 1 causes an event E_2 in mind No. 2, without any discoverable physical intermediary. It may be that E_2 resembles E_1 fairly closely. For instance, E_1 might be the seeing of a certain scene accompanied by a feeling of horror, and E_2 might be the imaging of a visual image closely resembling that scene, accompanied by a similar feeling of horror. But E_2 is not a *knowing* of E_1; just as, when you have scarlet fever and I catch it from you, my fever is not a knowing of yours.

But some advocates of the Intuitive Theory proceeded to take a further step, which we must now consider. We were told, and still are, that the problem before us was mis-stated. We started by assuming that every man has from the first a direct introspective awareness of himself, or of mental events in himself, and the problem was to justify his beliefs concerning other selves. The Analogical Theory said that they were justified by observation of other human bodies. The Intuitive Theory said that they were justified by occasional acts of extrospective acquaintance; or rather it said that some of them are not beliefs, but intuitive knowings, and that the rest (which *are* only beliefs) are justified by the evidence which these occasional extrospective knowings provide. But, it is now suggested, the problem has been stated the wrong way round; we are being puzzled at the wrong things. The really puzzling thing, it is suggested, is *self*-consciousness, not consciousness of other people. What comes first in the historical order is consciousness of one's neighbour, extrospective consciousness. Consciousness of oneself only come later, after considerable mental development; in some cases perhaps, say in the idiot or the very primitive savage, it never comes at all. Nor is the order merely historical. It is epistemological too. When I do come to know my own mind, I only come to know it by contrast with my neighbours' minds which I have been knowing from the first.

It may, however, be objected that this is only true of attentive and discriminating self-consciousness. Might I not have been *aware* of myself from the first, even though it required time and pain before I attended to this internal datum and discriminated it from other objects of my awareness? To meet this difficulty, the theory is sometimes stated in a still more radical way. It is suggested that the primary thing both in the historical and the epistemological order is a consciousness whose object is not "you" nor "me," but "us." This primitive *we-consciousness* can be called neither introspective nor extrospective, but is that out of which both introspection and extrospection have developed. Each man as he grows up gradually learns to distinguish between different parts of this orginally given we-object, and in particular to distinguish between "me," "you," and "the rest." But this achievement, it is suggested, is not an entirely stable one. In times of great emotional stress, as in a battle or a riot, it may break down. One then slips back into the primitive and undiscriminating we-consciousness, and is aware only that "we" are doing or feeling so and so. Such occasions are very rare in the life of the civilized man. But in the very primitive savage it may well be the other way round. Perhaps he only manages to distinguish between "me" and "you" once or twice in a lifetime.

We have now described several different forms of the Intuitive Theory. They differ as to the relation between introspective acquaintance and extrospective acquaintance, between self-consciousness and social consciousness. But they all have one very important contention in common. They all maintain that there is such an experience as extrospective acquaintance, a direct and intuitive knowing whose object is either another mind, or at any rate an event in or state of another mind. But *does* extrospective acquaintance ever occur? Am I ever acquainted with a feeling of anger or of fear which is not my own? I am sometimes acquainted with my own thinking-processes. Am I ever *acquainted* with thinking-processes which do not occur in myself and have nothing to do with me? It seems to me perfectly clear that the answer to these questions is, No. Of course I am constantly taking for granted the existence of all sorts of foreign emotions and foreign thinking-processes. I take their existence for granted without the least hesitation or doubt. But this is a very different thing indeed from knowing them by acquaintance. If anyone professes that he does sometimes have such extrospective acquaintance with his neighbour's mental processes, I do not see how to refute him. But I can easily conceive both of a strong motive, and of a plausible but inconclusive argument, which might lead him to claim that he had such acquaintance when in fact he had not.

First, the motive. As a distinguished philosopher has said, "we don't want inferred friends." But still, though one does not want them, one may have to put up with them for lack of anything better. Secondly, the argument. It may be urged that unless there is some extrospective acquaintance, the beliefs which each one of us holds concerning other minds could not have the high degree of probability which some of them obviously do have. For where else could the evidence come from which is to give them this high degree of probability? Mere observation of other human organisms, such as the Analogical Theory appeals to, provides but weak evidence, if it provides any at all. One might try to cut the knot by offering a Behaviouristic analysis of statements about other minds, as Logical Positivism did in its wilder youth, on the ground that otherwise these statements would be unverifiable and so nonsensical. If my belief about another mind is really only a belief about the behaviour of a certain human organism, then no doubt I can find abundant evidence to justify it. But then what about statements concerning my own mind? These can be verified or refuted by introspection; so they are *not* to be analysed in a purely Behaviouristic way. But this leaves us with an intolerable asymmetry between statements about myself and statements about my neighbour. It seems perfectly obvious that words like "hear," "see," "fear," "think," have exactly the same meaning when I apply them to my neighbour as when I apply them to myself. If "*I* see a cat" means simply "this retina here is being stimulated by light-rays and these muscles are adjusting themselves to respond to that stimulus" (*e.g.* by stroking the cat, or offering it a saucer of milk), well and good; then we may analyse "Smith sees a cat" in an analogous way. Only, what is sauce for Smith must be sauce for me as well. The Behaviouristic analysis must apply to both statements alike, or else to neither. But as a matter of fact it seems to me clear that "*I* see a cat" cannot be analysed in this way. However much truth we recognise in the detailed contentions of the Behaviourists—and for my part I am prepared to recognise a great deal—I do not understand how anyone can hold a purely Behaviouristic theory about himself. Much of what we are pleased to call our thinking is doubtless nothing but talking or twitching of throat-muscles, and much of what looks like deliberate action may well be nothing but a complicated chain of conditioned reflexes. But unless I sometimes do think in the literal and non-Behaviouristic sense, how could I discover that at other times my alleged thinking is only talking? How indeed could I *discover* anything at all, or even understand the statements which Behaviourists make to me?

For these reasons it is certainly plausible to argue that unless extrospective acquaintance sometimes occurs, one's beliefs about other minds could not have the high probability which some of them obviously do here. For if extrospective acquaintance be excluded, we must fall back on ordinary perceptual observation. And then it seems we must have recourse either to the Analogical Theory or to Behaviourism, and neither gives us what we want. But I think that this argument, though plausible, is not conclusive. For Behaviourism and the Analogical Theory are perhaps not the only alternatives available. There is at least one other which deserves to be considered, and I propose to devote the rest of this paper to the consideration of it.

2. The suggestion I wish to examine is that one's evidence for the existence of other minds is derived primarily from the understanding of language. I shall use the word "language" in a wide sense, to in-

clude not only speech and writing, but also signals such as waving a red flag, and gestures such as beckoning and pointing. One might say, the suggestion is that one's evidence for the existence of other minds comes from *communication*-situations. But this would be question-begging. For communication is by definition a relation between two or more minds. Thus if I have reason to believe that a communication is occurring, I must already have reason to believe that a mind other than my own exists. However, it would be true, according to the theory which I am about to consider, that the study of communication is of fundamental importance. For according to it one's most important evidence for the existence of another mind is always also evidence for the occurrence of communication between that mind and oneself. Even so, the word "communication" has to be taken in a wide sense, as the word "language" has to be. Utterances which I am not intended to hear, and writings or signals which I am not intended to see, will have to be counted as communications, provided I do in fact observe and understand them. In other words, we shall have to allow that there is such a thing as involuntary communication.

Let us consider some instances. Suppose I hear a foreign body[1] utter the noises "Look! there is the bus." I understand these noises. That is to say, they have for me a *symbolic* character, and on hearing them I find myself entertaining a certain proposition, or if you like entertaining a certain thought. (It does not matter how they came to have this symbolic character for me. The point is that they do have it now, however they got it.) As yet I only *entertain* what they symbolize, with perhaps some slight inclination towards belief; for as yet I have no decisive ground for either belief or disbelief. However, I now proceed to look round; and sure enough there is the bus, which I had not seen before, and perhaps was not expecting yet. This simple occurrence, of hearing an utterance, understanding it and then verifying it for one-self, provides some evidence that the foreign body which uttered the noises is animated by a mind like one's own. And at the same time it provides evidence that the mind in question is or recently has been in a determinate state. Either it has been itself observing the bus, or it has been observing some other physical object or event from which the advent of the bus could be inferred.

Now suppose that I frequently have experiences of this sort in connection with this particular foreign body. Suppose I am often in its neighbourhood, and it repeatedly produces utterances which I can understand, and which I then proceed to verify for myself. And suppose that this happens in many different kinds of situation. I think

---

[1] I use a phrase "a foreign body" to mean "a body other than my own." As we shall see, it need not be a *human* body.

that my evidence for believing that this body is animated by a mind like my own would then become very strong. It is true that it will never amount to demonstration. But in the sphere of matters of fact it is a mistake to expect demonstration. We may expect it in the spheres of Pure Mathematics and Formal Logic, but not elsewhere. So much at least we may learn from Hume. If I have no direct extrospective acquaintance with other minds, the most that can be demanded is adequate *evidence* for their existence. If anyone demands *proof* of it his demand is nonsensical, at least if the word "proof" is used in the strict sense which it bears in Pure Mathematics. It is not that the demand unfortunately cannot be fulfilled, owing to the limitations of human knowledge. It is that it cannot really be made at all. The words which purport to formulate it do not really formulate anything.

To return to our argument: the evidence will be strongest where the utterance I hear gives me new information; that is to say, where it symbolizes something which I do *not* already believe, but which I subsequently manage to verify for myself. For if I did already believe it at the time of hearing, I cannot exclude the possibility that it was my own believing which caused the foreign body to utter it. And this might happen even if my own believing were, as we say, "unconscious"; as when I have been believing for many hours that to-day is Saturday, though until this moment I have not thought about the matter. I know by experience that my believings can cause my own body to utter symbolic noises; and for all I can tell they may sometimes cause a foreign body to do the same. Indeed, there is some empirical evidence in favour of this suggestion. The utterances of an entranced medium at a spiritualistic séance do sometimes seem to be caused by the unspoken beliefs of the sitters. That one mind—my own —can animate two or more bodies at the same time is therefore not an absurd hypothesis, but only a queer one. It cannot be ruled out of court *a priori,* but must be refuted by specific empirical evidence.

It might, however, be suggested that we are demanding too much when we require that the foreign utterance should convey new information. Would it not be sufficient if the information, though not new, was, so to speak, *intrusive*—if it broke in upon my train of thought, and had no link, either logical or associative, with what I was thinking a moment before? Thus, suppose that while I am engaged in a mathematical calculation I suddenly hear a foreign body say "to-day is Saturday." I did in a sense believe this already. I have received no new information. Still, the uttterance has no logical relevance to the propositions which were occupying my mind, and there was nothing in them to suggest it by association. Would not the hearing of this utterance provide me with evidence for the existence of another mind? I admit that it would, but I think the evidence would be weak. For I know by experience that my powers of concentration are exceedingly limited. Sentences proceeding from my own unconscious sometimes break in upon my train of thought in just this intrusive way. It is true that they usually present themselves to my mind in the form of verbal images. But occasionally they are actually uttered in audible whispers, and sometimes they are uttered aloud. How can I tell that these same unconscious processes in myself may not sometimes cause a foreign body to utter such intrusive noises? Their intrusive character is no bar to their unconscious origin. What we require is that they should symbolize something which I did not believe beforehand at all, even unconsciously. It is still better if they symbolize something which I *could* not have believed beforehand because I was not in a position to make the relevant perceptual observations. For instance, I hear a foreign body say "there is a black cloud on the horizon" at a time when my back is turned to the window, and then I turn round and see the cloud for myself. Or I am walking in pitch darkness in a strange house, and hear someone say "there are three steps in front of you," which I had no means of guessing beforehand; and I then verify the proposition for myself by falling down the steps.

3. It follows from what has been said that if there were a foreign body which never uttered anything but platitudes, I should be very doubtful whether it was independently animated, no matter how closely it resembled my own. In the instance given ("to-day is Saturday," when I already believe that to-day *is* Saturday) the platitude was a *singular* platitude, stating a particular matter of fact. But there are also *general* platitudes. Among these some are empirical, such as "there is always a sky above us," "all cats have whiskers"; while others are *a priori,* such as "$2 + 2 = 4$," or "it is either raining or not raining," and are true at all times and in all possible worlds. If there was a body which uttered only singular platitudes, I should be inclined to conclude (as we have said) that it was not independently animated; I should suspect that its noises were caused by my own believings, conscious and unconscious. If it uttered nothing but general platitudes, I might doubt whether it was animated at all. I should be inclined to think that it was a mere mechanism, a sort of talking penny-in-the-slot machine, especially if its repertoire of platitudes was limited; though it might occur to me to wonder whether any intelligent being had constructed it.

So far, then, it appears that if the noises uttered by a foreign body (or its visible gesticulations) are to provide adequately strong evidence for the existence of another mind, they must give me information.

They must symbolize something which I did not know or believe beforehand, and which I then proceed to verify for myself. If these conditions are fulfilled, I have evidence of the occurrence of a foreign act of perceiving—an act of perceiving which did not form part of my own mental history. But it is not really necessary that the information conveyed should be a singular proposition, restricted to one single perceptible situation. It might be general, as if I hear a foreign body say "some cats have no tails," or "all gold dissolves in *aqua regia.*" Neither of these is restricted to one single perceptible object or situation. Still, they are both empirical, and there is a sense in which even the second can be empirically verified, or at any rate confirmed, by suitable observations and experiments. Clearly such utterances as these do give me evidence for the existence of another mind; but not in the way that the previous utterances did, such as "there is the bus," or "there is a black cloud on the horizon now." They do not show that a specific perceptual act falling outside my own mental history is now occurring, or has just occurred. In one way they show something less —merely that some perceivings of cats or of gold have occurred at some time or other. But in another way they show something more: namely, that a foreign act of *thinking* is occurring or has recently occurred, directed upon the *universals* "cat," "tail," "gold," and "aqua regia." (Or if it be objected that even perceiving involves some thinking, directed upon universals in abstraction from their instances.)

But further, the information I received need not be empirical at all. Suppose I hear a foreign body utter the noises "if 345 is added to 169, the result is 514." I understand these noises, but as yet I neither accept nor reject what they say. For I have never worked out that particular sum before, or if I have, I have forgotten the result. However, I now proceed to work it out, and sure enough the result *is* 514. This, too, gives me evidence of the existence of another mind. But this time I get evidence simply of a foreign act of thinking, and not of any foreign perceptual act at all.

Here, however, we encounter a difficulty. It may be objected that this argument for the existence of another mind is quite different from the one used hitherto, and even inconsistent with it. In the previous cases everything turned on the difference between utterances which give me information and utterances which do not. But a mathematical statement, it is often said, tells me nothing about the world. For it is true whatever state the world may be in. And the like holds of all other *a priori* statements. (Accordingly some philosophers have said that all *a priori* statements are *tautologies.*) If so, how can a mathematical statement be called informative? But if it is not informative, then according to our previous argument the hearing and understanding of it can give us no evidence for the existence of a foreign act of thinking. Indeed, we ourselves gave the utterance "$2 + 2 = 4$" as an instance of a platitude above.

To this I reply that there is a sense in which many mathematical and other *a priori* statements *are* informative. It is true that they do not give information about empirical matters of fact, in the way in which such statements as "it is now raining" do, or "some cats have no tails." But they do assert something. They assert certain *entailments* (or necessitations, if you will). And though any entailment, once you have seen it, may be called obvious or evident, it is not on that account necessarily a platitude. The term "platitude" is relative. That which is a platitude to you need not be a platitude to me; and that which is a platitude to me at one time of my life may have been non-platitudinous to me at another. A statement is only a platitude to me when its truth is *already* obvious to me, *before* I hear the statement. If the truth of it was not obvious beforehand, but only becomes so afterwards when I have attended to the meaning of the symbols and to their mode of combination, then it has certainly told me something new which I did not know before. At the time when I heard it, it was certainly not a platitude for me, though it will be one in future if my memory is good. Even "$2 + 2 = 4$," though it is a platitude to me now, perhaps was not always one. When I first heard it, perhaps it told me something new which I had not been able to work out for myself. As Mr. Russell says somewhere, even the Multiplication Table was probably exciting in the time of King Aahmes; for at that time it was not platitudinous to anybody.

It appears, then, that mathematical statements (and likewise other *a priori* statements) can very well be informative, in the sense that they can tell one something which one had not previously found out for oneself; though the something which they tell is an entailment, and not an empirical matter of fact. If it be said that such statements are tautologies, then we must insist that there are novel tautologies as well as stale ones; and the hearing and understanding of a novel one does give strong evidence for the existence of another mind, though the hearing of a stale one gives none or very little.

4. In the situations hitherto mentioned the noises which I hear and understand are uttered by a foreign organism which I observe. And the foreign organism is more or less similar to my own. But of course I need not actually observe it. It suffices if I hear an intelligible and informative utterance proceeding from a megaphone or a telephone, from the next room or from behind my back. It may, however, be thought that such a foreign organism must be in principle observable if I am to have evidence of the existence of another mind, and further

that it must be more or less similar to my own organism. But I believe that both of these opinions are mistaken, as I shall now try to show by examples.

There is a passage in the Old Testament which reads, "Thou shalt hear a voice behind thee saying, 'This is the way, walk ye in it.' " Now suppose that something like this did actually occur. For instance, I am lost on a mountain-top, and I hear a voice saying that on the other side of such-and-such a rock there is a sheep-track which leads down the mountain. After the best search that I can make, I can find no organism from which the voice could have proceeded. However, I go to the rock in question, and I do find a sheep-track which leads me down safely into the valley. Is it not clear that I should then have good evidence of the existence of another mind? The fact that so far as I can discover there was no organism, human or other, from which the voice proceeded makes no difference, provided I hear the noises, understand them, and verify the information which they convey. Now suppose I go up the mountain many times, and each time I hear an intelligible set of noises, conveying information which is new to me and subsequently verified; but I never find an organism from which they could have proceeded, search as I may. I should than have reason for concluding that the place was "haunted" by an unembodied mind. Such things do not happen, no doubt. But still there is no contradiction whatever in supposing them. The point is that if they did happen they would provide perfectly good evidence for the existence of another mind. And this is sufficient to show that the presence of an observable organism is not essential; *a fortiori,* the presence of an observable organism more or less resembling my own is not essential.

Now suppose an even more extravagant case. The clouds might form themselves into Chinese ideographs before my eyes. I might be able to read Chinese, and I might find that these ideographs made up intelligible sentences, conveying new information which I could verify by subsequent observation. Or I might find that they stated a geometrical theorem which I could follow when it was put before me, but could not have discovered for myself. Here, again, I should have good ground for thinking that there was another mind communicating to me. But I could not form the remotest notion of what sort of organism it had; and so far as I could tell, it might have none at all.

In the two cases just considered no body was observed to produce the words, but at least the words themselves were perceived by hearing or sight. But even this is not essential. It might be enough if they presented themselves to me in the form of mental imagery, auditory or visual. Suppose that a sentence came into my mind in this way which conveyed information entirely new to me, information which I could not have inferred from anything I already knew or believed; suppose further that there was nothing in the preceding train of thought to suggest it by association. Then I should be inclined to think that this image-sentence was produced by some unconscious process in myself. The sentence might be "there is a wrecked motor car round the next corner." Suppose that on turning the corner I did find a wrecked motor car. I should be somewhat astonished, especially if the sentence had been a long and circumstantial one (mentioning, say, the colour and make of the car, and the number of its number-plate), and was verified in all or most of its details. Still, I should stick to the hypothesis that it was produced by my own unconscious, and should attribute the verification to coincidence. But if such things happened to me several times, it would be reasonable to consider the hypothesis that there was another mind, or several, communicating to me telepathically. And if experiences of this sort went on happening, all giving me new information which was subsequently verified, the evidence might become very strong.

It appears then that I could conceivably get strong evidence of the existence of another mind even if there was no observable organism with which such a mind could be connected. This incidentally is a new and fatal argument against the old Analogical Theory which was referred to at the beginning of this paper. For that theory maintained that one's evidence of the existence of other minds could *only* come from observing foreign bodies which resemble one's own. It is also clear that even when I do observe a foreign body producing the relevant utterances, that body need not be in the least like my own. There is no logical absurdity in the hypothesis of a rational parrot or a rational caterpillar. And if there was such a creature, I could have as good evidence of its rationality as I have in the case of my human neighbours; better evidence indeed than I can have in the case of a human idiot. There is no *a priori* reason why even vegetable organisms should not give evidence of being animated by rational minds, though as it happens they never do. If the rustlings of the leaves of an oak formed intelligible words conveying new information to me, and if gorse-bushes made intelligible gestures, I should have evidence that the oak or the gorse-bush was animated by an intelligence like my own.

Here it may be well to consider the case of parrots more closely, for they appear to cause some difficulty to my thesis. Parrots do make intelligible utterances. But we do not usually think that they are animated by minds like our own; and some even hold that they are not animated at all in the sense in which human bodies are, but are simply behaving organisms which respond in a complicated way to environmental stimuli. It is true that the utterances of parrots do not usually tell us anything new. But it is quite conceivable that they might. Suppose that I do hear a parrot make an utterance which gives me new information. This certainly gives me evidence for the existence of a mind *somewhere,* an intelligent mind like my own. But I should usually assume that the mind in question does not animate the parrot-organism itself. Why should I assume this? In default of further evidence, it would be quite unreasonable to do so. But, as it happens, I have learned from observation of other parrots that when they make intelligible noises they are not, so to speak, the original sources of these noises, but are merely repeating the utterances which some human body has made in their neighbourhood. Thus, when I receive information from the utterances of *this* parrot, I have reason to think that the mind which is responsible for it does not animate the parrot-body itself, but does (or did) animate some human body in whose neighbourhood the parrot has lived. The case is parallel to that of an echo. An echo coming from a wall might consist of intelligible noises, and they might give me new information. But I should not conclude that the wall was animated by an intelligent mind, because I know that walls do not spontaneously produce noises of that sort, but only *re*produce noises which are going on in the neighbourhood. The parrot is merely a sort of delayed echo. The like holds for gramophones and telephones, and possibly also for human sleep-walkers.

It must, however, be noticed that my reasons for thinking that these things are *not* animated by intelligent minds are all, so to speak, extraneous reasons, drawn from observations falling outside the situation itself. Suppose one did not have this extraneous information: one might, for instance, be a savage who understood English but had had no previous experience of the behaviour of these particular sorts of objects. It would then be perfectly reasonable to believe that parrots, gramophones, and telephones *are* animated by intelligent minds. For since the noises they utter are *ex hypothesi* intelligible and informative, there is evidence for the existence of an intelligent mind which produced these noises. And as one would then have no evidence for thinking that the production was indirect, it would be perfectly reasonable to conclude that the object from which the noises emanate was itself directly controlled by the mind in question. The conclusion, though reasonable, would of course be mistaken. But perhaps we ourselves are sometimes mistaken in just the same way. For all we can tell, some of the human talkers we meet with may be nothing but living gramophones controlled by minds not their own. Indeed, there is reason to think that something of this kind does happen temporarily in hypnosis.

We have seen that one's evidence of the existence of another mind comes from the receiving of *information* by means of intelligible symbols. In the cases hitherto considered the information turned out to be true, and I discovered this by testing it for myself. But it is not really necessary that it should be true, nor that I should test it. False information is just as good, so long as it *is* information. What is required is that the utterance should convey something which goes beyond what is already present to my mind, something which I did not consciously think of for myself, and which could not (so far as I can tell) have been presented to me by some process in my own unconscious. A piece of true information which I did not previously possess has this "going beyond" character. But a piece of outrageous fiction may also have it. Of course some fictions are as familiar to me as some truths. These stand on the same footing as platitudes, and the hearing or reading of them gives me no decisive evidence of the existence of another mind. But when I read a novel which I did not write, or hear for the first time a tall story which I did not invent, then I do have good evidence for the occurrence of mental acts not forming part of my own mental history. These foreign mental acts of which I get evidence are primarily acts of thinking. But I can infer that the mind in which they occur must also have had perceptual experiences more or less like my own at some time or other. For one can only make up a fictitious narrative by conceiving of universals, and these must have been abstracted from perceived instances. Or if it be said that there are some universals which are not abstracted from perceived instances, but are known somehow else (innately perhaps?)—viz., such formal or categorical universals as "cause" and "substance"—we may reply that no narrative could consist wholly of these. If it is to be a narrative at all, it must also contain non-categorical universals, such as "cat," "green," "to the right of"; and these at any rate must have been abstracted from perceived instances.

5. I have now tried to show by a number of examples that it is the perceiving and understanding of noises and other symbols which gives one evidence for the existence of other minds. I think it is clear that the situations I have described do provide evidence for this conclusion. But exactly *how* they do so is not yet clear. Before we discuss this question, however, there are three preliminary points to be made.

First, it is necessary to insist that there is nothing recondite about this evidence for the existence of other minds. It is not the sort of evidence which only philosophers or scientists or other experts can discover. Perhaps I have spoken as if it were suddenly presented to the notice of an intelligent and reflective adult, who has reached years of discretion without ever finding any good reasons for believing in the existence of another mind, and now finds some for the first time. But of course this is not really the position. The evidence I have spoken of is available to anyone, however youthful and inexperienced, as soon as he has learned the use of language. All that is required is that he should be able to receive information by means of words or other symbols, and that he should be able to distinguish between observing something and being told about it. (Perhaps he is not *self*-conscious until he is able to draw this distinction. If so, we may agree with those who say that consciousness of self and consciousness of others come into being simultaneously, though not with their further contention that consciousness of others is a form of acquaintance or intuitive knowledge.) Thus by the time that he has reached years of discretion evidence of the sort described is exceedingly familiar to him, little though he may have reflected upon it.

The second point is more serious. It may be objected that one cannot learn to understand language unless one *already* believes (or knows?) that the noises one hears are produced by a mind other than oneself. For if not, how would it ever occur to one that those queer noises which one hears are symbols at all? Must one not assume from the start that these noises are *intended* to stand for something? Then, but not otherwise, one can proceed to discover what in particular they stand for.

To this I reply, at first it does not occur to one that the noises *are* symbols. One has to discover this for oneself. And one discovers it by learning to *use* them as symbols in one's own thinking. One begins by merely noticing a correlation between a certain type of object and a certain type of noise, as one might notice a correlation between any other two types of entities which are frequently combined, say, thunder and lightning. The correlation is at first far from complete, for one sometimes observes the object without hearing the noise. But gradually one comes to imitate the noise for oneself. And thus the correlation becomes more nearly complete; if no foreign body says "cat" when I see a cat, I shall say "cat" myself. Thus a strong association is set up in my mind between that type of noise and that type of object. The next step after this is certainly a mysterious one, the more so as it is perhaps not literally a "next" step, but merely the continuation and completion of something which has been going on from the start. But the mystery has nothing to do with awareness of other people's intentions. It has to do with what used to be called the abstraction of universals from particulars. We must suppose that all conscious beings have the power of recognising that two or more particulars are similar to each other. No consciousness devoid of this power would be of the faintest use to its possessor; so it must be assumed that the lower animals, if they are conscious at all, can recognise at least some similarities, namely, those which are important for their biological welfare. But only some conscious beings can single out within the similar particulars that common factor in respect of which they are similar, and can conceive of it in abstraction; that is, at times when they are not actually perceiving or remembering any particular of the sort in question. This conceiving of universals in the absence of their instances is what we commonly call thinking. And it is for this that symbols are required; conversely, noises and the like only become symbols in so far as they are used as means to such conceiving. For example, I have seen many cats, and for some time I have found that the noise "cat" occurs when I see one (whether it is uttered by a foreign body or by myself, or by both). I must now attend to the common feature of all these objects, and learn to associate the noise with that. Then, when I hear the noise in future, whether uttered by myself or not, it will bring that common feature—that universal—before my mind, even if no cat is actually being perceived by me. When this happens, and not till then, the noise "cat" has become a symbol for me. The process is very puzzling, and I do not profess to have given anything like an adequate account of it. But whatever difficulties there may be about it, it does not seem to presuppose at any stage that one has a prior knowledge of other minds, or even a prior belief in their existence.

Thirdly, a word must be said about so-called Primitive Animism. According to some Anthropologists, primitive men take for granted that all bodies whatever (or at any rate all striking and noticeable ones) are animated by minds; and if this is so, it is plausible to suppose that civilized infants do the same. In that case, have we not stated our problem the wrong way round? The problem will really be "What leads us to believe that most of the bodies in the universe are *not* animated by minds?" rather than "What leads us to believe that certain ones *are* so animated?"

This objection is difficult to discuss because the facts are in dispute. When people say that the savage or the infant is an animist, they seem to be attributing a kind of philosophical theory to him—a set of explicit and formulated beliefs about the universe. But this seems to be an over-rationalization. Beings so primitive and unreflective cannot be accused of subscribing to any kind of "ism." It would be nearer the mark to say that the savage or the infant *acts as if* he thought that most of the bodies he meets with are animated. But I suspect that even this goes too far. All we can be reasonably sure of is that he acts as if he *did not distinguish* between the animate and the inanimate—he speaks angrily to the chair-leg against which he bumps, or tries a stone for murder[2]—whereas we ourselves treat the animate in one way and the inanimate in another. If so, the question is this: what evidence has one got that this non-distinguishing treatment, which is observed in

[2] This is said to have happened in ancient Athens even in classical times.

savages and infants, is unreasonable; what reason is there for thinking that a human body differs in some very important way from a rock or a tree, or even from a cow? And the evidence is the sort of evidence already mentioned. Rocks and trees never utter noises which convey information to us, nor make informative gestures, and it is exceedingly doubtful whether cows ever do; but it is certain that human bodies do frequently utter informative noises and make informative gestures.

However, even if it is literally true that savages and infants hold explicit "animistic" beliefs, this need not worry us. It is just a curious psychological fact, if fact it be. It makes no difference to the logic of the matter. For the point is, what *reasons* has one got for believing the proposition that all bodies are animate? And the answer is that in the case of human bodies one has strong reasons, whereas in the case of other bodies one has not. One could perfectly well discover this even though one did *not* start by believing the proposition to begin with, as the "Primitive Animist" is supposed to do. The initial believing, if indeed it occurs, is not a logical presupposition of the discovery. The evidence for a proposition is neither strengthened nor weakened by the fact that I believed the proposition before I began my inquiry.

6. We may now return to the main argument. We have described a number of situations in which the perceiving and understanding of symbols gives one evidence of the existence of another mind. But how exactly do they provide evidence for this conclusion? Let us confine ourselves for simplicity to the cases in which the evidence comes from the hearing of sounds. Two conditions, we have seen, must be fulfilled. The first, and most important, is that they must have a symbolic character. And they must be symbolic *for me*. It is obvious that the characteristic of being symbolic is a relational character. An entity S is only a symbol in so far as it stands for some object—whatever the right analysis of "standing for" may be. It is no less obvious, though sometimes forgotten, that the relation is not a simple two-term relation. It involves at least three terms: the entity S, the object O, and in addition a mind or minds. S symbolizes O *to someone*. The relation is more like "to the right of" than it is like "larger than." A is to the right of B from somewhere, from a certain limited set of places. From other places it is not to the right of B, but to the left of it, or in front of it or behind it.

But if the hearing or seeing of S, or its presentation to me in the form of an image, is to provide me with evidence of the existence of another mind, it is not sufficient that S should symbolize some object to someone. It must symbolize some object *to me*. I myself must understand it. Otherwise all I know about it is that it is a noise or black mark having such-and-such sensible qualities. It is true that if I heard sounds uttered in the Arabic language, which I do not understand, I could reasonably conclude to the existence of another mind. But only by analogy. The sounds have some similarity to others which *are* symbolic to me; I therefore assume that they, too, might come to be symbolic to me if I took the trouble.

Secondly, it is essential, I think, that the sounds should symbolize to me something *true or false*. They must propound *propositions* to me. It is not, however, necessary that they should have the grammatical form of a statement. A single word may propound a proposition. Thus the word "snake" may be equivalent to "there is a snake in the immediate neighbourhood." Again, the phrase "the bus" may be equivalent to "the bus is now approaching." Must the proposition propounded be such that I can *test* it, whether in fact I do test it or not? It must certainly be such that I know what the world would be like if it were true. Otherwise I have not understood the symbols: for me they are not symbols at all. But it is not necessary that I should be able to discover by direct observation that the world is in fact like that, or is not. Otherwise I could not understand statements about the remote past, whereas actually I can understand them perfectly well.

The third condition is the one which we have already emphasized. The noises must not only be symbolic to me; they must give me information. The proposition which they propound must be new to me. That is, it must be new to me as a whole, though of course its constituents and their mode of combination must be familiar to me; otherwise I do not understand the utterance. If it is not new (i.e. new as a whole) the noises do still give evidence of the occurrence of a mental act other than the present act which understands them, and even of a mental act which is in a sense "foreign." But as we have seen, it might conceivably be an unconscious mental act of my own. And this greatly diminishes the evidential value of the utterance.

Now suppose these conditions are fulfilled. I hear noises which are symbolic to me; they propound to me something true or false; and what they propound is new to me. For instance, I hear the noises "here is a black cat" at a time when I do not myself see the cat and was not expecting it to appear. How exactly does this situation provide me with evidence of the existence of another mind? (It is well to insist once again that evidence, not proof, is all that can be demanded.)

It might be said: I have direct access to a number of cognitive acts by my own introspection. I find that these acts are usually accompanied by noises, audible or imaged. Moreover, I find by instrospection that an act directed upon one sort of object e.g. a cat, is usually accompanied by one sort of noise; and that an act directed upon another sort of object, e.g. blackness, is usually accompanied by another sort of noise. Thus there is a correspondence between the noises and the acts. Differences in the noises are accompanied by differences in the "direction" of the acts. When the object of the act is complex, I usually find a corresponding complexity in the noise. If n_1 usually accompanies an act directed upon O_1 and n_2 usually accompanies an act directed upon O_2, then I find that the complex noise n_1n_2 is usually accompanied by an act directed upon the complex object O_1O_2. And the structure of the complex noise (the way the constituent noises are arranged) varies with the structure of the object-complex upon which the accompanying act is directed. In this way, it may be said, I know from introspection that when the noise-complex "here is a black cat" occurs it is usually accompanied by a specific sort of cognitive act, namely, by the seeing and recognising of a black cat. But this time it cannot have been a cognitive act of my own, for *I* was not seeing any black cat at the time when the noise-complex occurred. It must therefore have been a foreign cognitive act, an act extraneous to myself, and therefore presumably forming part of the history of some *other* mind.

However, such an account of the matter is not altogether satisfactory. The relation between the noises and the mental acts is really much more intimate than this. It is not a mere accompanying. If it were, the noises would not be functioning as *symbols*. When I am thinking I am always aware of symbols of some sort or another. But they do not just occur along with the thinking. The occurrence of them, whether in a sensible or an imaged form, is an integral part of the thinking itself. One might even define thinking as awareness by means of symbols. Perhaps, indeed, I can *perceive* without symbols. But in fact symbols usually are present to my mind in perceiving as well. And if they are present, again they do not merely accompany the perceiving. They enable me to analyse what I perceive, to recognize and classify the various factors in it, so that the perceiving turns into what philosophers call perceptual judgment, a piece of intelligent or thoughtful perceiving.

Thus the argument should be restated as follows: I know from introspection that noises of this sort frequently function as *instruments to* a certain sort of mental act (not merely accompany it). Therefore they are probably functioning as instruments to an act of that sort in the present case. But in the present case the act is not mine.

But there is still a further amendment to be made. There is a sense in which the noises *are* functioning as symbolic instruments to a mental act of my own. For after all, I do understand them. It is true that I am not seeing the black cat. But I do entertain the thought that a black cat is in the neighbourhood. And I think this *by means of* the noises that I hear. But if the noises are in any case functioning as instruments to a mental act of my own, what need have I to suppose that there is also some other mental act—some foreign one—to which they are instrumental?

To clear up this point, we must distinguish two different ways in which symbols can be instrumental to cognitive acts. We must distinguish *spontaneous* thinking from *imposed* thinking. In the present case, my entertaining of the thought that there is a black cat in the room is *imposed* by the noises which I hear. What causes me to use these noises as symbols is the noises themselves, or rather my hearing of them. When I hear them, they arouse certain cognitive dispositions in me (dispositions arising from my learning of English, which are there whether I like it or not); and the result is that I am forced to use them for the entertaining of a certain determinate thought, one which but for them I should not on this occasion have entertained.

But how did these noises happen to present themselves to me? I did not originate them, either consciously, or—so far as I can discover—unconsciously either. And how did they happen to be arranged in just that way? They are so arranged that they make up a whole which is for me a single complex symbol, symbolizing something true or false about the world. That is how they manage to impose an act of thought upon me, which many of the noises I hear do not, striking and complicated though they be. How did this remarkable combination of events come about? How is it that each of the noises was for me a symbol, and how is it, moreover, that they were so combined as to make a single complex symbol, symbolizing something true or false? Well, I know from my own experience how it might have happened, because I know what happens in *spontaneous* thinking. In the spontaneous acts of thinking which introspection reveals to me, noises often function as symbolic instruments. And when they do, they are not usually found in isolation. They are ordered into complexes, each of which is symbolic as a whole and signifies something true or false. It would not be correct to say that I find two acts occurring at once: on the one hand, an act of spontaneous thinking, on the other an act of spontaneously producing symbols and ordering them into a symbol-complex which is true or false as a whole. What happens is that the producing of the significant symbol-complex occurs *in the process of performing* the spontaneous act of thinking. Sometimes this spontaneous act of thinking is concerned with something which I am perceiving. It is then a so-called perceptual judgment.

Thus I can now guess how the noises which I hear have come about, and how they have come to be such and so arranged that I am made to use them as instruments for an act of imposed thinking. For I know by introspection that just such noises, and just such an arrangement of them, are often produced in the course of acts of spontaneous thinking. This makes it likely that here, too, they were produced in the course of an act of spontaneous thinking. But in this case no spontanous thinking of that particular sort was occurring in myself. Therefore in this case the spontaneous act of thinking must have been a *foreign* act, occurring in some other mind. If the noises are "here is a black cat," the act was probably a perceptual judgment, occasioned by the perceiving of a black cat. But if on investigating the matter for myself I find no black cat, the evidence for a foreign act of thinking still stands. (As we pointed out earlier, false information is just as evidential as true.) Only I shall then have to conclude that this act of thinking was not a perceptual judgment after all, but a piece of fiction-making or story-telling.

In this instance the noise-complex was already familiar to me as a whole. I have often seen black cats and said to myself "here is a black cat." But this is not always so. When I hear a complex noise and find myself using it as an instrument for an act of imposed thinking, it frequently happens that the complex as a whole is one which I am not familiar with. Thus the noise-complex, "the steward of Common-Room keeps a tame mongoose," may be one which I have never myself made use of in an act of spontaneous thinking. Still, if I hear it, it will impose an act of thinking on me; not less so if I am sure that what I am being made to think of is false. And it will accordingly provide me with evidence of a foreign act of spontaneous thinking. This is because I often have used the *constituents* of the noise-complex in the course of my own spontaneous thinkings, for instance the noises "mongoose" and "steward" and "Common-Room." Moreover, although this actual combination of noises is new to me, the *manner* of combination, the structure which the noise-complex has, is perfectly familiar. I have often used it myself in the course of my spontaneous thinkings. Thus the noise-complex as a whole functions as a symbol for me, and imposes an act of thinking on me, even though I have never made use of it in any of my own spontaneous thinkings.

7. We must now raise certain general questions about this argument for the existence of other minds. Though very different in detail from the one used by the old Analogical Theory, it is clearly an argument from analogy. The form of the argument is: situations a and b resemble each other in respect of a characteristic C_1; situation a also has the characteristic C_2; therefore situation b probably has the characteristic C_2 likewise. The noises I am now aware of closely resemble certain ones which I have been aware of before (in technical phraseology, they are *tokens* of the same *type*), and the resemblance covers both their qualities and their manner of combination. Those which I was aware of before functioned as symbols in acts of spontaneous

thinking. Therefore these present ones probably resemble them in that respect too; they too probably function as instruments to an act of spontaneous thinking, which in this case is not my own.

But the argument is not only analogical. The hypothesis which it seeks to establish may also be considered in another way. It provides a simple *explanation* of an otherwise mysterious set of occurrences. It explains the curious fact that certain noises not originated by me nevertheless have for me a symbolic character, and moreover are combined in complexes which are symbolic for me as wholes (i.e. propound propositions). Many varieties of sounds occur in the world, and of these only a relatively small proportion are symbolic for me. Those which are symbolic for me can occur in a variety of combinations, and the number of mathematically possible combinations of them is very large; of these combinations only a small proportion "make sense," that is, result in noise-complexes which are symbolic for me *as wholes*. But if there is another mind which uses the same symbols as I do and combines them according to the same principles, and if this mind has produced these noises in the course of an act of spontaneous thinking: then I can account for the occurrence of these noises, and for the fact that they are combined in one of these mathematically-improbable combinations. When I say that these facts are "explained" or "accounted for" by our hypothesis, I mean that if the hypothesis is true these facts are instances of a rule which is already known to hold good in a large number of instances. The rule is, that symbolically-functioning noises combined in symbolically-functioning combinations are produced in the course of acts of spontaneous thinking; and the instances in which it is already known to hold good have been presented to me by introspection.

It may be objected by some that the hypothesis is worthless because it is *unverifiable*. Accordingly it may be said that it has no explanatory power at all, nor can any argument (analogical or other) do anything to increase its probability. For being unverifiable, it is nonsensical; that is, the words which purport to formulate it do not really formulate anything which could conceivably be true or even false.

Now it is true that the hypothesis of the existence of other minds is "unverifiable" in a very narrow sense of that word, namely, if verifying a proposition entails observing some event or situation which makes it true. I cannot *observe* another mind or its acts—unless extrospective acquaintance is possible, which there is no reason to believe it is. But the hypothesis is a perfectly conceivable one, in the sense that I know very well what the world would have to be like if the hypothesis were true—what sorts of entities there must be in it, and what sort of events must occur in them. I know from introspection what acts of thinking and perceiving are, and I know what it is for such acts to be combined into the unity of a single mind (however difficult it may be to give a satisfactory philosophical *theory* of such unity). Moreover, the hypothesis *is* verifiable in what is called the "weak" sense. I know what it would be like to find evidence to support it, because I have in fact found a great deal of evidence which does support it; and this evidence can be increased without assignable limit. It seems to me to be a mistake to demand that all the different types of hypothesis should be verifiable in the same manner. What is to be demanded is, first, that the hypothesis should be conceivable (otherwise certainly it is nonsense); and secondly that it should be verifiable or refutable in its own appropriate manner, in accordance with the methods suitable to that particular sort of subject-matter.

However, it is instructive to ask what one would be left with if one refused to entertain the hypothesis of the existence of other minds on the ground of its unverifiability. It would still remain the case that one thinks by means of symbols. Further, the distinction between spontaneous and imposed thinking would still hold good. Nor could one possibly deny that in imposed thinking one acquires information which one did not possess before. It is a rock-bottom fact, and one must accept it whatever philosophy one holds, that the thinking imposed by heard or seen symbols enlarges one's consciousness of the world far beyond the narrow limits to which one's own perception and one's own spontaneous thinking would confine it.[3] An extreme empiricist must accept this fact like anyone else. But the purity of his principles prevents him from attempting any explanation of it, since they force him to conclude that the hypothesis of other minds is nonsensical. So he must just be content to accept the fact itself. Or perhaps he may say: what I *mean* by asserting that there are other minds is simply this fact, that my own consciousness of the world is constantly being enlarged by the hearing of noises and the seeing of marks which are symbolic to me, and by the consequent acts of imposed thinking which go on in me; so that "you" is just a label for certain pieces of information which I get in this fashion, and "Jones" is a label for certain other pieces of information, and so on. In that case he, too, can admit that there are other minds. Indeed, he can say it is a certainty that there are, and not merely (as we have suggested) a hypothe-

---

[3] Here we may note that even the most rigorous course of Cartesian doubt requires the use of symbols. One cannot doubt without symbols to bring before one's mind the proposition which is to be doubted. And philosophical doubt, which is concerned with complicated and highly abstract matters, is scarcely conceivable without the use of *verbal* symbols. We may conjecture that Descartes himself conducted his doubt in French, with some admixture of Latin.

sis for which there is strong evidence. But obviously he is giving a very strange sense to the phrase "other minds," a sense utterly different from the one which he gives to the phrase "my own mind."

If I am right, there is no need to go to such lengths. One has evidence of the existence of other minds in the ordinary literal sense of the word "mind," the sense in which one applies the word to oneself. Nevertheless, the argument I have offered does have its sceptical side. Any mind whose existence is to be establishd by it must be subject to certain restrictive conditions, which follow from the nature of the argument itself. In the first place, it must use symbols which I can understand; and I shall only be able to do this if I am able to use them myself. It is true that I may be able to guess that certain noises or marks are symbolic even if I cannot myself understand them. But this, as we have seen, is because they have a fairly close resemblance to other noises or marks which I do understand. If I never understood *any* of the noises or marks which I hear or see, I should have no evidence for the existence of other minds. (Strictly speaking we ought to add "tactual data" as well. They, too, may be symbols for the person who feels them, as the case of Helen Keller shows.)

There is a second restriction of great importance: any mind whose existence is to be established by an argument must be aware of the same world as I am aware of. It must be such that the world which I am aware of is *public* to me and to it, *common* to both of us. This restriction really follows from the first. Unless the foreign symbols refer to objects which I too am aware of they will not be for me symbols at all. These public entities need not be sense-data. Sense-data might still be private, as many philosophers hold. It might even be, as some hold, that the sense-datum analysis of perception is mistaken from beginning to end, and that sensing is not a cognitive process at all, but is merely the being in a certain state ("seeing bluely," or the like). But still, if I am to have evidence of your existence, there must be publicity *somewhere*. Somehow or other we must both have access to one and the same world; if not by sensing, then by some other form of consciousness which sensing makes possible. Suppose this was not so. Suppose that there is another mind which is not aware of the same world which I am aware of, and suppose that it somehow produces noises which I hear or marks which I see. When it makes these noises, obviously I shall not have the faintest idea what it is talking about. How can I, since *ex hypothesi* the noises do not refer to any objects which I am aware of? But this is equivalent to saying that I have no reason whatever for thinking that it is *talking* at all. And so I shall have no reason whatever for believing that it exists, or even for suspecting that it does. The noises which I hear, even though in fact they

state the profoundest truths, will be for me mere noises, like the sough-
ing of the wind or the roaring of waves.

It appears, then, that any evidence which I can have of the existence
of another mind must also be evidence that the other mind is aware
of the same world as I am aware of myself. Philosophers have sometimes suggested that each mind perhaps lives in a private world of its
own. Probably no one believes this. But some people have been worried
by the suggestion. They have suspected that though incredible it could
not be rationally refuted, and have had recourse to mysterious acts of
faith to get them out of their difficulty. But the difficulty does not
exist, for this speculation of philosophers is nothing but a baseless
fancy. The theory is such that there could not conceivably be any
evidence in favour of it. Any relevant evidence one can get is bound
from the nature of the case to tell against it. Any evidence that I can
get of your existence is bound also to be evidence that you do *not* live
in a private world, but in the public world which is common to all
intelligences, or at least to all those which can have any good reason
to believe in one another's existence.

Another and less welcome restriction which our argument imposes
concerns the minds of the lower animals. It is commonly held that the
lower animals do not use symbols. Now this may be an overstatement.
Possibly some of the higher vertebrates do use them on some occasions.
It may be that some of their cries have a symbolic character (though
they would be extremely vague and ambiguous symbols), and some of
their bodily movements and postures may constitute a crude kind of
gesture-language. If this is so, then our evidence for consciousness in
them is the same in kind as our evidence for the consciousness of our
human neighbours, though it is very much smaller in extent. But there
is no reason to suppose that snails and oysters speak, even in the widest
sense of the word "speak," or that anyone has ever received information from a caterpillar; not that there is any *a priori* reason why these
things should not happen (cf. our remarks on parrots above), but so
far as we know they do not. However, these are empirical questions of
Natural History, which do not concern me. I only wish to insist that *if*
the lower animals do not use symbols—symbols which we can understand and which convey information to us—then our evidence for the
existence of animal minds is different in kind, and not merely in
degree, from our evidence for the existence of human minds. It can
only be evidence of a teleological sort, derived from observation of
their bodily behaviour. Much of the behaviour of animal bodies has
an apparently purposive character, and suggests that they are moved
by wishes and are adapting means to preconceived ends. But it is not
easy to say how strong this evidence is. How are we to distinguish be-

tween genuine purposiveness and mere *de facto* conduciveness to certain results, say to the survival of the animal or its species? The movements of the cat in the presence of a mouse are such as to increase the probability that the mouse will be caught. But is there more in the situation than this? Is it at all clear that the cat *wishes* to catch the mouse, and consciously controls its movements in accordance with this wish? Moreover, we find the same appearances of purposiveness in plants. We also find it in all sorts of biological phenomena which no one supposes to be under conscious control: in the anatomical structure of every type of organism, in the mutually co-ordinated growth of its parts, in the circulation of the blood, and in countless other cases. If once we start assuming that wherever there is purposiveness there is mind, we shall end with a most unplausible and extravagant form of Vitalism; every organism, even the humblest vegetable, will have to be endowed with an intelligence—an intelligence far exceeding our own in its scientific knowledge and its inventive capacity.

I shall not pursue these questions further. Perhaps the difficulties which I have mentioned can be met. I only wished to point out that when communication by means of symbols is lacking, the existence of foreign minds cannot be established in any simple or straightforward way; or if it can, it looks as if the word "mind" would have to be used in a sense somewhat different from that which it has when applied to beings who do communicate by means of symbols. (Cf. the difficulties which arise concerning "unconscious mind" in ourselves.) Thus, when Descartes maintained that human beings are conscious but the lower animals are not, this theory was by no means a foolish one, though it may be mistaken. Certainly there was no logical inconsistency in it. Our reasons for attributing consciousness to other human beings are radically different from our reasons (such as they are) for attributing it to the lower animals. Only he seems to have drawn the line in the wrong place. The line should really be drawn between those beings who use symbols and those who do not. If any animals do use symbols, they come above it; and if any human beings do not, they fall below it, even though they happen to walk on two legs.

8. My argument for the existence of other minds is an argument from language (in a wide sense of that word). It may, however, be objected that I have considered only the *informative* function of language. But of course language is not merely informative. It also has what is called an *emotive* function. This again may be subdivided. In so far as it gives vent to the emotional or conative attitude of the speaker—gives vent to it, not describes it—language may be called *expressive*. In so far as it is designed to arouse the emotions of others, or to influence their actions, it may be called *evocative*. Now many

would hold that in the language of everyday life (and it is this, not the language of science or philosophy, which concerns our present inquiry), the emotive function is quite as important as the informative, or, indeed, much more so. Would it not be very naïve to suppose that the main point of everyday language is to say things which are true or false? The main point of it surely is to express one's emotions and wishes, and to evoke those of others. Is it not this which makes language a *social* instrument? Or rather, since the word "instrument" suggests something which might conceivably be dispensed with and replaced by a substitute, let us say that language is the basis of society —a society is a set of minds which talk to one another. The contention then is that what makes it so is primarily its emotive function. Thus many who would agree that one's evidence for the existence of other minds comes from the perceiving and understanding of symbols would nevertheless complain that I have been approaching the problem from the wrong end. For I have been considering only the informative function of language, whereas according to them it is the emotive function which is of primary importance.

Now, of course, I agree that in any complete account of the nature and function of language great attention must be paid to the emotive side. But I am not concerned in this essay to suggest a theory of language, nor even the barest sketch of one. I am concerned simply with an *epistemological* problem: how the understanding of language gives each of us reason to believe in the existence of other minds. And for this purpose only the informative function of language is relevant. The reason for this is that one's access to another mind is not direct. One gets access to it indirectly by way of the *objects* which the other mind and oneself are aware of in common. If we like to speak of a "social relation" between one mind and another, then my contention is that this relation involves three terms, not two. It involves not merely the two minds, but also some object which they are both aware of. Or again: since I am never directly acquainted with another mind, my evidence for its existence can only be evidence for the existence of something satisfying a certain *description;* and the description must always contain a reference to some object or objects which we are aware of in common.

This primacy of the object is what makes the emotive function of language irrelevant to our present inquiry, however important it may be in other connections. Indeed, it is worse than irrelevant. If we allow it to intrude, we shall be involved in a vicious circle. For one can only understand the emotive aspect of an utterance (in that sense of the word "understand" which is here appropriate) if one has *already* got reason to think that the utterance was produced by a foreign mind. Once I have found out, by other means, that the foreign mind is there, I can get evidence that it has certain emotions and certain intentions, and I can discover certain rules for correlating these emotions and intentions with certain tones of voice and turns of phrase, as will be explained presently. But the evidence that it *is* there comes from the informative side of its utterances.

For what is the alternative? When people maintain that it is the emotive element in language which gives us our evidence for the existence of other minds, how are they going to work out this suggestion in detail? I think they must say that tone of voice, and likewise bodily bearing and facial conformation, *directly convey* to me the existence of foreign emotions and volitions. It is not enough to say that these features of utterances or of organisms "express" emotions or volitions, though doubtless they do. Your tone of voice may be ever so expressive. But the point is, how am I to *discover* that it is expressive, and what in particular it is expressive of? Why should I not be content to notice that the noise which this body utters has a peculiar raucous quality like the grating of a wheel, or a soft flowing quality like the sound of running water? And these facial grimaces— what makes me think that they are more than curious visible changes, like the flickering of a flame? No doubt these particular qualities of vocal noises do have what one may call a moving character. They give me so to speak a psycho-physical shake; and one may well suppose that the human organism has an innate tendency to be specially moved by them. But the fact that I myself am stirred by hearing a certain noise gives me no ground for inferring that someone else is feeling an emotion. Even if the emotion to which I am stirred happens to be just like the emotion which you felt when you uttered the noise, this does not help. It is not enough that there should in fact be a foreign mental state which my own mental state resembles—if indeed it does. For the question is, how am I to discover that there *is* this foreign mental state? So far this question has not been answered.

I can only think of one way in which it could be answered by those who hold that one's primary evidence for the existence of other minds comes from the emotive element in language. They must have recourse to a theory of "direct conveyance," as suggested above. They must say that the tone of a voice or the momentary configuration of a face enables me to be *directly aware* of the occurrence of a foreign emotion or volition. That is, they will have to hold that the experiencing of such-and-such auditory or visual qualities releases in me a certain cognitive capacity which cannot otherwise be exercised: a capacity for apprehending other minds, or their states, intuitively and immediately. They smuggle in this direct revelation under cover of the word "expressive," and so make their theory seem less paradoxical than it is. For it is really just a form of the Intuitive Theory, which was discussed earlier in this essay. The contention is that certain auditory or visual experiences—such as the hearing of a raucous tone of voice or the seeing of a facial grimace—enable me to perform an act of *extrospective acquaintance* whose object is a foreign emotion or volition. Perhaps the Intuitive Theory is more plausible in this form than in some others. But it is still open to fatal objections. How is it that I can be deceived by the voice or behaviour of an actor, who expresses emotions which he does not actually feel, or for that matter by ordinary everyday hypocrisy? Might there not be a moving wax-work whose face made lifelike grimaces, and which uttered noises in an angry tone of voice?

It appears then that important as the emotive element in language may be, it cannot provide one with one's evidence for the existence of other minds. But it still remains to ask how one does learn that other minds experience emotions and volitions. The evidence so far considered, derived from the informative side of language, shows only that they are percipients and thinkers. In other words, how does one learn that there *is* an emotive element in most or all of the utterances which one hears and understands, and likewise in writing and gesture?

Let us first consider utterances expressive of volitions. How do I get my evidence that other minds experience volitions? It is because I first get evidence that they are entertaining certain thoughts, and then find that the objective world is being altered in such a way as to conform to those thoughts. For instance, I am seeing a door and I notice that it is open. I then hear the words "that the door has got to be shut." At present, we are assuming, the expressive element in language conveys nothing to me (we are trying to explain by what process it comes to do so). So at present I can make nothing of the words "has got to," nor yet of the determined tone in which they are said. It is just a curious auditory quality which the noises have. But I *can* understand the words "that door" and "be shut," both of which refer to certain objective entities which I am aware of: the one to a certain material thing which I observe, the other to an objective universal which I am familiar with. Thus they bring before my mind *a proposition*, the proposition "the door is shut." Now this is a piece of information. It tells me something new which I did not believe before; I did not believe it before, because I believed the contrary, and indeed I still do. So far, then, I have merely received a piece of false information; still it *is* information, and therefore gives me evidence of the existence of a foreign mind which is holding a false belief, or at least entertaining a false proposition. But now a curious thing happens. The organism from which the utterance emanated proceeds to move in such a way that the door *is* shut. The situation is so altered that the information which was false before is now made true. Here, then, I have got evidence of the occurrence of a foreign thought which *affects the objective world*. There was a thought with which the objective state of affairs did not correspond; and immediately afterwards the objective state of affairs is altered so that it does correspond with this thought. Apparently this thought has somehow brought about its own verification. It was false when first uttered, but it has altered the situation in such a way as to make itself true.

Normally this alteration comes about by the intermediation of certain movements in the organism from which the utterances proceeded; it gets up and shuts the door. But even if I observed no organism, I could still get evidence of the existence of a foreign volition. Let us reconsider our previous instance of a disembodied voice. Suppose I heard such voice saying, "Let there be a thunderstorm"; and suppose there promptly was a thunderstorm, although hitherto there had been no sign that any such event was likely to happen (the sky, we will assume, was perfectly clear at the moment when the utterance occurred). And suppose that there were many instances of this sort of thing; many occasions when this voice made an utterance conveying a proposition which was false at the time, but was followed by an objective change which verified it—a surprising change, which no previously observable feature in the situation made probable. I should then have good evidence for thinking that the voice proceeded from a foreign thinker whose thoughts could directly alter the objective world. Such "telekinetic" action of unembodied minds does not in fact happen. But there is no logical absurdity in it. And it is no more difficult to understand how a mind can directly cause changes in the atmosphere than to understand how it can directly cause changes in an organism, which after all is only a complex material object.

We now see how one discovers that certain utterances are expressive of volitions. If one is to discover this, the utterance which expresses the volition must also have an *informative* side. It must among other things propound a proposition, one which is at the moment false. I learn that it is expressive of a volition because of the effects by which it is followed. And when I recognise that a sentence is expressive of a volition without actually observing the physical change which fulfils it, I do so by noticing that it resembles other utterances which *have* been observed to have such effects. It resembles them in respect of tone of voice, or in grammatical structure (by containing verbs in the imperative mood), or in respect of the gestures which accompany it. So I conclude that it, like them, is probably followed by an objective change which verifies it.

Thus it is quite wrong to suppose that the utterance "directly conveys" a foreign volition. There is no question of an immediate and infallible revelation, giving me direct insight into the volition of another person. The "conveying" is a misleading name for an induction which I have to do for myself, by observing that noises uttered in a certain tone of voice are frequently followed by objective changes which verify the propositions they propound.

Let us now turn to utterances expressive of emotion. Emotions are intimately related to thinking on the one hand, to action on the other; and in virtue of these two relations, they are also intimately related to the objective world. Every emotion includes some thinking, and this thinking is not a mere accompaniment, but is an integral part of the emotion itself. The thinking may consist in holding a false belief, as when one is afraid of a purely imaginary danger. But even so, certain objective universals must be present to the mind; else there could be no belief, not even a false one. I may be afraid of a lion outside a door, when in fact there is no lion within miles. But in order to have this "groundless" fear, I must conceive of *lionhood* and *outsideness*. It follows that any utterance which completely expresses an emotion must also propound a proposition, true or false. If someone says in a horror-struck voice, "Oh! a snake!" he is incidentally making a statement which gives me information; the information is, that there is a snake in the immediate neighbourhood. But how do I learn that the tone in which he speaks *is* a tone of horror? I answer, I learn it inductively. I discover by repeated observation that when an object is spoken of in that tone of voice, certain consequences are liable to follow. The objective situation is liable to change in a remarkable manner. The relation between the snake and the organism from which the noise proceeded does not usually remain what it was. The noise-making organism runs away, or strikes the snake with a stick. So when I hear that tone of voice again I conclude that such objective consequences are again likely to occur. We have seen that such utterances do propound propositions, and so give evidence of the occurrence of a foreign thought. But I have now found that when the utterance is in that tone of voice the foreign thought in question is a *tendencious* thought, one which tends to change the objective world in certain ways. And I can correlate differences in tone of voice (and in gesture or facial configuration) with different sorts of objective changes which are liable to follow. Thus I distinguish different sorts of tendencious thoughts, one tending to the avoidance of the object which the thought refers to, another tending to the pursuit of it, another to the destruction of it, and so on. And these are the different emotional attitudes.

It follows, and indeed is obvious in any case, that emotional attitudes and volitions are closely connected. Nevertheless, they are not expressed by the same sort of utterance. I discover that an utterance expresses a volition when I find that though false at the moment of its occurrence it results in an objective change which brings the facts into conformity with it. But utterances expressing emotions are related to subsequent objective changes in a more complex way than this. The objective change which follows varies with the specific quality of the utterance. This is not surprising. There is only one way of willing— setting yourself to bring into being the objective situation which you have thought of. But there are many different kinds of emotional attitude; one leads you to alter the objective world in one way, another in another way.

There are, however, certain emotional attitudes which appear not to influence conduct at all, and so do not affect the objective world; for instance, emotions about the past. How am I to discover that an emotion of this sterile kind is occurring in a foreign mind? The utterance which expresses it will indeed propound a proposition to me, and so give me evidence of the occurrence of a foreign thought. But it may seem that in this case the thought has no tendenciousness about it. To this I reply that if the foreign utterance really does express an emotion (and of course hypocrisy is always possible), then the thought of which it gives evidence *is* tendencious, though in rather a different way. Let us consider an emotion directed upon a historical character. Suppose that a man admires the Emperor Valentinian I. If he does, his thinking about that emperor does have effects, effects which it would not have if instead of admiring he disapproved of him. It does not affect the thinker's actions, but it does affect the course of his subsequent thoughts, and this will be revealed by subsequent utterances. We shall find, for instance, that he tends to talk about the good qualities of his hero rather than the bad ones: say, about his military efficiency rather than his atrocious bad temper. If we do not find this, we shall suspect that his utterance did not express emotion at all, but was merely a piece of hypocrisy. Thus in these cases the tendencious character of the thinking lies in the selective control which it exercises upon later thinkings, in directing the thinker's attention upon one set of facts rather than another, and even causing him to ignore certain facts altogether. Thus we may say that in these cases, as in the others, the emotion reveals itself by its tendency to affect one's subsequent relations with objects: only "objects" must be understood to include thinkable objects as well as perceived ones, and "relations" must cover cognitive relations as well as practical ones.

part three

CONCERNING
A PERSON'S KNOWLEDGE
OF PHYSICAL OBJECTS
IN HIS IMMEDIATE
VICINITY

A. J. AYER

Phenomenalism

~~~~~~

1

I shall be concerned in this paper with phenomenalism as a theory
of perception. In the form in which it is usually held nowadays, it is
the theory that physical objects are logical constructions out of sense-
data. Assuming that we understand what is meant by a physical object,
in the sense in which chairs and tables and match-boxes are physical
objects, we are left with the questions: What is a logical construction?
and What are sense-data? At the risk of repeating an excessively
familiar story, I shall begin with the sense-data.

I believe that the word 'sense-datum' was first used as a technical
term in philosophy by Bertrand Russell: and he defined sense-data as
objects of acquaintance. But this definition leaves us none the wiser
unless we know what is meant in this context by 'acquaintance.' In
the ordinary way, we talk of being acquainted with persons, or with
places, or even with facts: but this does not give us a sufficient indication of what it is to be acquainted with a sense-datum. When someone
tells me that he is glad to make my acquaintance, no doubt he is also
making the acquaintance of sense-data, in some sense, but the sense
in which he is supposed to be acquainted with them is not the same
as that in which he is acquainted with me. But in what sense, then, is
he acquainted with them? Some technical sense, presumably. But, if
so, it needs to be explained: and until it has been explained the
term 'sense-datum' has not been satisfactorily defined. Neither do
we escape this difficulty by defining sense-data as the objects of

From A J. Ayer, 'Phenomenalism,' *Proceedings of the Aristotelian Society,*
XLVII (1946–1947). Reprinted by permission of the author and by the Editor of The
Aristotelian Society.

'sensing' or 'direct apprehension' or 'direct awareness,' as various philosophers have proposed. For these also are technical terms, and there is no familiar usage of them by reference to which their meaning in this context is to be understood.

This may seem a trivial point, but I think that it is worth making because I suspect that behind these definitions lurks the suggestion that sense-data are objects of knowledge. That is, I suspect, that such artifical expressions as 'direct apprehension' or 'direct awareness,' or even the more natural 'acquaintance,' as they are used in this context, are euphemisms for the word 'knowledge,' which is itself too sacred, or too dangerous, to pronounce. But if sense-data are to be defined as objects of knowledge then I do not think that there are sense-data, because I do not think that there are objects of knowledge. And by this I do not mean that it is just not the case that we know any objects, though we might have known some if we had been luckier or cleverer. Nor, like some philosophers, am I using the word 'knowledge' so strictly that everything that is ordinarily taken for knowledge turns out really not to be so. What I mean is that there cannot be objects of knowledge, because to speak of knowing objects, in the sense here intended, is to commit a type fallacy. Admittedly, the word 'know' is often used as a transitive verb. I may say, for example, that I know a person if I have been in his company, and we recognize each other when we meet: or, in a slightly different sense, I may say that I know him if by being in his company I have learned how he is likely to behave. Again, I may say that I know a place if I have been there; or perhaps it may be required that I should have been there sufficiently often to be able to find my way about it, or for the various parts of it to be familiar to me. And many other examples could be given, in which the criteria for the proper use of 'know' as a transitive verb would be found to cover a fairly extensive range. But it is not this sort of thing that philosophers have in mind when they say, or imply, that there are objects of knowledge. The sense of 'know' with which they are concerned is the sense in which we speak of knowing that something or other is the case. And in this sense it is meaningless to speak of knowing objects. Failure to realize this has contributed, I think, to a famous piece of philosophical mythology, the act-object analysis of sensation. For once it is assumed that having a sensation involves knowing an object, then it may seem reasonable to apply to this case the principle that what is known must be independent of the knowing of it: and so we come to the fashionable refutations of Berkeley which consist in distinguishing the act of awareness, as a mental entity, from the object, not necessarily mental, which is the accusative of the act. But what are these acts of awareness supposed to be? No doubt sentences of the form '*A* is aware of *X*,' or '*A* is conscious of *X*,' are often given a meaning which is such that the propositions which they then express are found to be true: but it does not follow from this that the expressions 'being aware of' or 'being conscious of' are names for anything. And, indeed, not only do I not find any referents for such names when I analyse my sensations empirically, but I do not know what they are supposed to stand for. I do not know what it would be like to come upon an act of awareness. Consequently, if sense-data were defined as the objects of such acts, I should remain unconvinced that there were sense-data.

Professor Price, who has made himself the guardian of sense-data—he is not their parent but it is he who has chiefly interested himself in their welfare: it is to him more than anyone that they owe their present position of honour in the philosophical word—has another method of defining them. He says that when I look at a physical object, for instance a tomato, there is much that I can doubt. I can doubt whether it is not a reflection, or a cleverly painted piece of wax, or even a complete hallucination. But, he goes on to argue, there remains something that I cannot doubt. I cannot doubt that 'there exists a red patch of a round and somewhat bulgy shape, standing out from a background of other colour-patches, and having a certain visual depth, and that this whole field of colour is directly present to my consciousness.' And it is this object whose existence I cannot doubt that he proposes to call a sense-datum. But why can I not doubt it? What prevents me? It is not a question of my psychology. It is not just that I cannot now bring myself to doubt the existence of this bulgy patch, because that leaves open the possibility that I might. If I schooled myself in doubting, I might achieve it. But clearly this is not what Price means. He wants to say that the existence of what he calls the sense-datum is objectively beyond doubt: so that if anyone managed to deny it, he would necessarily be wrong. Thus, there is a sense in which, having accepted the premises of a valid deductive argument, I cannot doubt the conclusion, though there is also a sense in which I can doubt it, since I may not be sure that I have drawn the inference correctly. Similarly, I may be unsure of the truth of an analytic proposition, but there is also a sense in which it may be said that I cannot doubt it, if it is necessarily true. It is not in this sense, however, that I cannot doubt the existence of the bulgy patch. For it would not be self-contradictory to say that no such object existed. But perhaps what is meant when it is said that I cannot doubt the existence of the patch is that it does not make sense to say 'I doubt if this patch exists.' It may be suggested that the reason why I cannot doubt it is that one cannot properly speak of doubting in such a case. But the trouble with this is that there is a perfectly good sense in which it can be said that I doubt if this bulgy patch exists.

If I were not sure whether the appearance of the patch in question was not a constituent of a dream, it would be entirely proper to describe my situation by saying that I doubted whether the patch existed. Accordingly, one has to go on to explain that the sense in which it is meaningless to say 'I doubt if this patch exists' is the special sense that is appropriate to sense-data and not to physical objects. And thus we are once more brought back in a circle.

All the same, it is not very hard to see what Price and the other philosophers who talk about sense-data are getting at. For suppose that I am having an experience which it would be natural for me to describe by saying that I was holding a match-box in my hand and looking at it. In that case, assuming the experience to be veridical, there is a familiar sense of the words 'see' and 'touch' in which what I am now seeing and touching is simply 'this match-box.' And there is also a familiar sense of the words 'see' and 'touch' in which what I am now seeing and touching is not the whole match-box but only a part of its surface. Now, in both these senses, if it should happen that the match-box does not exist, if I am dreaming or having an illusion, then either I am seeing something, or a part of something, other than a match-box, something that I mistake for a match-box, or, in the case of a total hallucination, I am not seeing or touching anything. But it is also possible to use the words 'see' and 'touch' in such a way that even if I am dreaming or having a complete hallucination, so that there is no physical object there, it can still be said that there is some object that I am seeing or touching, and further, that this object really has the characteristics that the physical object, which I mistakenly think that I am seeing or touching, in the other senses of the words 'see' and 'touch,' appears to me to have. And what I am seeing in *this* sense may perhaps be a certain patch of colour, 'standing out from a background of other colour-patches and having a certain visual depth,' though I am inclined on psychological grounds to doubt whether this would be an accurate description of any normal visual experience. Let us then call the whole of what everyone sees in this sense at any given moment, his 'visual sense-field.' Then a visual sense-datum may be defined as anything that is the constituent of a visual sense-field. And, in general, a sense-datum may be defined as anything that is the constituent of a sense-field.

At this point it may be objected that I have not got away from the act-object analysis of sensation. For I have explained the use of the word 'sense-datum' in terms of a special use of words like 'touch' and 'see' and these are transitive verbs. But the answer is that there is no need to assume that such words as 'seeing' and 'touching,' in this usage, are names for mental acts. If the word 'sensing' be used to designate the experience of which seeing, touching, and the rest, in this usage, are the various modes, then to say of something that it is sensed need be taken to imply no more than that it is sensibly present, or, in other words, that it appears: and to specify that it is seen or touched is merely to indicate what manner of appearance is in question. We might therefore say that to be seen is to appear visually, that to be touched is to appear tactually, and so on, though we should still have to distinguish different senses of 'appear' as correlates of the different senses of 'touch' and 'see.' Thus what we obtain by introducing the term 'sense-datum' is a means of referring to appearances without prejudging the questions what it is, if anything, that they are appearances *of*, and what it is, if anything, that they appear *to*. And here it may be advisable to make the familiar point that the use of this term 'sense-datum' is not intended to carry any factual implications about the character of these appearances. It is not designed, for example, to beg the question in favour of an atomic as opposed to a *Gestalt* theory of sensation. Thus, when philosophers like Professor Stout make it an objection to 'the sense-datum theory,' and so to phenomenalism, that what is sensibly 'given' is something more substantial than a mere sense-datum, their argument is beside the mark. It is an empirical question whether the contents, say, of a visual-field are more accurately to be described as patches of colour or coloured 'objects.' But even if it is decided, on empirical grounds, that what is seen is, in some sense, a coloured 'object,' it will still be a sense-datum, according to our usage.

Now if the word 'sense-datum' is understood in this way, then if it is ever true that a physical object is being perceived, it must also be true that some sense-datum is being sensed. If, for example, it is a fact that I am seeing a match-box, in the appropriate sense of the word 'see,' then it *follows* that, in the appropriately different sense of the word 'see,' I am seeing some sense-datum. But the converse does not hold. I believe that I am now perceiving a match-box and this belief is directly based on the evidence of my senses. But from the fact that I am sensing the sense-data that I am now sensing it does not *follow* that I am perceiving a match-box. For if we disregard all the other evidence available to me, including the evidence of my memories, my having the sense-experiences that I am now having is compatible with there being no such match-box there; it is compatible with my being the victim of an illusion. Thus, when I say, truly as it happens, that I am now perceiving a match-box, part of what I am saying is that I am sensing sense-data of a certain kind; but only part. I am saying that and something more. But what more? That is our problem. And the phenomenalists' answer to it is that the more that I am saying is that further sense-data of the appropriate sort would, in the appropriate conditions, be obtainable.

If this answer is correct, then it seems to follow that the statement that I am perceiving this match-box, or whatever other physical object may be taken as an example, must be equivalent to some set of statements about sense-data. And since to say that I am perceiving a match-box entails saying that the match-box exists, the statement that this match-box exists must also, in that case, be equivalent to some set of statements about sense-data. And to say, as phenomenalists do, that physical objects are logical constructions out of sense-data is merely another way of expressing this. It does not mean that physical objects are literally composed of sense-data, or that physical objects are fictions and only sense-data real. It means simply that statements about physical objects are somehow reducible to statements about sense-data, or, as it is sometimes put, that to say anything about a physical object is to say something, though not necessarily the same thing, about sense-data. This, then, is the claim that we have to discuss.

2

The first point to be made is that if we confine ourselves to actual sense-data, this claim can evidently not be upheld. For to revert to our example, this match-box is not continuously perceived either by me or by anybody else. And yet at times when no one is perceiving it, that is, when there are no sense-data that are directly relevant to its existence, the match-box may still exist. In other words, it is not self-contradictory, though it may in certain cases be false, to say both that a given physical object exists in a certain place, and throughout a certain period of time, and that during that period of time no one was sensing any such sense-data as would constitute direct evidence for the existence of the physical object in question. Consequently, if the sense-datum language is to do the work that phenomenalists require of it, it must permit us to refer to possible sense-data. And what this means is that some at least of the statements about sense-data that are supposed to yield the equivalence of statements about physical objects will have to be hypothetical. They will have to state not that any sense-data have occurred, are occurring, or will occur, but that in certain specifiable conditions certain sense-data would occur. The difficulty, as we shall see, is to specify the conditions.

Now it would seem that the best way for a phenomenalist to prove his case would be to set about giving us some examples. We should expect him to take a statement like 'there is a flower-pot on the window sill,' and give us its equivalent in terms of sense-data. But this is something that no phenomenalist has ever yet done, or even, to my knowledge, seriously tried to do. We are told that statements about physical objects must be translatable into statements about sense-data, but we do not get any translations. The most we get are more or less vague descriptions of the sort of way such translations might run. We are given recipes for making translations; but they seem to be recipes that no one can ever put into use. One reason for this, of course, is the poverty of our sensory language. The vocabulary that we have for describing colours, shapes, and the rest is not sufficient for our purpose: so that we are constantly reduced to saying things like 'the sort of sense-data that you get when you look at a match-box' or 'the sort of sense-data that you get when you hear a telephone ring,' where the reference to the physical object is needed to identify the sense-data in question. But I suppose that a suitable vocabulary could be invented, if some ingenious person thought that it was worth his trouble: so that if this were all that stood in the phenomenalist's way he might be entitled to hold that his programme could be carried out, 'at least in principle.' But there are more serious difficulties.

One that is often brought forward is that no statement about a physical object can be conclusively verified, on the ground that, however much favourable evidence there may be for it, it is always conceivable that further evidence will show it to have been false all along. And from this premiss it is correctly deduced that no statement about a physical object can be equivalent to any finite set of statements about sense-data. For each of the statements about sense-data will be a description of a single piece of evidence in favour of the statement about the physical object; and if the evidence is to be sufficient the number of these descriptions must be infinite. I used to accept this argument but now I am inclined to reject it. The assumption is that if, for example, I am looking at my telephone and suddenly see it change into what appears to be a flower-pot, or vanish altogether, or what you will, that proves that it never was a telephone. To put the case more precisely, suppose that a series of visual and tactual sense-data were succeeded 'in the same place,' which here may be taken to mean 'in similar spatial relations to similar sense-data,' by sense-data characteristic of the appearance of a flower-pot, or that, while the surrounding conditions appear to remain unchanged, there cease to be any sense-data characteristic of the appearance of a physical object in the 'place' where the sense-data characteristic of the appearance of a telephone previously were, that proves that I must have been mistaken in taking these sense-data to be the appearances of a real telephone. But does it? The only way of deciding what it proves is to consider what one would say in such a case, that is, how one would describe such a situation. What I should, in fact, say would be that my present experience was hallucinatory: that the illusion lay not in the long series of my past 'perceptions' of a telephone, but in my present 'perception' of a flower-pot. But suppose that I applied the usual tests for hallucinations, and that they were negative. Suppose that the object that I seemed to be perceiving felt as well as looked like a flower-pot, and that it went on looking and feeling like a flower-pot, and that when I asked other people about it they said that they perceived a flower-pot too. In that case I should probably give up the idea that I was having a hallucination, though it may be remarked that if the evidence that previously led me to believe that I was perceiving a telephone was not conclusive, then the evidence that I was not subsequently having a hallucination with regard to the flower-pot would not be conclusive either. If no evidence is conclusive all the competing hypotheses remain open. But suppose that the evidence is such that I do, in fact, rule out the hypothesis that my 'perception' of the flower-pot is a sustained illusion. I *might* then say that I had been deceived all the time about the telephone. I might even start to distrust my memory, and wonder whether it had not always been the case that I perceived a flower-pot, though here the testimony of others would be a check. But what I think I *should* say is: 'It *was* a telephone and all of a sudden it changed into a flower-pot.' I should think this odd, certainly. I should probably write to the newspapers about it. And then if the ensuing correspondence showed me that other people had had similar experiences, I should begin to feel more comfortable. 'It has to be admitted,' I should say, 'that physical objects do sometimes undergo these abrupt changes. I wonder what the scientific explanation is.'

No doubt this example sounds excessively fanciful, but not long ago I did have a fountain pen that suddenly vanished. At one moment I was looking at it, touching it, writing with it, and the next moment it had disappeared. I could not find it any more and never have found it to this day. Of course, I do not really believe that it vanished. 'Pens do not just vanish,' I say, in default of stronger evidence that they do. But still less do I believe that it never was a pen. I do not say: 'The run of favourable evidence has come to an end as I was always warned that it might. My belief that it really was a pen that I was perceiving implied that the run of favourable evidence would continue indefinitely. Consequently my belief was false.' What I say is: 'There must be some explanation. Perhaps I turned my back on it for an instant, though I do not remember doing so, and somebody crept in and took it. Or, more probably, it dropped somewhere and I have not searched for it hard enough.' And from this I conclude that when I said, as I often have in the past, like other philosophers, that however strongly one's sense-data may support the hypothesis that one is perceiving a physical object of a certain sort, further experience may show one to have been mistaken, I was not serious. For when a situation arose which, on the face of it, supported this view, I did not interpret it in that way at all. I did not even seriously consider the possibility that what I had for so long been taking to be a pen never really had been a pen. Neither do I think that I am peculiar in this respect. I think that the explanation that it never really was a pen is one that, in the circumstances, nobody would consider seriously.

What bearing has this upon the phenomenalist's claim? As I said before, no single sense-experience, taken by itself, ever proves that a physical object exists. From the bare fact that I am sensing *these* visual sense-data it does not follow that this is a match-box. Nevertheless the occurrence of these visual sense-data, taken in conjunction with what I remember, fully justifies the statement that this is a match-box, and would justify it, I should now maintain, even if the 'match-box' were to vanish the next instant. By itself the occurrence of just these sense-data would not be sufficient, but in conjunction with previous experience it is. This previous experience may consist of previous perceptions of the physical object in question, that is, previous sensings of the appropriate sense-data, but it need not. In certain circumstances I might be fully justified in believing in the existence of a physical object that I had never before perceived: and in such cases the strength of the evidence would lie in the general character of my previous experience. For my belief that *this* is a physical object, and a physical object of a certain sort, is not based solely on the occurrence of sense-data which are manifestations of *this*: it is derived also from a more general belief that I live in a world of physical objects of which things that look like this are specimens: and this belief is supported by a mass of past experiences. So much so that if this assumption were to break down altogether, if, from this moment on, sense-data were to arrange themselves, as Price once suggested they might, in an eurythmic rather than a thing-like order,[1] I should not say: 'I was wrong all the time: there never were any physical objects.' I should say: 'The world has changed: there used to be physical objects, but now there are none any more.'

Does it follow then that at any rate some statements about a physical object can be translated into statements about sense-data, namely into those statements which describe the sense-data, past and present, the occurrence of which fully justifies us, on the occasions when we are so justified, in asserting that the physical object exists? Not necessarily. For in that case the truth of the statements referring to sense-data would be both a necessary and a sufficient condition of the truth

[1] Vide, *The Terminology of Sense-data*, p. 104.

of the statement about the physical object. And while I have argued that in certain cases it may be sufficient, I have not shown, nor do I think that it can be shown, that it is also necessary. No doubt the truth of some statement or other about sense-data is always a necessary condition of the truth of any statement which implies the existence of a physical object: but I do not think that it is ever possible to discover a finite set of statements about sense-data of which it can truly be said in a particular case that precisely these are necessary. In other words, though you may be able to discover sets of sufficient conditions, you cannot list them exhaustively. You cannot say, for example, exactly how much experience, nor exactly what type of experience, a child must have had in order to be fully justified, on the evidence available to him, in saying: 'This is a ball.' In a concrete case you can safely allow that he has sufficient evidence. But you cannot rightly say that it is necessary, because there will always be an indefinite number of other sensory experiences that would have done just as well. Thus, it makes no difference whether his general belief in the existence of physical objects is derived from the sense-data he has obtained when playing with rattles or when playing with teddy-bears: it makes no difference whether he punches the ball or strokes it, whether the angle from which he sees it makes it appear round to him or oval, whether the light is such that it seems to him to be red or orange. The sense-data that are sufficient, in conjunction with his previous experience, to establish the existence of the ball must all fall within a certain range: a sense-datum characteristic of the appearance of an alarm-clock would not fit the case: but the number of possible sense-data that fall within that range is indefinite, while the previous sensory experiences that may go to make the present evidence sufficient not only are indefinite in number, but themselves fall within a range that is extremely wide. And this is one reason why it is impossible to translate a statement about a physical object into any finite set of statements about sense-data. It is not, as has sometimes been suggested, that the physical object is eternally on probation, so that to try to establish its existence by sense-perception is like trying to fill a bottomless well. The reason is that all statements about physical objects are indefinite. The well can be filled, but there are an infinite number of ways of filling it. Consequently, the comparatively definite statements that one makes about sense-data, to the effect that such and such sense-data are being or have been obtained, or that in such and such conditions such and such sense-data would be obtained, cannot be exact translations of the indefinite statements that one makes about physical objects. And by this I mean not, of course, that a statement about a physical object is necessarily indefinite at its own level, but that it is necessarily indefinite at the level of sense-data.

3

If this be admitted, what becomes of the phenomenalist's case? What is there left for him to claim? It has been suggested that he should claim no more than that the direct evidence for the existence of a physical object is always the occurrence of some sense-datum. But if this were all there would be nothing to discuss. For, as I have already shown, the term 'sense-datum' may be defined in such a way that if anyone is perceiving a physical object it *follows* that he is sensing a sense-datum: and not only that but that all that his senses reveal to him is the presence of sense-data. This does not mean that his sensory experiences must be of the sort that we are all familiar with: they might be very queer indeed: but however queer they were they would still be experiences of sense-data. Now it is not to be disputed that the direct evidence for the existence of physical objects is sensory evidence: for any evidence that was not sensory would not be called direct. And clearly if you decide to call obtaining such evidence 'sensing sense-data' it will follow that you can obtain such evidence only by sensing sense-data. The only question then is whether you agree with the proposal to use the *word* 'sense-datum.' But surely those who have taken, or accepted, the title of phenomenalists have thought that they were doing more than extending their patronage to a word.

Yes, but what more? What is the point of introducing the sense-datum vocabulary? The idea is that it helps you to learn something about the nature of physical objects, not indeed in the way that doing science does, but that you come to understand better what is meant by propositions about physical objects, what these propositions amount to, what their 'cash value' is, by restating them in terms of sense-data. That is, the fact that you *can* restate them in this way, *if* you can, tells you something important about them. Furthermore, it is claimed that if you talk in terms of sense-data you are somehow getting deeper than if you are content to talk, as we all do in everyday life, in terms of physical objects. The naïve realist is not in error. Naïve realism is not a false theory of perception: it is a refusal to play this sort of game. And if a man will not play he cannot lose. But one is inclined to say that the naïve realist is missing something by refusing to play: that he is not getting to the root of the matter. And the justification for this is that there is a sense in which the sense-datum language is logically prior to the physical-object language. For it is impossible that a physical object should be perceived without its being true that some sense-datum is being sensed: but it is not impossible that any number of sense-data should be sensed without its ever being true that any physical object is perceived. For the relations between sense-data in virtue of which we are justified in claiming that we perceive physical objects are contingent: they might conceivably not have obtained.

But now it turns out that for the reasons I have given, statements about physical objects cannot be translated into statements about sense-data. Consequently, the phenomenalist is obliged to give up his original position. But he need modify it only slightly. He cannot show precisely what you are saying about sense-data when you make a given statement about a physical object, because you are not saying anything precise about sense-data. Nevertheless, he will maintain, what you are saying, though vague, still refers ultimately to sense-data and does not refer to anything other than sense-data. Consequently, he can hope to give a suitably vague translation. It should be possible to indicate at least what sort of thing we are saying about sense-data when we make a statement like 'there is a match-box on the table.' And if the phenomenalist can do this he may be allowed to have proved his case.

The *a priori* argument for supposing that this must be possible is that if we are not referring to sense-data, and exclusively to sense-data, when we talk about physical objects, it is difficult to see what we can be referring to. 'Physical objects,' is the unkind answer; and, of course, it is a correct answer, correct but unhelpful. For if we use the sense-datum language—and we have not found any good reason why we should not use it; it has not been shown that it necessarily involves any assumptions that are either logically or empirically mistaken— then it looks as if we are using it as a substitute for the physical-object language. The world does not contain sense-data *and* physical objects, in the sense in which it contains chairs *and* tables, or in the sense in which it contains colours *and* sounds. One is inclined to say, therefore, that phenomenalism must be true, on the ground that the only alternative to it, once we have agreed to use the sense-datum terminology, is the iron-curtain theory of perception: that physical objects are there sure enough but we can never get at them, because all we can observe is sense-data: and surely this theory at least can be shown to be untenable.

4

All the same, there are difficulties in the way of the phenomenalists. One, which I shall now try to meet, concerns the question of causation. Regarded by Professor Stout as a fatal objection to phenomenalism,[2] it led Professor Price to postulate, as the owners of causal prop-

[2] G. F. Stout, 'Phenomenalism,' *Proceedings of the Aristotelian Society*, 1938–39.

erties, a set of unobservable entities to which he gives the name of 'physical occupants,' [3] a piece of mythology which I understand that he has since repudiated—and it has recently been restated with force and clarity by Mr. W. F. R. Hardie.[4] The difficulty is this:

Our perceptions are fragmentary. We do not perceive all the physical objects that there are all the time: and yet we believe, and often have good reason to believe, that some of them exist when no one is perceiving them. And not only this, but we often have good reason to believe that they are causally efficacious when no one is perceiving them. An example that Price gives is that of a concealed magnet which causes the observed deflection of a compass needle. Now it may be held that what are described as causal relations between physical objects, or physical events, are analysable in terms of regularities among sense-data. But the trouble is that in a great many cases in which we postulate causal relationships, the required sensory regularities are not observed. Assuming that I perceive the deflection of Price's compass needle, then I am sensing certain visual sense-data, and the occurrence of these sense-data may, it is said, be described as an event. But the existence of the magnet throughout the relevant period of time is not an event in the same sense. For *ex hypothesi* no sense-data 'belonging to' the magnet are occurring. You may analyse the statement that the magnet exists into a hypothetical statement to the effect that if certain conditions were fulfilled, sense-data characteristic of the appearance of the magnet would be obtained. But since the conditions in question are not in fact fulfilled, the statement that the magnet exists does not, when analysed in sensory terms, describe any actual event. It does not, when so analysed, say that anything exists, but only, to quote Mr. Hardie, that given certain conditions something would exist which actually does not. But this is to fall into the absurdity, as Stout calls it, of supposing that 'actual occurrences depend upon mere possibilities.' For surely it is self-evident that actual events have actual causes. A mere possibility cannot be a cause.

Let me try to state this objection more clearly. The argument may be set out in the following way. It makes sense to say that physical objects exist and are causally efficacious at times when no one is perceiving them. There may, therefore, be unobserved physical events and they may stand in causal relations to other unobserved events, or to observed events. Now, if the phenomenalists are right, an unobserved physical event is reducible to a set of possible sensory events. But on an 'agency' view of causation this is incompatible with its being the cause, since a mere set of possibilities cannot *do* anything.

[3] H. H. Price, *Perception,* chaps. ix and x.
[4] W. F. R. Hardie, 'The Paradox of Phenomenalism,' *Proceedings of the Aristotelian Society,* 1945–46.

And the same is true even on a 'regularity' view of causation: for a possible sensory occurrence is not an event in the sense in which an actual sensory occurrence is an event, and the regularities must be assumed to hold between events of the same type. It is impossible, therefore, for the phenomenalists to explain how unobserved physical events can be causes. Consequently phenomenalism is false.

As Mr. Hardie has pointed out to me, the argument may be made independent of the empirical premiss that our perceptions are fragmentary, or, in other words, that some physical events are unobserved. For whether or not a physical event is observed, the observation of it is not logically necessary to its occurrence. That is to say, the statement that it occurs does not entail the statement that it is observed to occur. Consequently, the phenomenalist's analysis of a statement which describes the occurrence of a physical event need refer only to possible sense-data, though actual sense-data may have to be brought in if the statement at the physical level itself involves a reference to a percipient. Furthermore, the causal properties of physical objects adhere to them whether they are observed or not. If, therefore, the phenomenalist is to allow that any physical events are causes he must maintain that a set of possibilities can be a cause. And this, in the eyes of those who raise this objection, is a manifest absurdity.

This argument has convinced many people, but I think that it is fallacious, and that the fallacy lies partly in a confusion over the use of the word 'cause,' and partly in an ambiguity in the use of the word 'event.' I am perfectly willing to admit that an actual event, if it has a cause at all, must have an actual cause, though even here there is a play on the word 'actual,' since in many cases what is called the cause will be a past event, and so, in a sense, no longer 'actual.' Still I will grant that, if an event has a cause, that cause must itself be an event which is 'actual' in the sense that it either is actually occurring or has at some time actually occurred. But in this proposition the word 'event' is being used as a term at the physical level. I do not mean by this that an event, in this sense of the word, must be physical: it may be also mental: but it is at the physical level inasmuch as it occupies a position in physical time, as opposed to sensory time, and inasmuch as it occupies a position in physical space, as opposed to sensory space, if it is spatially located at all. In this sense both the deflection of the needle, to recur to Price's example, and the state of the magnet are actual events, whether they are observed or not. The magnet actually exercises the causal properties in virtue of which the needle is deflected: and that is to say, the deflection of the needle can be explained by reference to the properties of the magnet. But this is in no way incompatible with the phenomenalist's view that a proposition asserting the existence of the magnet and describing its causal properties is equivalent to a set of purely hypothetical properties about sense-data. Again, the actual event which is my observing the deflection of the compass needle also has actual causes, including certain processes in my nervous system, which are not themselves observed. Or, in other words, the truth of the proposition that I am observing a compass needle is connected by a well-established theory with the truth of certain other propositions, themselves not directly verified on this occasion, which refer among other things to processes in my nervous system. These propositions are all at the physical level. They are categorical, and consequently they describe actual events, in the appropriate sense of 'event.' But once more this is perfectly compatible with their being analysable into hypothetical propositions about sense-data. Only—and this is the important point—the sense-datum propositions, even those that are categorical, do not describe events in the same sense of the word 'event.' The 'events' that they describe are not in physical time or in physical space. And it is only at the physical level that causal relations hold between actual events. It is indeed only at the physical level that events can properly be said to have causes at all.

This being so, the trouble arises when, instead of asking what is the cause of my observing the compass needle, which is a legitimate question, or even what is the cause of my sensing sense-data 'belonging to' the compass needle, which is still a legitimate question, so long as 'my sensing the sense-data' is taken as the description of a process which takes place in physical time, we ask what is the cause of the sense-data themselves. For this is a nonsensical question. It is nonsensical because the sense-data are not events in the sense in which the deflection of the needle is an event, so that the term 'cause' which is understood as a relation between events at the physical level, does not apply to them. Unfortunately phenomenalists, among whom I must here include myself, have usually failed to see this and so have fallen into the trap of meeting the question 'What is the cause of these sense-data?' with the answer 'Other sense-data.' And in this way they have gratuitously laid themselves open to the sort of objection that Stout and Hardie raise.

To make it clear that such objections are invalid, we may restate the phenomenalist's answer as follows: There are well-established theories, or hypotheses, which connect different propositions at the physical level. There is, for example, a well-established theory of electromagnetics through which a proposition describing the deflection of a compass needle can be connected with a proposition describing the state of a magnet; that is, the proposition referring to the needle will, give certain conditions, be deducible from the proposition about the magnet in conjunction with the propositions of the theory. When this is so, then, if the hypotheses in question are of certain specifiable types, we say that the event described by one of these propositions is a cause of the event described by the other. This is not by any means the only sense in which we used the word 'cause,' but it is the sense that is relevant to the present argument. Both events are actual, in the sense that the propositions which describe them are categorical, but these propositions, which are categorical at the physical level, are reducible to hypothetical propositions about sense-data. This may be expressed by saying that the physical events in question are analysable into sets of possible sensory occurrences; but these sensory occurrences are not events, in the same sense of 'event'; neither can they have, or be, causes in the same sense of 'cause.' It is therefore misleading to say that sense-data depend upon one another: for this suggests that they can possess causal properties in the same way as physical objects, which is not the case. They can, however, be correlated with one another, and it is only because they can be so correlated that we have any reason to believe in the existence of causal connections between physical events. Indeed to say that there is a causal connection between physical events is, in the last analysis, to make a very complicated statement about correlations between sense-data. The sense-data which are correlated may be actual, but they need not be. For the basis of the correlation is always a hypothetical proposition to the effect that a sense-datum of a certain sort occurs if in certain conditions a sense-datum of a certain other sort occurs, and it is not necessary for the truth of such a proposition either that the protasis or that the apodosis should be actually fulfilled. Thus a proposition of the form 'if, if p then q, then, if r then s' may very well be true even though p, q, r, and s are all false. Consequently in the case of sense-data, there is no absurdity in making actual occurrences 'depend upon' mere possibilities: for there is no absurdity in saying that a categorical proposition would not be true unless some hypothetical proposition were true. This hypothetical proposition states that such and such an event would occur if certain conditions were fulfilled, and there is no absurdity in holding that it may still be true even if the requisite conditions happen not to be fulfilled. But this is all that the 'dependence' of actual upon possible sense-data comes to. What makes it seem an absurdity is the misleading terminology of 'causes' and 'events.'

5

So far, I hope, so good: but the conception of 'possible sense-data' still involves certain difficulties. It is usually illustrated by some such example as "the 'family' of sense-data which constitutes the table in the next room is possible in the sense that if I were there I should be sensing one of its members": and with that we are supposed to be content. But I do not think that we should be content with anything so simple as that. To begin with, the choice of such an example covers two very important assumptions. It is assumed both that the introduction of myself as an observer would not affect what I am supposed to observe, and that the conditions would be such as to allow of my observing: and neither of these assumptions will be justified in all cases. Consider, for example, the proposition that Dr. Crippen murdered his wife in his house in Camden Town in the year 1910. Now the suggestion is that this means that if I had been there at the appropriate time I should have sensed certain sense-data, namely, such as would constitute a sensory manifestation of a man, answering to the description of Dr. Crippen, engaged in murdering his wife. But even allowing that there is a sense in which I logically *could* have been there, although in actual fact I was not yet born, the answer is that even if I had been there I almost certainly should not have sensed anything of the kind. It is most unlikely that Dr. Crippen would have murdered his wife while I was looking on. But here it may be objected that the word 'I' in this context does not refer explicitly to me. It is a variable, not a constant. What is meant is that if *anybody* had been there, he would have sensed the requisite sense-data. But it is most unlikely that Dr. Crippen would have murdered his wife while anybody, other than an accomplice, was looking on. Besides why do we have to say 'If anybody had been there.' Somebody *was* there. Dr. Crippen was. And he must have sensed a host of sense-data while he was murdering his wife and subsequently dismembering her. So, up to a certain point in the story, did his wife. So why should we not just say that a number of interesting sense-data occurred in such and such a part of Camden Town on such and such a day in the year 1910? We shall see later on why this will not do either.

Again, take the proposition that the sun, though it may look no larger than a man's hand, is really very large indeed, so many thousand miles in diameter. Does this mean that if I were very close to it I should see it stretching out enormously in all directions, or that if I laid measuring rods along it of the requisite sort I should sense the required coincidences of sense-data? But if I were very close to it I should not see anything at all, I should be shrivelled up: and my operation with the measuring rods could not be carried out. Of course it is possible to carry out some operations with a view to determining the dimensions of the sun: for how else should we, in fact, determine them? But these operations are ordinarily thought to provide only indirect, and not direct, evidence for the conclusions that they establish. Whereas what the phenomenalist is seeking to describe is an observation that would constitute direct evidence: and the objection is that in the conditions that he postulates such direct evidence may not be physically obtainable.

Professor Price has suggested to me that these difficulties can be overcome by making suitable assumptions about the character of the observer. Thus it is not necessary, he supposes, that the hypothetical witness of Dr. Crippen's act should be a human being; it might be a mouse. Or, if a human being be insisted upon, the observer might be assumed to be looking through the keyhole, or surveying the proceedings from afar through a telescope. Or it might be made a supplementary condition that Dr. Crippen should be affected with psychic blindness, so that he would have gone about his business just as if no intruder had been there, in exactly the way, in fact, in which he *did* go about his business, since no intruder *was* there. Similarly, in the example of the sun, I might credit myself hypothetically with an uninflammable body, so that I could make my observations without being shrivelled up. And in this case it can also be argued that all that is required is that the observations should be 'possible in principle': so that it is not a fatal objection to the analysis that they would not be made in fact.

But if the fact is that the desired observations would not be made in the stated conditions then the hypothetical proposition in which it is affirmed that they would be made are false: and since the categorical proposition of which they are offered as an analysis may nevertheless be true, the analysis is incorrect. To say that the observations are 'possible in principle' is merely to say that one can conceive of the conditions being such that they would be made: but it is just the specification of the conditions that constitutes our problem. Neither do I think that the difficulty can be met in the sort of way that Price suggests. For, in his examples, the truth of the hypothetical proposition is dependent upon the truth of some physical or psychological law, as that murderers are not deterred by the presence of mice or that gaseous bodies are not shrivelled by great heat: and while these laws may be valid, their validity is not involved in that of the propositions which we are trying to analyse. After all, Dr. Crippen *might* have been put off by the presence of a mouse: it *might* be the case that when Professor Price approached the sun in his gaseous body he still could not make the required observations. But, however this might be, it would remain true that Dr. Crippen *did* murder his wife, and that the sun has the diameter that it has. And this means that even if we recast our hypothetical propositions in such agreeably fantastic forms as Price suggests, they will still not be equivalent to the propositions of which they are supposed to be the analyses.

Neither is this the only difficulty. So far, in referring to the conditions which go to constitute the 'possibility' of sense-data, in any given case, I have used such phrases as 'if I were in the next room,' or 'if any observer had been there': and it is in such terms as these that phenomenalists do usually talk when they try to indicate the sort of way in which they would analyse propositions about unperceived physical objects. Thus Berkeley, for once ignoring God, says that "the question whether the earth moves amounts in reality to no more than this, to wit, whether we have reason to conclude from what has been observed by astronomers, that if we were placed in such and such circumstances, and such or such a position and distance, both from the earth and sun, we should perceive the former to move." [5] But to speak of 'my' or 'our' being in a certain position is to speak about a physical object, namely a human body, and to speak of its position involves a reference to other physical objects, in Berkeley's example the earth and the sun. No doubt he is 'speaking with the vulgar': he has to in order to make himself intelligible; so do we all. But how do 'the learned' speak in this case? If the phenomenalist is to make good his claim that categorical propositions about physical objects are reducible to hypothetical propositions about sense-data, it is not enough that he should indicate what the apodoses of his hypotheticals come to in sensory terms: he must do the same with the protases also. But how is this to be done?

Professor Price deals with this point in the fifth chapter of his book on *Hume's Theory of the External World.*[6] He remarks truly that the phenomenalistic analysis of any 'material-object statement' is extremely complex, since it involves in each case an indefinite number of statements to the effect that if someone were at a place P_1, he would be sensing a sense-datum S_1, if he were at a place P_2 he would be sensing S_2 . . . if he were at place P_n he would be sensing S_n, and he goes on to consider what the phenomenalist must mean by someone's being at a place P. His answer is that he must mean 'so far from here' and 'in such and such a direction' and that these expressions 'refer to the sensational route, so to speak, which anyone would have to traverse if he were to pass from P, to the place where the speaker is.' "Thus the phenomenalistic analysis of 'x is at P' will be something like the following: 'X is sensing a visual or tactual field such that *if* he had replaced it by another spatially adjoined to it, and *if* he had replaced that by another spatially adjoined to it, and *if* he had replaced that in turn by still another, and so on, then eventually he would have been sensing the visual or tactual field which is actually

[5] *Principles of Human Knowledge* lviii.
[6] Pp. 183–88.

being sensed by the speaker at this moment.' " Presumably some reference to kinaesthetic data would be needed to bring out the point that it is the person X that is supposed to be moving: and certainly one would require some description of the contents of the visual and tactual fields 'through' which X is supposed to pass. For otherwise neither his starting-point nor his route would be identifiable.

A similar treatment is given to the question of position in time. The first stage of the analysis will yield hypothetical propositions such as 'If anyone had been at place P_1, at time t, he would have sensed S_1; if anyone had been at place P_2, at time t_2, he would have sensed S_2. . . .' And here 'at time t' will mean, according to Price, 'so many minutes or hours, or days before *now*,' which again must be 'analysed in terms of a sensational route.' So, " 'X had a sense-experience at a past date t' (*e.g.* 3000 years ago) must be equivalent to something like the following: 'he sensed a sense-field such that *if* he had been going to sense a later one spatio-temporally adjoining it, and if he had been going to sense a still later one spatio-temporally adjoining that one and so on, then eventually he *would* have been going to sense the sense-field which is at present being sensed by the speaker.' "

Price goes on to make the further point that the observer must be supposed *really* to travel along his sensational route, both in space and time, and not merely to dream or have a hallucinatory experience of doing so. And this means that the phenomenalist must include in his analysis the possibility of obtaining innumerable bye-series 'branching off from the main one' as a guarantee that the main series is veridical. Accordingly, Price concludes that although he may not have shown that the phenomenalistic analysis is false he has at least shown it to be very much more complex than is usually realized.

But is it only a question of complexity? I think that the analysis which Price attributes to the phenomenalist is open to a far more serious objection. For it implies that the description of any event which is remote in space or time from the speaker contains as part of its meaning not only a description of the sense-field that the speaker is actually sensing, but also a description of a long series of intervening sense-fields. And surely this is incorrect. Suppose, for example, that I make some remark about the South Pole, say that there is a colony of penguins so many miles to the north of it, engaged in some activity or other. It seems clear that this remark will not contain any reference whatsoever either to what I am sensing now or to what I should sense on my way to the place in question. I have, indeed, only a very vague idea of the way to get from here to the South Pole, and a still vaguer idea of what I should observe on my journey, but I do not think that this impairs my understanding of my original proposition. Of course, if I am allowed to take an aeroplane it will be easier: there will be fewer sense-fields to traverse and they are likely to be more homogeneous in content, assuming that the aeroplane does not crash. But even aeroplanes take time to travel, and by the time I get to the South Pole the colony of penguins may have dispersed. So I shall have to make myself start earlier. 'If I had taken an aeroplane so many hours ago'—whatever this may come to in sensory terms—'then I should now be sensing sense-data characteristic of the appearance of penguins, preceded by sense-data . . .' and here there follows a step by step description in reverse of all my experiences *en route*. Surely as an analysis of my original proposition this is most unplausible.

Again, it is to be noticed that Price's phenomenalistic analysis of the proposition about someone's having an experience in the past ends with the words: 'eventually he would have been going to sense the sense-field which is at present being sensed by the speaker.' But it is characteristic of the sense-field that is now being sensed by me, the speaker, that it is somato-centric to my body: and for anyone to sense it he must, as it were, be 'in' my body. That is, he must be having sense-data that are identical with those that are now being obtained 'from' my body. And this adds a further touch of strangeness to what is already a very strange fashion of dealing with the past. Consider, for example, the proposition that Julius Caesar crossed the Rubicon in the year 49 B.C. Resurrecting Caesar after the Ides of March, or ignoring the Ides of March altogether, which we are presumably entitled to do since the whole of our story will be hypothetical, we carry him through two thousand years of history, second by second or minute by minute, according to our estimate of the average duration of a sense-field, and finally bring his wanderings to an end by making him occupy my body. I cannot believe that when I say that Julius Caesar crossed the Rubicon in the year 49 B.C. I am implying quite so much as this.

6

These are serious difficulties: and they might well be thought to be fatal to the phenomenalist, if he were committed to holding the views that Price attributes to him: but I do not think that he is. I do not think that he is bound to claim that the analysis of a proposition referring to an event which is remote in space or time from the speaker involves tracing the sensory route from 'there' and 'then' to 'here' and 'now.' There would in any case be no *one* sensory route to trace. I think rather that he would hope to describe the 'setting' of the event directly in sensory terms, without including what would have to happen for this setting to become the speaker's own. Thus he would try to reproduce 'being at the South Pole' in sensory terms without saying anything about *this* sense-field, or about the other sense-fields that, in a suitably Pickwickian sense of 'between,' may lie between this sense-field and the sense-field that 'presents' the South Pole. Similarly, he would try to give a sensory version of 'Caesar crossed the Rubicon in 49 B.C.,' without referring to *this* sense-field or to the long series of sense-fields that might be supposed to fill the gap between that time and this. But how could this be done? The answer is, I think, that one would have to describe both places and times in terms of the local scenery. Thus, it should be possible to indicate a series of sensory experiences which were such as would entitle anyone who had them to assert 'I am so many miles north of the South Pole,' and in that case the analysis of our proposition about the penguins would be that if such sensory experiences were occurring they would be accompanied by other sense-experiences, which were such as would entitle anyone who had them to assert 'here is a colony of penguins, behaving in such and such a fashion.' It is true, indeed, that not all places are identifiable by obvious landmarks—I imagine, for example, that the South Pole looks very much like the North Pole—so that the descriptions of the 'local scenery' would often have to be rather complicated. In the case of the South Pole I suppose that it would involve a hypothetical reference to the results of making certain measurements. But the fact remains that people do contrive to orient themselves, and that they do so by having certain sense-experiences. Consequently, it seems reasonable for the phenomenalist to set out to define positions in space in terms of the sense-experiences by which they would actually be identified.

There is, however, still a difficulty about time. For the expression 'if such and such sense-experiences were occurring' means 'if they were occurring *now*,' and the use of the word 'now' involves a reference to physical time. Consequently, some phrase will have to be added to the effect that these sense-experiences are, or rather would be, sensibly contemporaneous with some standard sense-experiences which fix the moment of time. And this too will be rather complicated: Given such sense-experiences as would entitle anyone who had them to assert that he was was looking at a watch, and given such sense-experiences as would entitle anyone who had them to assert that the watch was going properly, and given such sense-experiences as would entitle anyone who had them to assert that the watch showed such and such a reading, and given that these last experiences were sensibly contemporaneous with the experiences described in the final apodosis of the long series of 'if-clauses' involved in the identification of the place, then (there would be) such sense-experiences as would entitle anyone who had them to assert that there was 'there and then' a colony of penguins, behaving in such a fashion. And even this is a considerable over-simplification since each of the hypothetical clauses conceals an indefinite number of subsidiary hypotheticals. But once again the phenomenalist might appeal to the fact that people do identify times and that they do so by having certain sense-experiences. And an analysis of this sort, though very far from simple, is at any rate not quite so complex as the analysis in terms of sensory routes.

The same problem arises in the case of propositions about the past. Take Dr. Crippen again. I suppose that one could describe a series of experiences which would be such as to justify the assertion 'this is the year A.D. 1910,' without having to go back to the birth of Christ, which anyhow is wrongly dated. One might, for example, invoke calendars or newspapers, though this would not do so well for such a date as 49 B.C. Still we do manage to determine dates without having to refer explicitly to history or astronomy, though there is a sense in which dating involves both. Consequently, the phenomenalist might try to deal with Crippen on the following lines. "If a certain set of sense-experiences, namely such as would entitle anyone who had them to assert 'this is such and such a room in such and such a street in Camden Town' had been sensibly contemporaneous with a series of sense-experiences of such a character as would entitle anyone who had them to assert 'this is such and such an hour of such and such a day in the year 1910,' they would have been accompanied by a series of sense-experiences of such a character as would entitle anyone who had them to assert 'here is a man called Dr. Crippen engaged in murdering his wife.' " But the defect of this formulation is that it provokes the question: *When* would all this have happened? to which the only answer is that the question is illegitimate. For all the wheres and whens are supposed to be included *in* the sensory story: so that there can be no where and when *of* the story. It was for this reason that in dealing just now with my example of the penguins at the South Pole I introduced the conditional clauses with the word "given" instead of the customary "if." My object was to avoid the use of verbs which, by reason of their tenses, would have referred unwarrantably to physical time.

Another defect of the formulation: 'If a series A of sense-experiences had been sensibly contemporaneous with a series B, they would have been accompanied, or followed, by a series C' is that in certain cases it may be that they *were* so accompanied, so that it is idle to say that they *would* have been. Thus, in the Crippen example, it may be objected, as I remarked before, that it is silly to say '*if* anybody were to have had certain experiences' when we can reasonably assume that somebody, namely Crippen himself, *did* have them. But the answer to this is that it is a mistake to say either that certain sense-experiences *were* obtained, or that they would have been obtained, if this is understood, as it naturally would be, to involve a reference to physical time. The protasis of our hypothetical is supposed to describe, in sensory terms, the 'setting' of the event of which the apodosis contains the sensory description. Consequently, there is no need to put the setting itself into space and time: and not only is there no need to do this, but the attempt to do it leads to a vicious confusion of the physical and sensory levels of language.

A similar confusion arises if it is said, or implied, that the sense-data, which supply the phenomenalist with the materials for his analyses, are, or would be, sensed *by* anyone, whether it be myself, the speaker, or anybody else. For not only does this involve an illegitimate reference to physical bodies, and so to physical space and time, but it leads also to the difficulties which I mentioned earlier, concerning the possibility of physical interaction between the observer and the event that he is put there to observe. The way to meet these difficulties, I now suggest, is not to choose some apparently inoffensive observer, such as a mouse, or a man with a telescope, but to exclude from the analysis any reference to an observer at all. Admittedly, it is necessary, in practice, to refer to an observer in order to explain what is meant by a sense-datum: for it is only in terms of what is relatively familiar that an unfamiliar term can be understood. But once the sense-datum language has been accepted as basic, then observers, like everything else at the physical level, must be reduced to sense-data. For to allow them to stand outside 'having' or 'sensing' the sense-data would be to bring sense-data themselves up to the physical level and so vitiate the whole phenomenalistic programme.

That no explicit reference to a physical body should occur in the phenomenalist's analysis would be generally admitted: but it seems usually to have been thought that an observer of some sort must always figure in the protases, not indeed baldly as his physical self, but in the correct sensory disguise. It does not appear to me, however, that this is necessary. I do not see, for example, why the phenomenalist's version of such a proposition as 'there is a book-case in the dining-room' should contain the description of any sensory manifestation of a human body. It has to identify the dining-room in question and also to specify some period of time, but that should be enough. It may, indeed, be argued that unless some human body were present no sense-experiences would occur at all. But the analysis does not state that any sense-experiences do occur: only that given certain sense-experiences, then . . . certain others. That no experiences at all would be 'given' unless there were an observer is indeed a physical fact: but there is no reason why that physical fact should be prefixed to every sensory analysis. On the contrary, the phenomenalist must hold that it is itself to be analysed in purely sensory terms. The only cases, therefore, in which the analysis will contain a sensory description of an observer are those in which there is some reference to an observer in the proposition which is to be analysed. In such case the observer will figure *in* the sensory story, but in no case will there be an observer *of* the story. The phenomenalist's tale does not include the author: it is, in that respect, a tale that tells itself.

7

I suggest then that the phenomenalist's analysis of a simple proposition about a physical object, say a proposition to the effect that there exists a physical object of a certain sort in a certain place throughout a certain period of time, should take the following form. A protasis, which will itself include a number of subsidiary hypotheticals, describing such sense-experiences as would be sufficient to identify the place and time in question, or in other words, to put the physical object in its proper setting: followed by an apodosis which would describe such sense-experiences as would be sufficient to verify the presence of the physical object in question: and this apodosis will also have to contain a number of subsidiary hypotheticals to rule out the possibility of an illusion. If this were done, the truth of the whole hypothetical might, I think, pass as a sufficient condition of the truth of the proposition which it was intended to analyse. It would not, however, be a necessary condition, because of the relative indefiniteness of the proposition at the physical level. But as has already been shown, to formulate a sufficient condition in purely sensory terms is the most that the phenomenalist can reasonably hope for: and I cannot claim to have done more than give a very rough sketch of the way in which this might be achieved.

The fact is that so long as he confines himself to giving a *general* account of the way in which physical objects are 'constructed' out of sense-data, or a *general* account of the way in which physical space and time are 'constructed' out of sensory spaces and times, the phenomenalist does not appear to meet any insuperable obstacles. But directly he tries to reduce any particular statement about a physical object, even the simplest, to a statement, or set of statements, about sense-data, he runs into difficulties which, however he may make light of them in theory, in practice overwhelm him. The reason for this may lie only in the extreme complexity of his undertaking. But I think that there may be a more serious reason. I think that it might be argued that he was setting himself a task that could not, by its very nature, be satisfactorily fulfilled. For the language in which we refer to physical objects has its own logic. Now the sensory language to which the phenomenalist seeks to reduce the other must also have its logic, and this logic must be either the same as that of the physical language or different. If it is made the same—if, for example, the phenomenalist allows himself to speak of 'sensibilia' having a continued and distinct existence in space and time—then we are inclined to say that he has not carried out his programme, because these sensibilia are only physical objects, or attenuated physical objects, in disguise. But if the logic of the sensory language is different, then we are inclined to say that the statements which are expressed in it are not perfect translations of the statements at the physical level, just because their logic is different. So what is the phenomenalist to do?

If this line of argument is correct, then the solution of the 'problem of perception' may be to treat our beliefs about physical objects as constituting a theory, the function of which is to explain the course of our sensory experiences. The statements which are expressed in terms of the theory may not then be capable of being reproduced exactly as statements about sense-data; that is, it may not be possible wholly to rewrite them as statements about sense-data. Nevertheless, they will function only as means of grouping sense-data: and it will be a contingent fact that sense-data are so organized that the theory is valid. It may then be required of the philosopher to make clear in what this organization consists: that is, to show in a general way what relations must obtain between sense-data for the demands of the theory to be met. Thus, to echo Kant, he may be represented as trying to answer the question How is the physical-object language possible? And to this question the phenomenalist has, I think, the makings of a satisfactory answer.

R. J. HIRST

The Representative
Theory of Perception

~~~~~~

I. MODERN NEUROLOGISTS' STATEMENTS OF THE THEORY

We have now seen that the main current philosophical theories and
methods do not provide a satisfactory solution to the central problems of perception. They can neither refute nor supersede a careful
restatement and amplification of our common-sense notions, though
the discussion has revealed some inadequacies in the latter. It is therefore time to re-examine the traditional causal theory of perception,
usually called the Representative Theory, to see whether it is in fact
so easily refuted as is commonly supposed by modern philosophers
and whether a study of its failings can point the way to a fully satisfactory treatment of the problems.

This reconsideration is advisable on other grounds. First, the Representative Theory is a notable attempt to explain the causal processes
involved in perception and to take account of the scientific evidence
concerning the sense organs and nervous system. As our chief aim
is a comprehensive theory of perception which will cover all the facts,
we must naturally pay great attention to this evidence. An excellent
introduction to this task is the study of classical attempts to explain
it, for although the detailed study of these processes has made great
advances, their general principle is much the same as in Locke's day;
the philosophical difficulties lie mainly in the existence of a transmission system or causal chain, not in the composition of the links.
Secondly and consequently, modern neurologists tend to assert theories
which are in essentials the old Representative Theory though under

From R. J. Hirst, 'The Representative Theory of Perception,' *The Problems
of Perception* (London: George Allen and Unwin, Ltd., 1959), pp. 145–80. Reprinted
by permission of the author and George Allen and Unwin, Ltd.

different names like 'Physiological Idealism' or 'The Two-world Theory.' We can thus use versions of impeccable modernity in outlining and discussing the traditional theory.[1] Its very persistence and the perennial appeal it makes to those who consider carefully the scientific facts of perception render the theory of fundamental importance; indeed many philosophers who have tried to show its absurdity have been unable to disentangle themselves completely from it. Hume inconsistently advances arguments based on experiments on the nervous system and sense organs,[2] while Berkeley, after proclaiming the absurdity of unobservable matter as a cause of perceptions, goes on to offer a different unobservable cause. Kant's 'thing-in-itself' and Price's 'physical occupant' are also unknown causes of perceptions, while the latter's Generative Theory can only avoid the traditional difficulties by paradoxes about sense-data. And that Phenomenalists or Linguistic Philosophers avoid them is only because they ignore or fail to appreciate fully the problems posed by the scientific evidence.

It will be convenient to divide a modernized exposition of the Representative Theory into four stages, considering first the nature of the physical and physiological transmission.

(i) If for example we look from directly above at a circular plate, light rays reflected from it strike the eyes and are focused on to the two retinae and set up a roughly circular pattern of stimulation on the mosaic of sensitive cells of each retina. (We may neglect the complication due to slight eye movements.) This stimulation causes a discharge of impulses along the nerve fibres leading to the brain, and eventually evokes a specific spatio-temporal pattern of impulses in the cerebral cortex. Apparently, however, this final pattern will not be circular from a circular object, but will consist of four flattened semicircular areas of excitation; as Brain puts it with more verve than syntax (p. 9), 'when we perceive a two-dimensional circle we do so by means of an activity in the brain which is halved, reduplicated, transposed, inverted, distorted and three-dimensional.' In sound a different type of cortical representation seems to occur: if one hears a note of say 3,000 cycles a second, sound waves of this frequency strike the ear and set vibrating the part of the cochlea responsive to it. This vibration sets up impulses in the auditory nerve fibres, and the impulses in turn excite a special area of the cerebral cortex. A note of a different frequency would set up activity in a slightly different area, and the range of frequencies that can be heard is represented by a series of excitation areas along a strip of the brain, though the situation is complicated

[1] For a modern outline of the theory I have followed J. C. Eccles, *The Neurophysiological Basis of Mind,* pp. 279–81, and Sir W. R. Brain, *Mind, Perception and Science.* J. R. Smythies' *Analysis of Perception* I discuss in Chap. vi, § 6.

[2] *Treatise* I, iv, 2 (Everyman edition, p. 203).

by secondary areas of excitation. For touch also the various parts of the body seem to have a spatial representation, though a very distorted one, in the brain. The situation for taste and smell is understandably obscure as they are more difficult to test.

One must note that the impulses which travel along the nerves do not resemble their stimulus, either in themselves or in their frequency. The nerve impulses in the auditory and optic nerves seem to be of similar type, and the frequency with which the impulses follow each other seems to depend on the intensity of the stimulus and to bear no relationship to the frequency of the light or sound waves responsible. But the transmission of impulses is not along a single path or fibre. The optic and auditory nerves are each a bundle of very many fibres, and each fibre is connected to a different sensitive cell in the retina or cochlea at the one end and a different part of the cortex at the other (at least approximately, for there are complicating interconnections). The transmission of perceived qualities thus seems to depend on the set of paths or fibres by which the impulses travel and on their destination in the cortex. Attempts have been made to represent perceived qualities by a 'cortical map' of corresponding patterns in the brain,[3] but in so far as this is possible the 'map' is either a very distorted representation (if it is of seen or touched shape) or one in another medium (when a strip of the brain 'maps' a sound or colour spectrum).

(ii) As a consequence of one of these patterns of activity in the brain we experience a sensation or group of sensations, e.g. a colour patch of circular shape or a high-pitched sound. The occurrence of the brain activity is the necessary condition of the experience of the appropriate sensation: thus if the visual cortex of the brain is destroyed visual sensations do not occur. But more interestingly, it seems to be also a sufficient condition of the sensation. Admittedly it is commonly supposed that the proper working of the causal chain antecedent to brain activity is a necessary condition of perception—if the eye is damaged sight is lost. On the Representative Theory this must be reinterpreted: damage to the eye prevents the brain from being stimulated by the object and so prevents sensations caused by it; injury thus prevents a necessary condition of the sensation, viz. brain activity, but the eye is not a necessary condition of visual sensation for if the brain activity were otherwise caused the sensation would follow. This important point has been supported by experiment. Sensations can be produced by direct electrical stimulation of the appropriate part of the cortex, and the information thus gained has been used for drawing 'cortical maps,' as a sensation of touch, for example, will appear to come from the part of the body which is related to the stimulated point on the

[3] See E. D. Adrian, *The Physical Background of Perception*.

cortex. The sensation thus caused is unlike the normal tactile sensation and is difficult to describe; but the difference would seem to be adequately accounted for by the difference between direct electrical stimulation (excitation of a large group of cells at a fixed frequency) and the normal impulses from the skin (trains of impulses rising and falling in frequency and confined to fewer nerve endings). Sensations of colour and sound from direct stimulation are similarly vague owing to the unavoidable crudity of the stimulus. However, on the assumption that a closer reproduction of normal activity in the brain would give more life-like sensations, one can even explain dreams, hallucinations and mental images: they are due to activity in the visual cortex, and perhaps also the afferent nerves, activity not caused by stimulation due to the external object but similar to activity so caused. And one can at least deal with the classic case of the 'phantom limb'; if one's foot is amputated one may afterwards feel that it is still there and feel pain in the non-existent toes; this is apparently because the nerves which previously connected toe to brain and which remain in the untouched part of the limb, are still sending impulses like those normally due to external excitation.

(iii) Upholders of the theory seem generally agreed that we pass from the awareness of sensations caused by brain events to the awareness of percepts, i.e. of ostensible objects, which, though in fact private to the percipient, are regarded by him as public and external, or at least as externally caused. But they disagree as to how this projection or interpretation of sensations occurs. We may distinguish Actual Inference and Justificatory Inference views. On the former we actually proceed from sensations perceived as private to infer or construct a public world of objects. This seems to be the view of Eccles: The observers 'each with his own private and unique perceptual world come to agree on the existence of a single physical world' which explains them; 'Personal experiment from earliest childhood onwards, and communications with others, are the standard procedures' by which we interpret private experiences 'as events in a single physical world.' Others hold that the private data are inferred to be effects, not parts, of the external world. The second type of view denies that any such inference occurs; our private world is always accepted as external or externally caused. The proper role of inference is thus the justification of this acceptance as far as possible, i.e. to the extent of showing that the private sensations or percepts do have public external causes which they represent and which are as described in science. Despite some contrary suggestions this alternative seems to be the one chiefly favoured by Brain, who claims (p. 76) that experiences 'reach consciousness already stamped with externality'; it is also apparently the view of Locke, who, however, exaggerates the extent to which we see things as externally caused rather than external. He says 'the actual receiving of ideas from without gives us notice of the existence of other things, and makes us know, that something doth exist at that time without us, which causes that idea in us,' [4] and he supports this 'sensitive knowledge' by 'concurrent reason.'

This divergence of view is complicated by a similar disagreement about synthetic or constructive activity on the part of the percipient. Some hold that an actual synthesis occurs: our sensations are basically atomic and have to be combined into percepts and objects. Thus Eccles says 'all kinds of diverse patterned inputs are coordinated and linked together to give some coherent synthesis,' though it is not easy to distinguish the various types of activity he supposes to occur. But if we reject the notion of atomic sensations and regard the unit of visual sensation as the whole of one view of an object, like Price's sense-datum, then we already have a percept in this respect, and the synthetic activity is not necessary to a single act of perception. Its place is then in the Justificatory Inference, as part of the process of showing that these percepts belong to external objects or families. It is thus the same sort of process as that which Price developed for showing that a sense-datum belonged to an external object and so advancing from 'perceptual acceptance' to 'perceptual assurance,' but is added to a theory which interprets 'belong to' as 'caused by.'

(iv) Despite these differences, however, there is general agreement on the relation between the private world of percepts and sensations and the public world of external objects. The former is a representation or symbolization, rather like a map, of the latter;[5] this is the main representation which gives the theory its name and any additional representation by cortical patterns is ancillary to the main one and is the means by which it occurs. The old distinction of primary and secondary qualities is revived as well: some of the features of the private world, e.g. spatial relations, reproduce the external world fairly closely, but many of them, e.g. colours, sounds and smells, no more copy the external original than do the conventional symbols of maps, music or other representational systems.

Plus ça change plus c'est la même chose. In this modern neurological account appear all the key features of the seventeenth-century Representative Theory: hence it seems equally liable to the traditional charge of self-refutation. In steps (i) and (ii) it is assumed that we can observe and know the operation of physical objects such as nerves and brains; in steps (iii) and (iv) we are told we perceive only a private world, which is moreover widely different from the external physical world.

---

[4] *Essay* IV, xi, 2. The concurrent reasons are given in IV, xi, 4–7.
[5] Eccles, *loc. cit.*; Brain, *op. cit.*, pp. 58 ff., cf. p. 21.

If therefore our supposed observation of nerves and sense organs is it-self merely experiencing a private and biased perceptual world, what justification have we for supposing that it is valid and gives a true account of their working? The last stages of the theory would seem to jeopardize the first and to destroy the evidence on which it is based. Indeed if we are thus enclosed within the barrier of our private world, how do we know what the real physical world is like, how far it differs from the private one, or even that there is an external world at all? We have no means of checking our theories about it, for the observations which we might suppose to verify them are in fact only more glimpses of our private world. The theory adopts what has been called the 'angel's view': it seems to assume we can observe both our mental experiences and the external world they represent, and can compare the two. This is impossible on the theory, and its supposition is due to a confusion of immanent and external viewpoints.

This basic epistemological difficulty may be put in other ways. One is to point out the weakness of the map analogy. We can make and understand maps because we can see directly the country that is mapped as well as its representation on the map; if we could only see the representation and had never seen the reality or anything like it, the map would be meaningless to us and we should not realize that it was a map. Again, whenever we assert or infer a causal relation be-tween two things, we have either observed them both or have observed analogous cases of cause and effect. Here, however, we are asked to infer the cause from the effect without *ex hypothesi* being able to ob-serve it, and that too in a causal situation which is *sui generis*. This illegitimate inference from the known to the unknown is concealed by the assumption in the first stage of the theory that we can observe ex-ternal objects and their action on the senses; but the conclusion of the theory shows that this was an illusion—it was only observation of more private data.

Such a refutation has proved quite sufficient for many philosophers, but we must give the theory further consideration to see how it may be defended or improved on. Mere refutation is not enough as the scientific data will still require interpretation and explanation.

2. UNPLAUSIBLE VARIANTS REJECTED

To be fair to the Representative Theory we must take it in its most plausible form. We must therefore reject at the outset the Actual In-ference variants with their suggestion that we do in fact infer the existence of an external world from private data perceived as such.

In Chapter IV of his *Perception* Price has given a convincing refutation of this kind of view, which he calls the Causal Theory, and here we need only briefly show its weakness. Eccles claims that by personal experiment and communication with others we come to interpret our private world as events in a single physical world; but unfortunately he gives no details by which we could judge the adequacy of these means. Perhaps he is relying on some suggestions of Brain,[6] who in answer to the question "If the observer's knowledge of any 'world' is limited to his perceptions, how does he ever discover that there is any other 'world'?" mentions inference based on the observation of others and experiments such as, (i) stimulating a person's brain and asking for his sensations, or (ii) inferring the speed of sound by observing a man hammering and noticing the increasing discrepancy between sight and sound of each blow as you move away. But these already accept the existence of physical objects like brains, hammers and electrical apparatus, and so could only be for discovering what the external world is like, not that there is one. And like 'communication with others' they beg the question in that to assume one is really talking to another person is already to put oneself outside the alleged private world. Some childhood experiments may perhaps more readily be put forward, e.g. dropping things, putting things to the mouth, poking the finger through the holes in the fireguard. But they can be interpreted more plausibly than as attempts to infer from private to public world: they may be accidental, or from other motives, e.g. to attract attention, and if exploratory they are most likely attempts to find out what happens if one does X or to discover what Y is like.

But the real objection to Eccles' suggestion is twofold: (i) We are not conscious of having performed such experiments and feats of interpretation. It might be replied that we did in fact perform these activities in childhood but have forgotten it, or that the activities have become so swift and automatic as not to be noticed. But this is pure speculation without evidence and puts a terrible load on the infant mind. It is too much to suppose that the small child, to whom the distinction of public and private world would be meaningless, spends his time in such interpretations, many of which would have to be complex to be convincing. (ii) To interpret A as B you must first be conscious of A as A: if you interpret a pattering sound as rain on the roof, you must first have been aware of it as a pattering sound. But why assume that the private world of sensations ever appears as private to adult or infant? Even with efforts of introspection it is hard, if not impossible, to regard colours as private and mental; they seem undeniably external, and so probably have always seemed external, at least in so far as the external/internal distinction is appreciated at all. This might be due to the nature of their causation. In our experience pains, tickles and similar bodily sensations are almost always roughly located, e.g. one has not just a pain but a pain in the leg; and this may be an essential feature of sensations not originating in the brain, due to the fact that with sensations of different origin different sensory areas are activated. Hence an apparent externality, or at least a placing at the sense organ, might be an essential feature of the content of visual, auditory and similar sensations, since they are caused by nerve impulses from externally activated sense organs. That this physiological placing is not inference may be seen from referred pains, which are not felt to be at the place where their true cause is, even when this is known to the sufferer.

The supposition of Actual Synthesis must also be rejected on similar grounds: we are not aware of performing it and are not aware of sensations as atomic or as small elements out of which objects may be constructed. As the result of binocular vision and of our awareness of depth, our world, even if private, probably appears from the first as roughly differentiated into objects;[7] or at least it is an undifferentiated whole in which objects are gradually distinguished, not a set of discrete elements to be combined.

Nor can we accept a further variant of the theory which Brain finally adopts in an attempt to avoid the obvious danger of self-refutation.[8] He suggests that the two 'worlds' are not distinct worlds or series of events, nor is one the representation and the other the real original, but they are both symbolic representations or languages. (He specifically likens this theory to Ayer's two language view.) Thus the perceptual world is a private sensuous representation of an underlying reality or series of events, and the physical world of science is an alternative and conceptual representation of the same reality. The second representation may seem to be more real and to be the cause of the former, but that is an illusion due to its greater accuracy.

Despite Brain's statement that he agrees with Ayer's two language view his own theory seems quite different. Ayer's languages are at least verbal systems and the facts they symbolize are sensory experiences; the sense-datum language describes these directly, while the material object language is a convenient way of referring to their grouping and sequences. So what Ayer regards as the one set of facts symbolized by his two languages corresponds exactly to one of Brain's languages or sym-

---

[7] R. J. Hirst, *The Problems of Perception* (London: George Allen and Unwin, Ltd., 1959) Chap. ix, 2.

[8] *Op. cit.*, Chaps. v–vii, esp. pp. 78 ff.

bolic systems, namely his perceptual world. Brain's other language, his scientific conceptual system, would seem to be a sub-class of Ayer's material object language.

More important, as any symbolic representation or map must represent some original, Brain has to postulate a reality or system of events of which both sensations and science are symbols. Apart from being unlikely to appeal to Ayer, this postulation means that Brain has failed to solve the epistemological problem. The whole question at issue is how, if we are all along aware only of representation or effects, do we know that they are representations and effects, or learn what are the originals or causes. To be told that the supposed original, the physical world of science, is yet another symbol system is no help at all, for one then has to postulate a third factor, the unknown reality they are both supposed to symbolize. Again, if the public physical world is to be regarded as part of this conceptual symbolic system, then so must the events in the sense organs and nervous system discovered by physiology. Hence these events, being mere representations, cannot act as causes, and the initial stages of the theory are jeopardized. The main reason for supposing that the perceptual world was a representation and not reality was that it seemed to be the effect of a causal chain from external object to brain; if the object and causal chain dissolve into symbols we are left with theoretical chaos.

We must conclude then that these modern neurologists have not found a satisfactory way out of the epistemological difficulties. Nor are the traditional philosophical attempts, even to support the more plausible Justificatory Inference view, any more successful. Locke, for example, offers as 'concurrent reasons' to confirm our supposed assurance that ideas or sensations have external causes:

(i) The sense organs are necessary for the production of sensations, but do not produce them on their own; sensations must therefore be due to external causes acting on the senses.

(ii) Sensations obtrude and often cannot be avoided; I cannot help hearing a certain sound or, if my eyes are open, seeing certain sights.

(iii) Sensations, e.g. of heat, may be produced with pain; this distinguishes the actual sensation from the memory of it which is not accompanied by pain.

(iv) The senses confirm each other; if you see a fire you can feel it too, and you can see yourself write. In discussing this Locke adds what should really be regarded as another reason (v), that others too can see what you have written; i.e. that genuine sensations, as opposed to dreams, are shared or public in that others can have similar or qualitatively identical sensations at the same time.

The difficulty facing Locke is a double one: partly that while genuine sensations do have a feeling of externality, a 'tang of reality,'[9] so do many illusions and hallucinations; and partly that he wants to show, not that colours, shapes, etc., are external (which is what we normally assume), but that they are private mental data whose cause is external. But his concurrent reasons scarcely support these points. The first and fourth do not take us outside the private world of ideas or sensations; all our evidence about sense organs is based on observation, on having further sensations, and the sense organs themselves are thus, on the theory, groups of sensations. The most the first reason proves is that unless certain sensations are experienced or obtainable no sensations of another type are obtainable; if an observer does not or cannot get sense-data of X's eyes being open, then X cannot get the normal visual sensations of his private world. And the fourth reason only shows that two sets of ideas go together, that sensations of sight are supplemented by those of touch, not that they have an exernal cause; thus we may in a dream feel the fire that we see or see what we write. The fifth point, that genuine sensations may be shared, is stronger—you can see what I see in a way in which you do not dream what I dream, and this suggests some external cause. But the tough-minded objector can still argue that my only evidence that you exist and see what I see is my observation of your actions or my hearing of your utterances, i.e. further observations of mine, and so I have still not crossed the barrier of sensations. The second and third reasons are also unconvincing. Involuntariness or obtrusion is no criterion of external reality, for some mental imagery, many thoughts, and all dreams and hallucinations, come to us involuntarily and are not summoned up at will. Nor is occurrence with pain a good test, for it is not applicable to the great majority of genuine sensations, which occur without pain, and pain may attend hallucinations or nightmares, e.g. in cases of 'phantom limbs' and psychic illness. Hence the concurrent reasons fail to prove that certain sensations have an external cause; alternative explanations are always possible.

3. THE THEORY AS THE BEST HYPOTHESIS

Although it is difficult to see how even its Justificatory Inference version can be given a watertight proof, the Representative Theory can and should adopt a different line of defence, arguing simply that the supposition of external causes is the best explanation of the uniformities and sequences of sensations or percepts. It must therefore be regarded as truly a theory, an explanation of the given facts, not as new facts

[9] Cf. R. I. Aaron, *John Locke,* 2nd ed., p. 245.

deduced from them: as such it must be tested by the criteria applicable to theories and explanations, and must be compared in point of plausibility with the possible alternatives.

One such criterion is the successful prediction of new facts or experiences, but, as we have seen, that is a very difficult test for any philosophical theory and cannot always be applied to the more general scientific theories. Other criteria of an explanation thus become of prime importance, namely comprehensiveness, systematic unity and simplicity. The best explanation will cover all the facts, and will include them as part of its systematic whole and not as stray coincidences; it will do this with the smallest number of basic concepts and axioms, with the postulation of the fewest types of entity and without the introduction of *ad hoc* hypotheses to meet awkward discoveries.

Several attempts have been made to defend the Representative Theory on these lines. Thus Professor Montague argues:[10] "The dualist's contention that the data of his experience are the effects of something beyond his experience is based on the fact that the data of experience do not themselves afford an explanation for their occurrence and behaviour." Bertrand Russell's attempts to justify the inference from percepts to physical objects in his *Human Knowledge* are probably meant and are certainly best understood this way, while the recent work by the neurologist J. R. Smythies is more explicit in advocating the Representative Theory as the "best explanation of the world." [11] These writers differ widely on details, however, and I shall therefore discuss this rehabilitation of the theory in general terms.

The defence means that not only does one give up the fruitless search for a proof of the existence of external objects from the evidence of sensations—something which would make the Representative Theory not a theory but demonstrable fact—but also that the taint of circularity in defensive arguments is avoided. If one were trying to deduce the existence of a public world from premises about private sensations, then the introduction of arguments from the observations of other persons would be circular in its assumption that there were other persons; but if one's aim is to provide the simplest and most convincing explanation of the occurrence of those sensations, then it is legitimate to include as part of the explanation the hypothesis that what we take to be utterances of other people are in fact just that, and to build on this.

The Representative Theory is thus offered as an attempt to improve on ordinary notions or 'theories' of perception and to avoid their inconsistencies. A common criticism of its claim to be the most plausible

[10] W. P. Montague, *Ways of Knowing,* p. 258.
[11] *Analysis of Perception,* p. 35.

hypothesis is that it is difficult to see how, if we were aware only of private ideas, the hypothesis that they had external causes would ever occur to us. This criticism has force against the Actual Inference view with its assumption that we start with sensations perceived as private, but it hardly holds against this present defence if, like the Justificatory Inference approach, it assumes from the start that we perceive our in fact private percepts as external, and if it suggests that this is explained by their causation from without and by the general tendency to locate sensations at their approximate origin. The theory must nevertheless challenge the widespread assumption that colours, shapes, sounds and so on are external; it must point to the physiological data and the occurrence of dreams, hallucinations and perceptual relativity, and must claim that the best, in fact the only, explanation of all these is that what we treat as external are only externally caused private sensations and percepts.

Similarly the danger of self-refutation is apparently avoided, for though the final statement of the theory involves modification of the original conception of the physiological observation on which the first stages depend, it does not undermine it. This observation cannot on the theory be regarded as direct awareness of a part cause of the subject's perception since it likewise involves a causal chain, but it can be claimed that the best explanation of the data it gives and of their correlation with experiences of the percipient subject is that the percepts we are directly aware of do reproduce the structure and primary qualities of their external causes. In this way observation of the sense organs of a percipient subject, though strictly only direct awareness of percepts caused by them, does give sufficient essential information about them to support the evidence of physiological transmission.

Rehabilitation of the theory thus involves the claim that science, by correlating percepts, can discover much about the real nature of their external causes. This has in fact always been an integral part of the theory, and one can but suppose that the failure of its earlier adherents to realize the epistemological difficulties of their version was due to a robust faith in the validating power of science. Very often this faith has gone further than our present supposition that, granted there are external causes of our percepts, science can be held to discover their basic nature; it has been also supposed that it can justify the inference from private data to public physical objects and can show that though our observation is limited to awareness of private data nevertheless such objects exist. Science, it is thought, stands or falls with this inference and science must be true because of its very success. The effective development of the atomic bomb and other devices could only have been achieved on the basis of a theory about the ultimate constituents of matter that was largely correct; but such a theory cannot be isolated from the rest of science, which forms one interlocking system guarantee-ing both the existence of external objects and the limitation of our direct awareness to private data.

There are two difficulties in this wider appeal to science. The first is that practical success is no guarantee of theoretical accuracy. One may succeed by accident or for the wrong reasons or on the basis of incorrect theory, just as astronomers calculated and sailors navigated successfully for years on the basis of the Ptolemaic Theory; and even today Newton and Euclid are of more practical value than Einstein. And there are various rivals to the Representative Theory which also claim to give the best explanation of the world and to account for the success of science on other grounds.

One might argue, for example, that the success of science is simply due to scientists' having discovered the general laws linking perceptions and the rules for predicting them. 'Matter,' 'atoms' and 'electrons' are therefore at best only useful co-ordinating concepts, devices to help us predict further sense experiences; there is no need to suppose that they stand for anything real, indeed the only realities are the sense-data to be co-ordinated. The difficulty of conceiving the nature of electrons and similar scientific entities has made this kind of explanation popular today among scientists and philosophers of science. They claim that physics should, in the light of present advances, be regarded not 'as a study of the nature of the external world' but 'as an attempt to find rational relations between elements of our experience.' 'When they are expressed as characteristics of a world existing outside us and inde-pendently of us (which causes our experience by its impact on our sense organs), these discoveries require such a world to have contradictory properties.' [12] This view is in fact the Phenomenalist one, but defenders of the Representative Theory on scientific grounds would have to show that it was a less satisfactory hypothesis than theirs.

A rival explanation on Kantian lines might also be attempted. The Phenomenalist explanation held that, whereas the ideas or sensations are private and their quality subjective, nevertheless the order of their sequences and coexistence was objective and could be discovered by science and so explained their successful predictions. But the Kantian one would go further and claim that this order also was subjective, was a character of our private worlds of ideas only and not of external reality. The mind imposes its own forms of synthesis on the unorganized representations that it receives; thus the spatial and temporal relations of the world as perceived are all due to the knowing mind, as are its categories, e.g. the apparent division into subject and attribute, cause

[12] H. Dingle in *The Listener*, November 18, 1948, cf. his article in *Nature*, 1951, p. 630.

and effect. Hence the success of science is understandable, almost inevitable, for it amounts merely to discovering the way in which sensations are organized by our minds. Its laws seem to be objectve and public and so be knowledge of the external world which causes our ideas; but this is illusion in that these causes are unknown and unknowable. The laws are only objective for us, revealing the kind of order that the human mind must impose on the raw material of sensation. Thus again defence of the Representative Theory must include reasons for preferring it to these alternatives.

Secondly, it is no part of science to put forward its results as correlations of private sense-data and to argue from them to the existence of public physical objects as their causes; rather it is an attempt to correlate observations and experiments on public objects and to argue from these to the real nature of the objects or to the laws explaining their behaviour. It thus accepts as implicit premisses, that there are public objects to be observed, measured and experimented on, and that different persons can observe and measure the same object, so that their results confirm each other. In this way it begs the fundamental question at issue—how if we are aware only of private ideas or sense-data can we justifiably infer that there are external objects?—and can hardly be used to answer it. If the Representative Theory is to be regarded as a hypothesis to explain the course of our sensations, confirmaton of this part of it must be sought rather in the various communications with other persons and the multifarious activities of social life, which are prior to scientific experiment and hypothesis.

We must therefore divide our assessment of the theory into two parts, considering first the pre-scientific belief in the existence of public external objects, and secondly the claims of science to discover the nature of these objects, in particular the claim that they consist of primary qualities only, the secondary ones being purely subjective.

4. EXTERNAL CAUSES

For the first part then of this double justification the Representative Theory must be held to claim that the best, simplest and most coherent explanation of the course of our sense-data is that they are actually caused by the public and persistent external objects to which they seem to belong. And for this Locke's 'concurrent reasons' take on a new importance as typical cases of the kind of pattern of sense-data which is best explained in this way. The first of these reasons only showed that unless one group of sense-data is obtainable another does not occur. The second of these groups consists of general visual experiences of a percipient P, and the first may be expanded to include sensations of the opthalmologist X normally taken to be due to the proper functioning of P's eye and sensations of a third observer Z which would normally be regarded as data of P's eye being open. Now granted that P, X and Z are only aware each of his own private sensations, this correlation between them is all that is proved; it is not demonstrably due to causal relations between P's eye (as a material object, not simply a group of sense-data) and the persons concerned. But the most plausible explanation of the correlations is that the data of X and Z are caused by P's eye, a public material object which also in a different way enables P to have data caused by other external objects. A detailed justification of this would be lengthy, but we may refer for support to the attempt by Price to show how, starting from private sense-data, a percipient could reasonably conclude that they were generated by sense organs.[13] This part of his work could well be taken over by this defence of the Representative Theory, despite disagreements on other points.

The second of Locke's reasons would be simpler to restate: just the claim that the best explanation of the involuntariness and obtrusion of sensations is that they are externally caused. There would be some weakness about thoughts, but the obtrusiveness of dreams and imagery could be put down to their being caused outside the mind, though in the brain; they are caused within the body because not shared with other persons, whereas the obtrusive sensations are more plausibly due to external objects because very similar sensations may simultaneously obtrude on other persons. The third reason can hardly be improved much, but the fourth is strengthened in that the simplest explanation of the way ideas of sight and touch go together in many situations is that they there have a common external cause.

Even so Locke is hardly adequate; he scarcely appreciates the most cogent reason, namely that very often closely similar sense-experiences are simultaneously enjoyed by several people; we have already had to introduce this to support the second of his reasons, but it deserves to stand on its own. The theory must point to the apparent publicity of sense-data, to the way people can see, hear or feel the same object, and argue that this is best explained by there being a common external cause of the various private sense-data. A special case of this is the possibility of communicating with each other about the data thus obtained; Locke hints at this, the example of writing, without realizing its importance.

To show that the Representative Theory gives the best explanation of these correlations of data (granted *pace* common sense that they are private data), we must compare it with rivals. One of these is solipsism, the view that only one's own stream of ideas or sensations exists. This

[13] *Perception,* Chap. x.

has the basic weakness that the only reason anyone could have for rejecting the almost irresistible common-sense assumption that we are aware of other persons and public objects is that the evidence of physiology and hallucinations shows that such awareness is really only of sensations; but such evidence rests almost entirely on the evidence of other people, e.g. of neurologists or, in the case of the more spectacular hallucinations, those who have had the experience. Furthermore the sequence of experiences involved in what would ordinarily be described as being given information by another person and then verifying it for oneself is not easy to explain on solipsistic lines; one would have to suppose that one only dreamt or imagined that there was another person, and this would amount to denying the distinction between dreaming (or imagining) and reality, with the resultant difficulty of explaining away the tests and differences on which the distinction is normally based (e.g. the continuity of causal law between two waking states but not between two dream states). All this would mean a loss in simplicity and coherence. In fact, of course, no one believes solipsism is satisfactory, and philosophers would not give it a moment's thought were it not for the difficulty of conclusively refuting it, as opposed to showing that it is not plausible.

The next alternative, Phenomenalism, has already been discussed at length and its special application to science will be considered briefly in the next section, so it is only necessary here to mention its points of inferiority to the Representative Theory.

They arise out of the apparent publicity and persistence of physical objects and the continuance of their causal properties even when unobserved. The types of situation involved, e.g. our leaving the room for a minute and returning to see the table and chair just as before, the support of the floor by unseen joists, the deflection of the compass by the magnet in the pocket, or the operation of the sense organs and nerves, may perhaps all be described in terms of correlations of sense-data, though this would be difficult and complex; but to suppose that these correlated sense-data alone exist creates many paradoxes, as we have seen, and is a much less simple and plausible explanation than the supposition of the Representative Theory that the correlated data are due to continuing, public and causally efficacious physical objects.

We may point the contrast by taking an example of communication and exchange with other persons, namely when I go into a shop to buy a pound of sausages, hand over the money and receive the goods. On the Representative Theory the series of sense-data I and the shopkeeper get here is simply explained by supposing that material objects, public and external to our minds (viz. sausages and money), pass from one material object (person's body) to another, and in doing so affect our sense organs and cause the sense-data concerned. But if there are only persons and sense-data (or worse still only sense-data) and no material things, one is at a loss to explain the sequence of experiences I and the shopkeeper have during the transaction. That he and I should at the same time get a sequence of sense-data apparently of the interchange of objects, yet nothing in fact be exchanged, seems to be a strange and unexplained coincidence. Why should he get sense-data of receiving coins from me, indeed what am I doing in the shop at all, if I do not really hand over coins to him in exchange for goods, but I merely get sense-data of doing so? Why does he not get data of receiving the money if I only dream or imagine giving it to him? Phenomenalism seems quite incoherent on this and the only possible explanation of the situation seems to be that actual physical objects do change hands.

As to the complaint that the Representative Theory has to postulate unobservables, in that we are not directly aware of its physical objects, many of its rivals have to do the same. Berkeley has to bring in God as a *deus ex machina* to save him from the paradox of the continual annihilation and re-creation of objects, the Sensibilist postulates unsensed sense-data whose existence cannot be tested by observation, while the paradoxical possible sense-data of the Factual Phenomenalist are no better. If the Linguistic Phenomenalist avoids these postulations it is only at the cost of other paradoxes and implausibilities.

The main force of the Kantian alternative is directed against the second or scientific part of the Representative Theory; so far as the belief in the existence of physical objects is concerned, it seems to get the worst of both worlds. In so far as it regards material things as phenomenal, as constructs from our experiences, it is open to the objections levelled against Phenomenalism, quite apart from the difficulty of supposing an Actual Synthesis; and in so far as it regards them as noumenal, as the ultimate causes of our representations, they are mere unknown things-in-themselves, and it is open to the charge of postulating unobserved causes, without the advantages of crediting these causes with being, so far as primary qualities at least are concerned, the objects they seem to be.

5. PRIMARY AND SECONDARY QUALITIES

We may accept for the present that the Representative Theory is more plausible than its traditional rivals in supposing that our sensations are caused by the external objects to which they seem to belong; the second part of its justification as the best hypothesis rests on the claim that by science we can discover the fundamental characteristics of these causes. Historically this is bound up with the distinction of Primary and Secondary Qualities, viz. that the perceived qualities of sensations or percepts are of two kinds: the primary ones like shape, size, number and motion, which characterize the external causes as well as percepts; and the secondary ones like colours, sounds, smells and warmth, which are purely subjective and characterize only our experiences: their causes in objects are quite unlike them and possess only primary qualities. (This way of putting it is a little loose but is far more convenient than reserving the term 'quality' for properties of the external objects alone; that was Locke's way, but it means that one has to refer to colours as 'representations of secondary qualities,' which is pedantic and almost impossible to keep up in practice.)

The main arguments for this distinction are:

(i) That science can explain and describe the physical world solely in terms of primary qualities, therefore only they belong to it. The objection may be made that this mistakenly identifies science with physics, for colour and smell are important in biology; but what is important there is strictly the perception of colour or smell as affecting behaviour, and so does not touch the argument which concerns the real nature of physical objects. The main objection is that the science of one's day is not final and its account may not be the whole truth; so even if secondary qualities have no place in science they may still be real properties of matter.

(ii) Neurologists claim that there is nothing in the conduction of nerve impulses from sense organ to brain that could correspond to or transmit qualities such as colour, warmth or sound. As the nerves from the different sense organs are all similar, the only variables seem spatial (the different pathways and cortical destinations) and temporal (the frequency of the impulses, which anyhow seems only a mark of intensity). Thus though the spatial patterns in the cortex, and the sensations they cause, can be regarded as reproductions, if distorted ones, of the spatial patterns of the stimulus, secondary qualities cannot have been transmitted and must somehow arise out of the excitation of the cortex: it is unlikely, therefore, that they exist in the inorganic world outside the brain. One might object that sound can be transmitted by radio and colours by television without travelling as such through the air or along the aerial: they are converted into electrical impulses at the transmitter and converted back at the receiver. So the fact that colours and sounds do not travel along the nerves as such is no proof they are not transmitted; they may be converted into spatio-temporal patterns of impulses at the sense organ and reconverted at the brain.

Perhaps the real neurological argument is that, so far as we can judge, it is the physical correlates of colour, warmth and sound which activate the sense organs. The ear responds to different frequencies of sound waves, not to pitches and tones, and the retina to different frequencies of light waves, not to colours. But it would be difficult to prove this: and no waves are involved in taste and smell; there seems no evidence that the small particles which there activate the sense organs do not possess the properties of taste and smell.

In general this second argument reduces to one like the first; it claims that the causation of perception, as well as the nature of physical objects, is adequately explained in terms of primary qualities alone. This is no *proof* that secondary qualities do not characterize physical objects; but it suggests that there is no need to suppose that they do, and that account of the physical world which postulates the smallest range of fundamental properties is presumably simplest and best.

(iii) The most important argument for the distinction is the relativity one. The secondary qualities of our sensations are affected by the state of our sense organs and nervous system, by the temperature of our body, by our position with respect to the external object and by the medium separating us from it. As they thus vary according to conditions quite external to the object they cannot be intrinsic properties of it. I suggested in Chapter ii that all this meant was that the accuracy of our perception of the object varied: and though what was said there is true as far as it goes and is adequate against theories like the Sense-datum Theory, it can hardly survive as a final explanation once the scientific data of the causal process have been introduced. A comprehensive theory must not only take this process into account but must explain how this variability in the quality and accuracy of perception comes about; and that cannot be done on simple common-sense lines. I shall offer my own explanation later, but here need only point out that the Representative Theory is offering a plausible one. If the physiological evidence is to be explained by supposing we perceive percepts which are caused by external objects, then these so-called variations in the perception of external objects are variations in the percepts or representations caused by them: and these variations in turn are due to the way the conditions mentioned affect the brain activity that is the immediate cause of the representations. This means that the old argument from relativity is not really an independent one; it is secondary to the causal argument that claims that both primary and secondary qualities are in the first instance, i.e. *qua* perceived, qualities of percepts.

What then remains of the distinction? Simply that the primary qualities also characterize physical objects—the table is square as, in favourable circumstances, is the percept or representation of it; but it is not brown in the sense that it possesses what one can only call the sensuous quality of brownness; it can only be called brown in the sense of causing a representation of that nature. This claim can hardly be established by the relativity or variability of perception; such considerations are subordinate to the causal argument, and, as Berkeley pointed out, perceived shape, size and motion vary as much as colour or warmth. On these grounds then both types of quality are alike and are equally subjective. The essential point, however, is the distinction between perceived and measured shape, size, or motion. The former, including but not limited to 'apparent' shape, size, etc., are variable and characterize percepts as do colours. But it is the real measured qualities that are the concern of science; they are what it attributes to physical objects and they do not vary with the percipient's health or position. The penny may look elliptical but its measured shape is round—any two diameters at right angles to each other are equal in length and not of differing lengths as in an ellipse. Similarly one tree many look taller than another, but their measured height may be the same and does not vary with distance. Motion is in some ways relative, but with respect to a given frame of reference it is objectively determinable. This criterion of measurement gives us more invariant qualities than Locke envisaged, e.g. measured temperature is objective while felt warmth is not; but once the distinction of qualities is accepted, the extent of the 'primary' or rather 'fundamental' list will be influenced by scientific theory, and temperature would probably be reduced to mass and motion.

The relativity argument should therefore be recast. All immediately perceived or 'sensible' qualities are relative to the percipient and hence subjective, characterizing percepts only; this being confirmed by consideration of the causal process. Measured or scientific qualities are invariant and thus are objective intrinsic properties of physical objects. Also there is sufficient similarity between certain sensible qualities (size, shape, motion and number at least) and their counterparts and causes in scientific properties for them to be distinguished from others like colours or sounds. We may still call the first group 'primary' and the other 'secondary' if the reinterpretation is realized.

Before considering further the notion of measurement on which this depends, one might note that this amended distinction is still open to, though may survive, Berkeley's other main criticisms of Locke.[14] They were (i) that an idea can only be like an idea—i.e. that a sensible quality cannot resemble a scientific property of matter; and (ii) that matter consisting only of primary or scientific properties is inconceivable. The first seems to run counter to the obvious fact that percepts have shape and spatial properties; but it had strong *ad hominen* force against the older Representative Theory which claimed that mind was unextended and so had difficulty in explaining how mental percepts could have spatial properties. Modern versions like those of Russell

---

[14] Berkeley, *Principles of Human Knowledge*, viii ff.

and Smythies avoid that difficulty by allowing mind extension in some space other than physical space.[15] As to the second objection, whether we can conceive anything in Berkeley's sense of 'conceive,' namely 'imagine' or 'picture to oneself,' is a matter of past experience and powers of imagination, and is relative to what we can perceive. Thus one can allow to Berkeley that we could not immediately perceive or imagine ourselves perceiving anything which possessed only scientific properties and no sensible or secondary ones, but this in fact analytic statement is quite irrelevant to whether anything exists possessing only intrinsic scientific properties. Many things are commonplace in science which cannot be pictured or imagined, e.g. the dual wave/particle behaviour of electrons, the working of a band-pass filter, or four- or n-dimensional manifolds.

An examination of the notion of measurement suggests that the basic distinction is between the sensible qualities, which seem to characterize an object as viewed in a single perceptual act, and the properties which are ascertained as the result of co-ordinating a series of perceptions. Thus colour, taste, smell and apparent shape are each the content of a single perceptual act and are revealed by one; they are therefore particularly liable to distortion introduced by the health or position of the percipient. But measured size, shape and speed are discovered by reading meters or noting the coincidence of the ends of objects with marks on measuring rods, and by calculating from a number of such readings. In this series of operations the effect of distorting factors is cut to a minimum; the variations in a reading due to vagaries of the reader are within a small range, and checks by several persons can be made and an average taken of their results; nor are the calculations affected by sensory factors. Hence by a roundabout method which gives less scope for major error and more scope for checks, objective agreed answers can be obtained which are not open to attack by the traditional relativity argument.

Measurement is still a perceptual process, however, and reliance on it may seem to raise again the old bogy of the Representative Theory; perhaps in measurement, one is still confined to the private world of sensations; one is merely getting the percept of the coincidence of certain lines, not seeing the coincidence of external objects. But it must be remembered that at this stage the existence of external causes of our sensations and percepts has been accepted as the result of the first part of the justification. Hence it must be maintained that the simplest explanation of the percept of coinciding lines or objects is that it is caused by actually coinciding objects, especially when the senses confirm each other. Thus one may place the end of the ruler at the end

---

[15] But see H. H. Hirst, *Problems of Perception,* pp. 178 ff.

of the object, see them coincide, bring up one's hand and then feel that they coincide. *Ex hypothesi* one's direct awareness here is only of a series of data externally caused; but the best explanation of the nature and sequence of the data is that they reproduce in essentials, and are caused by, actually coinciding objects.

It has been suggested that measurement is not the only way to discover objective properties, and that one might adopt a method akin to the gradual-transition series and spatial synthesis proposed by Price for discovering nuclear sense-data. Thus if one considers all the various circular and elliptical sense-data obtainable from a penny and arranges them in order, the circle seems to be the central one from which all the others diverge; hence it is the real or 'proper' shape of the penny. This would be another and supporting method of co-ordinating single perceptions, but measurement of diameters of the penny would seem to be a primary and more reliable way of establishing its real shape. For the observed nuclear 'proper' shape is not the actual shape of the object but is the sense-datum caused by and corresponding to it (assuming the Representative Theory, not Price's); that they are similar may only be true of shape and size, and one needs the support of general scientific theory or of measurement to guarantee the similarity. Thus one can apply Price's method to colour and arrive at the nuclear or standard colour, but the scientific counterpart and cause of that is something very different—a wave frequency.

The main aim of the second part of the justification of the Representative Theory is not, however, the defence of the distinction of primary and secondary qualities, but the support of the claim that science can discover real properties of objects. The defence seemed necessary here not only because the distinction is normally made part of the theory but in order to show how measurement and co-ordination of perceptions can surmount the relativity of perception, so far as the primary qualities at least are concerned. In support of the more general claim it is appropriate here to introduce the argument from the predictive success of science. As science progresses it cannot advance by measurement and calculation alone, but develops hypotheses and far-reaching theories; but the success of the predictions based on these must be regarded as verifying them and so confirming and extending our knowledge of objects. This success cannot reasonably be explained in any other way, and so the Representative Theory can claim that, though in a single perceptual act we are limited in direct awareness to sensations or percepts, nevertheless science, by measurement and experiment, by framing and testing hypotheses, has succeeded in discovering the essential properties of the external causes.

This argument was out of place before, but can be used now that the existence of external material objects has been justified on pre-scientific grounds. A little more remains to be said, however, about alternative philosophical explanations of this success. The Phenomenalist one has been largely disposed of at a pre-scientific level; but a truncated form of it can survive as an account of atomic science; it might still be held that, though there are macroscopic physical objects, unobservable postulated entities like electrons must be regarded as co-ordinating concepts not real existents, because they are in principle unobservable, and contradictory properties are attributed to them. But that involves a very specialized controversy and we can do little but note that the non-Phenomenalist view of their reality is held also by many physicists.[16] It is a question more of what science really claims than of whether its claims are in general justified, and so whichever answer is the correct one it will involve only a qualification, not a refutation, of the Representative Theory. The essentials of the latter still remain in the acceptance of the claim that there are external physical objects to cause our perceptions and that their macroscopic properties at least can be readily and reliably discovered by science.

More dangerous to this position is the Kantian thesis, that the causal relations established by experimental methods and the spatial ones revealed by measurement and calculation are properties of phenomena only, and that they do not characterize the ultimate and unknowable causes of our experiences, the things-in-themselves.

The best way to deal with this view is to attack the arguments on which it is based. It rests ultimately on the belief that in mathematics and the basic principles of science we have knowledge which is *a priori*, and so necessarily and universally true, but which is not simply analytic or logically certain. Kant asks how this is possible, how we know that all experience will conform to the principles of mathematics and science. He answers that it is because these principles are features of the way we organize the data of experience—otherwise they would not be inseparable from our observing it; but since they are thus contributed by us there is no reason to suppose they characterize the causes of the data of experience, the unknown external things-in-themselves. If then we can show that these mathematical and scientific principles are not necessary and universal, the basic claim of the Kantian thesis fails; and the Representative Theory could argue that this is possible. Thus spatial relations do not necessarily or universally conform to Euclidean geometry as Kant thought they did:[17] not necessarily, because there are alternative non-Euclidean geometries which might conceivably hold good of our space, and not universally, because scientists claim that neither interstellar space nor the spatial relations

[16] E.g. Max Born in *Philosophical Quarterly*, 1953, pp. 139 ff.

[17] Cf. my paper "Mathematics and Truth," *Philosophical Quarterly*, 1953.

of protons and electrons are Euclidean. There is also reason to doubt the necessary and universal applicability in science of two categories Kant stressed as *a priori* and contributed by us. One is that of causation, expressible in the principle that every event has a cause. How far this holds good at the sub-atomic level is a subject of dispute among physicists, some holding that statistical laws are fundamental; but at least the fact that it can be seriously entertained and argued that the principle of causality does not hold there shows that it cannot be part of the way we inevitably organize our experience—an alternative is conceivable. The modern stress on probability and statistical laws was not envisaged at all by Kant, and is a sign that it is the facts that force us to amend our categories and concepts to conform to them—not *vice versa*. To attempt to force the material of experience to conform to our mental mould is a bad habit rather than unavoidable necessity. Much the same applies to the category of substance: the problem of the duality of waves and particles, for example, suggests that the old category of substance may be inadequate to the discoveries of modern physics; we seem forced to new ways of thought that should be neither necessary nor possible if Kant is right.

This is unavoidably a mere sketch of an answer to Kant; and I may mention even more briefly that the Representative Theory could make various additional counter-attacks: it could dwell on the notorious difficulties in the Kantian position, e.g. the mysterious nature of the thing-in-itself or of the human self on his view. Indeed, apart from the dubiety of its basic assumptions, the working out of the Kantian doctrine involves the postulation of so many unobservables as to make it a less simple and plausible explanation than the Representative Theory.

6. ITS REJECTION AS AN EXPLANATORY HYPOTHESIS

The Representative Theory can thus be rehabilitated to a considerable extent and can be defended against certain traditional alternatives. Nevertheless its new guise as a hypothesis to explain the nature and order of our sense experiences lays it open to criticism from a different quarter and to the charge of being itself unnecessarily complicated, in fact incoherent, as an explanation.

Note first how it differs from the actual assumptions which we unthinkingly make and which I outlined in Chapter i. We take it for granted that what we perceive are external objects; indeed not only are the cats, cabbages and chairs we are aware of taken to be public and external, but so are sounds and smells. Yet the Representative Theory still apparently has to maintain that this is an illusion. We

are aware only of sensations or percepts that are in the mind not outside the body, even though it is a reasonable hypothesis to suppose
that they are the effects of external objects resembling them in certain
ways. But why then are we so chronically deluded, and even when
the error is pointed out to us why do we incorrigibly cling to the belief that we are perceiving the external table itself, not just its private
effects on us? The Representative Theory would be a better hypothesis
if it could give a convincing explanation of this, and a much better
one if it could allow us to be partially or wholly right.

Furthermore this claim to be the best hypothesis was advanced as a
way of saving the conclusion of the usual version of the theory, 'we
perceive only private ideas or percepts,' from epistemological disaster.
In reply to a common objection it showed how one could proceed from
that conclusion to the belief that ideas or percepts have external
causes whose nature science can discover by methods other than simple
perception. But this is only valid granted that conclusion or as an *ad
hominem* argument against philosophies like Phenomenalism which
claim as given merely sequences of sense-data. It is not therefore clear
that it escapes the self-refutation charge, namely that the conclusion
denies both what it set out to explain, our perception of external objects, and its premiss, that we observe certain facts about sense organs.
One might argue that if we did not perceive external objects, including nerves and sense organs, then the theory could never get started
and if it did it would defeat its own purpose. For the 'facts' of the
physiological causation of perception which it sets out to explain would
themselves dissolve into sensations and hypotheses.

Hence if the theory is to survive, it must maintain that in some way
we perceive or observe external objects as well as the sensations or percepts that they cause; and this observation of external objects must be
supposed to be more than making inferences or hypotheses from the
perception of private data. The best way to accommodate the two
perceptions would be to regard the one as the means to the other. The
way we perceive public objects, i.e. get to know of their presence and
of their characteristics, is by perceiving private ideas or percepts
caused by them and representing them. The double use of the word
'perceive' is awkward, but this could be avoided by synonyms 'observe' or 'aware of.' The amended theory would not be just juggling
with words: it could claim to fit the facts. If I seem to be perceiving a
tomato, i.e. am aware of a percept which I take to be or to be caused
by a tomato, and the best hypothesis to explain my experience is that
there is an actual tomato there causing it and resembling the percept
in primary qualities, then surely I am perceiving the tomato; I am ascertaining its existence before me and its essential properties, even if
I do not realize that I am doing so only indirectly by means of a rep-

resentation. At least a possible sense has been given to 'perception of external objects,' and the Representative Theory is now a better hypothesis for allowing the kernel at least of the common-sense assumption, as indeed its own starting point requires it should. Thus even if they might disagree with this suggested linkage, the best modern versions of the Representative Theory carefully and explicitly distinguish these two kinds of perceiving or awareness.

But this seems to lay the theory open to the very criticisms, of duplicating seeing and supposing that we see sensations, which Ryle levelled against the Sense-datum Theory. In an attempt to explain our perception of the world it offers two kinds of perceiving: the original perception of objects it set out to explain and a new perception of sensations or percepts caused by external objects. This duplication seriously weakens the claim to simplicity and coherence in explanation for we are offered two to account for one. This leads to a dilemma: either this perception of percepts is similar to the perception of external objects, in which case it must contain within it an inner perception of inner percepts, and so *ad infinitum*; or else it must be a radically different kind of awareness in not requiring causal process and inner awareness. This is the alternative usually adopted, but then this new kind of perception needs explanation. How does it occur without causal process and awareness of its effects? Why don't we need eyes to see percepts?

This dilemma is particularly pointed because seeing (or 'having' or 'being aware of') percepts seems in other respects just like seeing physical objects, especially as that is commonly conceived. Thus it is apparently of a transitive act/object nature like perceiving tables or tomatoes, percepts being regarded as distinct private objects or existents; it is in fact assumed to be an immediate confrontation with the percept, a direct awareness of it. It is as though, having rejected supposed immediate confrontation with physical objects on account of the causal process, the theory reintroduces it at the end of the process with different, private objects. But what is the evidence for it there? It would be illegitimate to rely on the fact that perceiving seems to the percipient to be immediate and direct in this way, for to him it seems to be direct awareness of public external objects, not of private ones.

Furthermore the very supposition of a host of private objects is a serious weakness in any theory which claims to be the simplest in a technical sense, i.e. to explain phenomena with the least postulation of types or orders of entity. And once these private percepts have been postulated there arises the problem of where to put them—there is no room for them in the head or in physical space.

Some of these points have been anticipated and turned by a traditional thesis which is integral to the theory but which in turn greatly reduces its value as an explanation. This is that percepts are mental; they are objects in the mind not in physical space, and the seeing of them is mental also, it is perception by the mind in the mind. Mental awareness is a direct intuitive confrontation which does not need material intermediaries such as sense organs. But this is a queer ending for what set out to be a scientific explanation of the facts. In the first place it seems to take us out of the sphere of natural science and of publicly observable entities and processes. For what is the evidence for this novel mental seeing? Neither the private world of sensations, nor the mind as the perceiver of it, not yet its perceiving of it, can be observed as part of the physiological causal chain. This mental seeing cannot be inferred as a further but so far unobserved link in the chain because it is something *ex hypothesi* quite different from all the other material and publicly observable links. It may be said that the evidence comes from the percipient—we stimulate the brain and ask the patient for his sensations. But then his answer is evidence only of the quality of his experience, not of its ontological or epistemological status. He can say that he sees a red glow or flashing lights or hears a tinkling sound, but his experience is not labelled 'private and mental, sensation only.' And brain stimulation is a special case; in perception generally, even in hallucination, the percipient is convinced that he is seeing external objects and so his evidence contradicts the theory.

Secondly, 'mind' and 'mental awareness' tell us so little that we are in effect being offered an explanation *per obscurius*. What is mind and how does it see directly? How is it related to the person and his body? The hypothesis raises more difficulties than it solves, and we must investigate the various theories of mind to elucidate it, let alone assess its value as an explanation.

Lastly, despite its introduction of 'mind,' the theory does not deal adequately with the non-sensory mental activities that occur in perceiving. This is most clearly shown in the case of misperception, but is also illustrated by various psychological phenomena, such as attention. Consider a situation where the object present is a wax imitation of a tomato, and observer A takes it to be a tomato while observer B, next to him, takes it to be a piece of wax. The theory may say that B sees the wax by seeing a percept caused by and representing it, but this cannot be said of A for he 'sees' a tomato. And how is A's error to be explained? Not by difference in the percept or sense-data directly seen, for there is no reason to suppose that they differ for A and B as they would if A were colour-blind or were seeing the object from a long way off; the wax presumably causes similar activity in the sensory areas of the brain, and similar corresponding mental effects, in both observers. There would then seem to be two suggestions: the difference may lie in the way the percept or datum is seen—A does not see it properly, misperceives it—or it may be that some interpretation or judgment or taking-for-granted is necessary for perceiving objects. The first would destroy the assumption of a direct seeing of percepts—if the seeing varies so much it cannot be an immediate confrontation. Furthermore we wish to know how this mental seeing can vary so much; it can hardly be explained in the way varying perspectival distortion is explained, as being due to differing brain activity which causes different mental data. On the second suggestion misperception is taking the percept caused by object X to be, or be caused by, object Y. All perception must be regarded as taking-for-granted or judging that a directly seen percept is, or is caused by, a certain physical object, and I allowed for this in my initial account of the two types of seeing. But the problem for the theory then is how to explain this without being reduced to an unplausible Actual Inference view, which would treat seeing external objects as merely inferring from or interpreting a true inner seeing of percepts.

Similar difficulties arise over other psychological factors: we have already mentioned the dilemma of attention in Chapter iii, and it would seem to apply also to the Representative Theory and suggest that the seeing of percepts must be variable in character and not direct confrontation; and stereoscopic vision, object constancy and the effects of past experience on perception all raise similar questions. I shall discuss these points in Chapters viii and ix, and it is a pity that the recent exponents of the Representative Theory, especially the neurologists, say so little about them.

We may illustrate these objections to the modified Representative Theory by considering their application to a recent version put forward by J. R. Smythies in his *Analysis of Perception*. One might call it the 'Television Version' for he quotes with approval, and tries to justify, the dictum of Grey Walter that 'the televisual system behaves very much like the neuro-visual one.' Seventeenth-century versions of the Representative Theory had to be content with simple analogies, that the mind perceiving ideas was like the king in his audience chamber; the rise of the cinema suggested that sensing sense-data was like seeing a private film of the outside world, and now there is television. However Smythies claims that it is not just an analogy and that it would not be misleading to take it literally (p. 41). Since the complex patterns one sees on looking at a flashing light in a stroboscope are similar to those which appear on a T.V. screen when the light is being televised, it is argued that they are produced in each case by a scanning mechanism, and that the private visual field of sense-data is constructed by such a mechanism in our brain or retina, just as the picture on the T.V. set is constructed by the electron beam travelling regularly over the screen (pp. 68 ff.). ('Scanning' in these contexts does not mean or entail 'seeing'; it means 'travelling regularly over an area, scene or surface.')

Now there are various special objections to this version, e.g. that there is no physiological evidence of such mechanism in the person, that neither the light waves striking the eye nor the resultant nerve impulses seen like a modulated radio wave, that there is nothing like the T.V. camera to scan the seen picture and convert it into impulses that could work the equivalent of the T.V. receiver. (The theory only mentions the latter, but it would surely need: the eye = camera, nerve impulses = radio waves, and brain = receiver and screen—which is even more speculative.) Further, even if there is a scanning mechanism in the brain (the alpha rhythm has been suggested), the simplest hypothesis would not be that seeing an object consists in inner seeing of a picture of that object constructed by a scanning mechanism— which would duplicate seeing—but that it consists in scanning, i.e. having a special impulse travel over, the pattern of brain activity caused by the external object. Furthermore, whereas a T.V. set only reproduces a few of the characteristics of the external object (no colour usually, no smell, taste, touch or warmth), the T.V. reproducer on this theory will have to *add* all these secondary qualities since the outside world has only primary ones.

But it is with the general epistemological objections that we are chiefly concerned here. As on the older Representative Theory we or our minds could directly perceive only ideas, so on this modern version we (or our 'pure egos') can directly observe only the T.V. picture consisting of sense-data which represent the external world which causes them. Hence we are all incorrigibly mistaken in thinking that we directly observe external objects. How then can we know about the latter or justify our observational premisses about sense organs, stroboscopes and television sets? Smythies answers by emphasizing that the existence of external causes is a hypothesis, though one offering 'the best explanation of the world' (p. 35), and by distinguishing between direct and indirect observation:

"We can say that "directly to observe an object or event" is synonymous with 'to sense a sense-datum (or examine an image)' and that 'indirectly to observe an entity or event' is synonymous with 'to perceive a material thing.' The causal theory of perception does not then require us to say that physical objects are *unobservable* things-in-themselves. It has only to postulate that physical objects are ontologically distinct from sense-data (are things-in-themselves), and that the relations between sense-data and physical objects are such that by sensing some sense-data (not hallucinations) we perceive material things and so gain knowledge about the physical world" (pp. 33–34).

If we take this at its face value we have two kinds of observation instead of one—a clear duplication. Moreover how is it that observation (= perception) requires sense organs and scanning mechanisms, while observation (= sensing) does not and is apparently immediate. After all we need eyes to look at a T.V. screen, the same eyes that we need to see the scene being televised if we are present in the studio. So if the analogy were pressed we should need a further T.V. set to enable us to see the images produced by the retina/brain T.V. set, and so on.

To avoid this infinite regress direct observation is made mental, but there is no appreciation of the problems posed by the psychological processes in perceiving and misperceiving. There are some novelties, however. Mind is defined as 'a complex composite of sense-data organized into sense-fields, together with images, thoughts, affects and perhaps a Pure Ego,' and is made spatial as sense-data are spatial (p. 28). But it is not thought to be in the same space as physical objects, and three resultant hypotheses, Theories I, IIA and IIB, are offered concerning the relations between minds (including sense-data) and objects. The first is that they have no mutual spatial relation; the last two are elaborate suggestions of higher-dimensional spatial relations between them, and theory IIA involves postulating a system of unsensed psychical entities. Most of the suggestions are so speculative and complex as greatly to weaken the claim to be the best explanation, even assuming one can decide which theory to adopt. Yet the main epistemological difficulty still remains: causal relations are still supposed to hold between physical objects and sense-data, but it is not clear how they can do this. As Smythies says 'The general problem is how may one group of spatio-temporal events affect another group of spatio-temporal events when the members of one group either bear no spatial relations or higher-dimensional spatial relations to members of the other group?' (p. 59). He thinks it may be solved if one can construct an n-dimensional physics based on an n-dimensional geometry, but he does not attempt the construction. This is very chimerical and I should have thought that all scientifically recognized causal relations hold between entities in the same spatio-temporal system. The idea of cause in one space and effect in another is a paradoxical novelty; in fact it is usually supposed that cause and effect are spatially continuous within the one space, action at a distance being rejected.

It would be no help to say that we already have an example of such inter-spatial causal relations in the causation of mental images by brain activity; that would pre-judge the question, for the occurrence of mental images is just another instance of the fundamental difficulty of explaining the relations between brain events and our experiences. Indeed it may be that there is no *causal* relationship between sense-data and events in the physical world. There is a causal chain within physical space from external objects to brain activity, but it may extend no further; the sense-data may be aspects in one space of the perceptual activity of the person, activity which in physical space presents the aspect of brain activity. Indeed there is a danger of interpreting 'the space of sense-data' too physically, as though sense-data are different objects, and are analogues of physical objects but in a different physical space or extension; whereas strictly all one can say is that sense-data are *spatially ordered* differently from physical objects, and this may only mean that they are events in ordinary physical space (brain events) as revealed on a different mode of access or observation from perception or scientific observation. I shall suggest a theory on these lines in Chapters vii and x.

Our general conclusion must be then that even in its most plausible forms the Representative or Causal Theory is unsatisfactory. On the credit side it does at least try to explain the puzzling physiological facts, which is more than some philosophical theories have done, and it is the explanation to which generation after generation of investigators are first drawn. To avoid self-refutation it must simply claim to be the best hypothesis to deal with the facts. But it is then unsatisfactory in accusing us all of ineradicable and inexplicable error, and in duplicating the perception of external objects it set out to explain by postulating a second and inner perception of inner objects—one that mysteriously needs no sense organs. It seems forced in fact to use 'mind' and 'mental awareness' as a *refugium ignorantiae* for this second inner awareness, and this not only leaves much unsolved but is really an abandonment of scientific principles, for all the modern sophistication it may acquire.

This last charge raises wider issues, but they must be faced if we are to achieve a theory of perception which will account more satisfactorily for the scientific evidence. As an essential preliminary we must examine and attempt to improve on the current theories of mind, an examination which should also support our criticism of the Representative Theory as an explanation of perception.

Physical Objects

The problem I shall discuss is What reason have we for believing that there are physical objects? My purpose is not either to raise or to dispel doubts as to the existence of physical objects; this doubt constitutes a medical rather than a philosophical problem. The point of asking the question is that, while there can be no reasonable difference of opinion as to whether there are physical objects, there can be and is reasonable difference of opinion as to how the notion of a physical object is to be analysed; and if we are clear as to what grounds there are for believing in physical objects, we shall also be clearer as to what sort of physical objects we have grounds for believing in. Also, it is worth while to inquire which other beliefs are logically connected with, and which are logically independent of, the belief in physical objects.

I make one important assumption at the outset: namely, that by a physical object or process we mean something that exists or occurs apart from and independently of our perceptions, and of our experiences of other kinds. The distinction between the physical or "real" world and the "subjective" or "imaginary"—illusions, hallucinations, after-images, shadows, rainbows, mental pictures, what we merely suppose, imagine or expect—is a distinction between things and events which exist or occur whether anybody is aware of them or not, and things and events which have their being only as and when somebody is aware of them. A belief in physical objects is a belief in things which are sometimes at least unobserved by the believer.

It is obvious that the existence of such things is not a question to be settled by sense-perception alone. That there is a material world can-

From C. H. Whiteley, "Physical Objects," *Philosophy,* 34 (1959). Reprinted by permission of the author and the Editor from *Philosophy.*

not be established or even made plausible merely by looking, listening, touching; it is not *given* in the way in which the existence of something red and something round, of sounds, smells, aches, feelings of sadness, can be given. I do not mean that the something red or round cannot be a physical object; I mean that it cannot be known to be a physical object just by looking at it or otherwise perceiving it. For I cannot, simply by perceiving something, tell whether that something continues to exist when I cease to perceive it. This logical necessity is not evaded by naive realism, which holds that the something red or round which appears to sight is (usually at least) identical with a physical object; for though this may be so, we cannot know it just by looking. Nor is it evaded by phenomenalism; for no phenomenalist does or plausibly could analyse statements about physical objects into statements asserting the *actual* occurrence of sense-data; he must add statements about what sense-data *would* be sensed if certain conditions were fulfilled; and this fact is not given by sense-perception, but reasons for it are required. That there are physical objects is not something we observe or perceive, but something we suppose or assume (to call it a "hypothesis" or "postulate" is to suggest something rather too deliberate and self-conscious). In old-fashioned language, it is a transcendent belief; it goes beyond the evidence.

Thus there is no logical absurdity in denying or refusing to admit the existence of a material world. To say that there are no physical objects, while doubtless very foolish, does not involve a man in any logical contradiction, nor does it force him to shut his eyes to any patent and indisputable facts. An intellectually indolent percipient, whose few wants were supplied independently of his own efforts, might well abstain from supposing that there was a physical world. There is some evidence that young babies, who are more or less in this situation, do not believe that there are any material things—do not believe, for instance, that the rattle just dropped from the hand and the visitor just departed from the room are now anywhere at all.

If somebody did behave like this, in what way would he be worse off, and what other beliefs would he be debarred from entertaining? I answer—and this is my principal point—that he would be unable to make valid generalizations, or reliable forecasts of his future experience. He would have to do without the belief in an order in nature, in regular sequences of events, in causal laws. For if I confine myself to what I myself observe or am aware of, I can make no valid generalizations concerning the concomitance or sequence of types of phenomena. I find only that phenomena of one type are quite often accompanied or followed by phenomena of another type, but sometimes not. There is no type of sense-datum A of which it is true that whenever it occurs another type of sense-datum B accompanies or follows or precedes it. And this is the case however complex you make your A and your B. This point has often been overlooked. People know quite well that lightning is always accompanied by thunder, barking by the presence of dogs, that green apples are always sour, and the ground always gets dark and sticky after a heavy fall of rain; and they talk about these as though they were *phenomenal* regularities—as though the seeing of lightning always went along with the hearing of thunder, and so forth. But this is of course not the case. If, as some people have said, it was the business of science to disclose the order or regularity in phenomena, meaning by phenomena what we see and hear and feel, science would be a very unrewarding pursuit. For phenomena are disorderly and irregular, and scientists cannot make them out any different.

Many philosophers have indeed thought that natural regularities could be conceived without the postulation of actual unobserved things and events, if instead we postulate that certain phenomena would occur or would have occurred, given certain unfulfilled conditions. Instead of saying that whenever I hear barking there exists an actual dog, perceived or unperceived, I am to say that whenever I hear barking, I should perceive a dog if certain conditions were fulfilled— if my eyes were open and my sight normal, if there was an adequate amount of light, if I looked in the right direction and there was no opaque obstacle in my line of vision etc. Such an interpretation in terms of possible phenomena would relieve us of any need to postulate another order of physical events over and above perceptual events, and would in this way be more economical. There are, however, three ways in which phenomenal generalizations of this kind cannot take the place of physical generalizations.

(1) A physical generalization associates one uniform property with another uniform property: I mean that when something is asserted to be universally true of dogs, or pieces of iron, or cases of pneumonia, or falling bodies of a weight of ten pounds, it is assumed that there is some physical property or group of properties which is common to all dogs, pieces of iron, etc. Phenomenal generalizations, however, concern associations between sets of diverse phenomena. If we wish to correlate the auditory phenomenon of barking with visual phenomena we must specify a set of canine sense-data, or views of dogs, which are not all alike in any sensory property, but form one class only in virtue of a very complex set of relations.

(2) A physical generalization applies to *all* cases of a given type, and the study of nature aims at reducing to laws all events and all features of events. But phenomenal generalizations can never apply to all cases of a given type, but only to some of them, namely to those cases in which the supplementary conditions for observation are fulfilled. The

physical generalization "There's no smoke without fire" applies to all instances of smoke, whether or not either the smoke or the fire is observed. But the corresponding phenomenal generalization brings under a uniformity-rule only those cases in which both the smoke and the fire are observed. Observed smoke can be correlated with observed fire; but when I observe the smoke but not the fire, the observed smoke is correlated with nothing, and is an instance of no natural law (except in the forced and trivial sense in which a white cat with brown eyes and quick hearing is an instance of the law that all white cats with blue eyes are deaf); it forms no part of the order of nature.

(3) A phenomenal generalization must always include a reference to conditions of observation, whereas physical generalizations are independent of these. We can say without qualification "Whenever it thunders, it lightens." But we can say "Whenever thunder is heard, lightning is seen" only if we add "provided that there is an observer with adequate eyesight, facing in the appropriate direction, having his eyes open and his view not obscured by any opaque object, etc." This difference does not merely prevent the phenomenal generalization from adequately replacing the physical one. It also means that there can be no generalizations on the phenomenal level which are universally valid. For it is impossible to give in purely phenomenal terms an adequate statement of all the conditions required for perceiving lightning besides the occurrence of lightning. It is curious that the analysis of physical-object statements in terms of sense-data and the analysis of causation in terms of regular sequence should have been so often advocated by the same philosophers. For if we restrict our attention to phenomena, we can find no instances for the regular-sequence concept of cause to apply to.

If, therefore, I am to make reliable generalizations about the course of events, and reliable forecasts about my future experiences, I must suppose that there are unperceived as well as perceived events. Thus the connection between the category of substance and that of cause is, as Kant suggested, not fortuitous but necessary. We do not discover that there are (perfect) regularities in nature, that is, in the physical world, as we discover that there are (imperfect) regularities amongst phenomena. On the contrary, the regularity is essential to the concept of nature; the assumption that the physical world is orderly is inseparable from the assumption that the physical world exists. It is only to the extent that I assume it to be orderly that I have any grounds for believing that there is a physical world at all. This may help to account for our strong inclination to regard physical determinism as a necessary *a priori* truth.

What, then, is the sort of supposition which will make it possible to believe in regular sequences and concomitances in the world, and to regulate our expectations accordingly? A simple and comprehensive answer cannot be given to this question. The precise character of the suppositions we make about physical objects and processes is subject to variation for different kinds of cases, and to modification with the improvement of our knowledge. One can, however, indicate the general line which must be followed.

There are, amongst the events which we are aware of, certain associations of characteristics which, while not invariable, are very common: for example, the association between the sound of barking and the sight of dogs, between the visual appearance of oranges and their characteristic flavour, between the brightness of sunshine and felt warmth, between the kinaesthetic sensations of speech and the sound of my own voice, between the visible immersion of a lump of sugar in a cup of tea and its gradual disappearance, between the various members of the visible sequence black-coal . . . flame . . . red-coal . . . ashes, between the patter of raindrops, the sight of rain falling, the feeling of dampness on exposed parts of the body, and the darkening of the soil or pavement. (These are, of course, examples of several different kinds of association.)

The supposition required has two parts: (1) That to these imperfect phenomenal regularities there corresponds in each case a perfect physical regularity, that is, in each case in which there is a frequent association between phenomenal characteristics there are some corresponding physical characteristics which are invariably associated. Whereas the sound of barking is often but not always accompanied by the sight of a dog, there is some type of event, physical barking, which is always accompanied by the presence of some one type of physical object, a dog. Whereas the visual brightness of sunshine is only sometimes accompanied by a feeling of warmth, there is a physical entity, sunlight, and a physical entity, heat, which always goes with it. Whereas a person may be seen setting off from A and arriving at B without being seen at intermediate places at intermediate times, physical passage from A to B involves the temporally continuous traversing of a spatially continuous path. In general, whenever there is an imperfect but frequent association between a phenomenal characteristic A and a phenomenal characteristic B, there is a thing or process having a characteristic corresponding to A which is invariably associated with a thing or process having a characteristic corresponding to B. Thus whenever I hear barking, there exists a physical dog, whether or not there also occurs the experience of my seeing him.

(2) The existence of the corresponding physical thing, or the occurrence of the corresponding physical process, is a necessary but not a sufficient condition for the awareness of the phenomenal characteristic. There can be no hearing of barks without there being (physical)

barks; but there can be barks without the hearing of barks. The further conditions, other than the existence of the dog or the occurrence of the bark, which are required if I am to have the corresponding perception of the dog or the bark, may be called the observation-conditions. Some of these conditions are pretty easy to discover. For instance, if I am to see anything at all, there must be a certain amount of light (but not enough to dazzle), and my vision must not be blocked by any obstacle. Other observation-conditions can only be discovered by much experimental research: for instance, the need for air or some other transmitting medium in the case of hearing, the need for integrity of the optic nerves in the case of sight. The occurrence of the appropriate sense-experience is determined jointly by the corresponding physical process and the relevant observation-conditions. (These conditions, of course, concern the properties of other physical things and processes, so that we cannot say just what they are without knowing something about physical things other than the one to be perceived. Learning about the properties of dogs, and learning about the properties of light and the human sense-organs, go hand in hand.) Thus the assumption of a physical world involves two supposed sets of regularities: an association between one physical characteristic and another, and an association between physical processes together with observation-conditions on the one hand and sense-experiences on the other.

So far, the physical world has been presented as a set of processes which occur independently of perceptions, which are related by laws of sequence and concomitance to other processes, and which together with the relevant observation-conditions determine specific sense-experiences of ours. These are purely relational properties; and nothing has been said so far about any other properties that physical objects may possess. On the view here advocated, namely that the justification of a belief in a physical world is that it makes possible the formulation of laws of nature, the only positive reason for attributing a property to physical objects would be that by assuming physical objects to possess this property we can account for the character of our perceptions, and explain how we come to perceive this rather than that, now rather than then. One way of accounting for the character of our perceptions would be to suppose that the sensory qualities which are present in them (the particular colours, sounds, tastes, etc.) are properties of physical objects, and persist unperceived just as they appear when perceived. This is naive realism. A completely naive-realist theory would hold that all sensory qualities are properties of physical objects, and exist independently of perception; other theories are naively realistic to the extent that they identify the properties of physical things with those properties which are present in sense-experience.

Now the investigation of the properties of physical things is the business of the science of physics. And contemporary physics is not naively realistic in any degree. The properties which it attributes to physical objects are not sensory properties, but hypothetical properties defined by their relations to one another and to certain kinds of perceptions. The reason for this is often misunderstood. Philosophical criticism of naive realism is apt to concentrate on the "argument from illusion," that is, on the *deceptiveness* of sense-perception. This is the wrong sort of criticism. Our perceptions can sometimes mislead us (that is, lead us to form false expectations about other perceptions to come) only because they also, and more often, lead us to form true expectations; perception could not be systematically misleading. But the question whether our perceptions induce in us true or false expectations is quite independent of the question whether they show us the permanent characteristics of material things. The damaging criticisms of naive realism rest on this principle: given that the physical object corresponding to a given sense-datum is something which, in conjunction with the relevant observation-conditions, determines the characteristics of that sense-datum, then if a given characteristic can be shown to be determined by the observation-conditions, there can be no reason for attributing it to the corresponding physical object. The successive modifications in our concept of the physical world arise from our increasing knowledge of the dependence of sensory properties upon observation-conditions. The challenge to naive realism with respect to colours comes from optics. The challenge to naive realism with respect to space and time comes from relativity-theory. The challenge to naive realism with respect to beauty and ugliness comes from our understanding of the dependence of aesthetic delight and disgust upon the dispositions and past experiences of the subject.

In abandoning naive realism, scientific theory only carries further a process which pre-scientific common sense has already begun. The common-sense view of the physical world is by no means a purely naive-realist view. When I look at an object from different angles and in different lights successively, the sensory properties which appear to me are many and various. Common sense does not hold that all these various sensory properties belong to the physical object and exist apart from my perception. Were that so, there would have to be either a multitude of physical objects or a constantly changing object to possess all these different properties. Common sense holds, on the contrary, that there is but one object with one shape, size, colour etc., which are unchanging throughout my changing perceptions. This postulation of a single set of physical properties corresponding to a multiplicity of sensory properties is the first and fundamental step away from naive realism. A Berkeleian analysis, which reverses this step, is a greater affront to common sense and provokes more resistance from it than a Lockean analysis which takes a step or two further in the same direction.

It is a belief of common sense that at least some sensory properties are *not* properties of physical objects, but are due to conditions of observation (quantity and quality of light, distance, defects of vision, etc.). As to whether *any* sensory properties are also physical properties, I am not convinced that common sense has any clear and consistent view. Of course we say that grass is green and roses are red. But does this mean more than that if we look at them under suitable conditions green and red are the colours we shall see? It is not clear to me that common sense is committed to the belief that objects have any colours when unperceived. (Examining the way we talk about the matter is of no help. Given that a certain piece of cloth looks bluish in artificial light and greyish in daylight, are we to presume that its colour changes with changes in the light, and say "It *is* blue in artificial light and grey in daylight," or are we to presume that it has a colour independently of the light, and say "It is really grey, but it looks blue in artificial light"? Ordinary idiom allows us to say either of these things indifferently.) By contrast, there are some properties which common sense does attribute to physical objects apart from perception—size and weight, for instance. When I conclude that this brick must have made that hole in the window, though nobody saw it do so, I credit the brick with having a size and weight at a time when it was not being perceived. But size and weight are not sensory properties. Blueness is a way things look; but heaviness is not a way things look or feel. A thing can, of course, look or feel heavy; but its *being* heavy is something different—it is heavy if it will hold down or make dents in other objects, if you can't lift it with one hand, and so on; and these casual characteristics are not ways of looking or feeling. Properties like size and weight, which common sense does attribute to unperceived objects, bear the same sort of relation to sense-experience as the concepts of modern physics. Thus it seems to me that one can abandon naive realism in all its forms without abandoning any belief to which common sense is committed.

To sum up. That there are physical objects is a supposition, not a datum. The use of the supposition is to account for the regularities in sensory phenomena, to enable the course of events to be set in a framework of regular sequences and concomitances. It is confirmed by the success we achieve in ordering our experiences by its aid, in making our generalizations continually more extensive and more exact. Being a supposition, and not an inevitable and invariable category of thought, it is subject to modification as we learn more about the conditions under which perception takes place. Scientific concepts are related to sense-experience in a remoter and more complex fashion than common-sense concepts of physical objects. But they are not of an entirely different order. The common-sense concept of "table" is not, like "blue" or "bang" or "stench," a merely phenomenal concept; it is explanatory and theoretical.

Bibliographical Essay

~~~~~~

I. CONCERNING A PERSON'S KNOWLEDGE OF PAST EVENTS IN HIS LIFE

Three good short introductions to some of the philosophical problems sur-
rounding our concept of memory, remembering, a person's knowledge of
past events in his life, and related matters are: A. D. WOOZLEY's *Theory of
Knowledge* (New York: Barnes & Noble, Inc., 1966), Chaps. ii and iii, paperback; A. J. AYER's *The Problem of Knowledge* (London: Macmillan & Co.
Ltd., 1956 and Baltimore: Penguin Books, Inc., 1956), Chap. iv; and SYDNEY
SHOEMAKER's "Memory," *The Encyclopedia of Philosophy,* edited by Paul
Edwards (New York: The Macmillan Company and New York: The Free
Press, 1967). A considerably more detailed discussion of these problems is
found in the following, all written by philosophers: E. J. FURLONG's *A Study
of Memory* (Camden, N.J.: Thomas Nelson & Sons, 1951); W. VON LEYDEN's
Remembering (London: Gerald Duckworth & Co. Ltd., 1961); BRIAN SMITH's
Memory (London: George Allen and Unwin Ltd., 1966); and STANLEY
MUNSAT's *The Concept of Memory* (New York: Random House, Inc., 1967),
paperback. IAN M. L. HUNTER, a psychologist, has written a good introductory book, *Memory* (Baltimore: Penguin Books, Inc., 1957), paperback. Bibliographies are included in VON LEYDEN's *Remembering* and in MUNSAT's *The
Concept of Memory.*

An empiricist theory of memory is presented in: DAVID HUME's *A Treatise
of Human Nature* (London: Oxford University Press, 1888), Book I, Part I,
§ 3 and Book I, Part III, § 4 and 5; THOMAS REID's *Essays on the Intellectual
Powers of Man* (Cambridge, Mass.: The M.I.T. Press, 1969), Essay III;
BERTRAND RUSSELL's *The Analysis of Mind* (London: George Allen and Unwin
Ltd., 1921), Chap. ix; and H. H. PRICE's "Memory-Knowledge," *Proceedings
of the Aristotelian Society,* Supplementary Vol. XV (1936). The latter essay is
discussed in: J. LAIRD's "Memory-Knowledge," *Proceedings of the Aristotelian
Society,* Supplementary Vol. XV (1936) and J. N. WRIGHT's "Memory-Knowl-
edge," *Proceedings of the Aristotelian Society,* Supplementary Vol. XV

(1936). R. F. HOLLAND's "The Empiricist Theory of Memory," the first essay in this book is discussed in: E. J. FURLONG's "The Empiricist Theory of Memory," *Mind*, LXV (1956); PHILLIP P. HALLIE's "Empiricism, Memory, and Verification," *Mind*, LXVI (1957); and JOHN TURK SAUNDERS's "Scepticism and Memory," *The Philosophical Review*, LXXII (1963).

Some of the conclusions that WILLIAM EARLE defended in his essay "Memory" are very much like those upheld in: SAMUEL ALEXANDER's *Space, Time and Deity* (New York: Humanities Press, Inc., 1920), Vol. I, Chap. iv; and J. W. HARVEY's "Knowledge of the Past," *Proceedings of the Aristotelian Society*, XLI (1940–41). Arguments against these conclusions can be found in: the introductory essays on memory by A. J. AYER AND A. D. WOOZLEY mentioned at the beginning of this bibliography; C. D. BROAD's *The Mind and Its Place in Nature* (London: Routledge & Kegan Paul Ltd., 1925), Chap. v; and R. F. HARROD's "Memory," *Mind*, LI (1942). Harrod argues for a view similar to that defended by E. J. Furlong in his essay "Memory."

Alternative theories of memory and discussions of how it is related to our knowledge of our past are presented in RICHARD TAYLOR's "The 'Justification' of Memories and the Analogy of Vision," *The Philosophical Review*, LXV (1956). Taylor attempts to solve the problem of justifying our memory-beliefs by showing that this is no more than a special instance of the problem of justifying our beliefs in the existence of distant objects. In "Philosophical Problems of Memory," *The Journal of Philosophy*, LIX (1962), CHARLES LANDESMAN argues that however we come to know something about our past we do not come to know it by remembering, for in remembering an event, say, we are simply exercising our knowledge that the event occurred. JOHN O. NELSON, in "The Validation of Memory and Our Conception of a Past," *The Philosophical Review*, LXXII (1963), suggests that generally a person's memory of a past event in his life is reliable, and that this can be shown to be true without assuming that it is. He contends that some philosophers have thought otherwise because they were confused about the kinds of events that it is possible to remember, and they have overlooked the role of some statements about a person's past in the person's rational life.

An attempt to put some of the philosophical problems discussed in the first part of the book into a broader perspective can be found in R. B. BRANDT's "The Epistemological Status of Memory Beliefs," *The Philosophical Review*, LXV (1955).

II. CONCERNING A PERSON'S KNOWLEDGE OF OTHER MINDS

A brief survey of many of the philosophical problems concerning a person's knowledge of other minds, as well as a survey of proposed solutions to these problems can be found in J. M. SHORTER's "Other Minds," *The Encyclopedia of Philosophy*, edited by Paul Edwards (New York: The Macmillan Company and New York: The Free Press, 1967). For a more detailed account of some of these matters, see DON LOCKE's *Myself and Others* (London: Oxford University Press, Inc., 1968). A sophisticated discussion of one fairly recent attempt to deal with the problem of other minds can be found in the col-

lection of essays *Wittgenstein and the Problem of Other Minds,* edited by
Harold Morick (New York: McGraw-Hill Book Company, 1967), paperback.
An extensive bibliography on the philosophical problems of other minds is
included at the end of JOHN TURK SAUNDERS and DONALD F. HENZE's *The
Private-Language Problem* (New York: Random House, Inc., 1967), paper-
back.

A statement of the view that an argument by analogy is our justification
for believing what we do about other minds is found in: JOHN STUART MILL's
An Examination of Sir William Hamilton's Philosophy (London: Longmans,
Green & Co., Ltd., 1899) pp. 243–44; BERTRAND RUSSELL's *Human Knowledge: Its Scope and Limits* (New York: Simon and Schuster, Inc., 1948), Part
VI, Chap. viii. An attack on this view is in MARTIN SHEARN's "Other People's
Sense Data," *Proceedings of the Aristotelian Society,* L (1949–50). Shearn's
article is discussed in PETER ALEXANDER's "Other People's Experience," *Proceedings of the Aristotelian Society,* LI (1950–51). ALVIN PLANTINGA in "Induction and Other Minds," *The Review of Metaphysics,* XIX (1966), presents
a much more advanced and formal attack on the argument by analogy. This
article is discussed in MICHAEL ANTHONY SLOTE's "Induction and Other
Minds," *The Review of Metaphysics,* XX (1966). Plantinga replied to Slote
in "Induction and Other Minds, II," *The Review of Metaphysics,* XXI (1968).
NORMAN MALCOLM's "Knowledge of Other Minds," *The Journal of Philosophy,* LV (1958) further attacks the argument by analogy. Malcolm's
essay is discussed in HECTOR-NERI CASTANEDA's "Criteria, Analogy and Knowledge of Other Minds," *The Journal of Philosophy,* LIX (1962). STUART HAMP-
SHIRE provides a sophisticated defense of the argument by analogy in "The
Analogy of Feeling," *Mind,* LXI (1952). And a reply to Hampshire's article
is in W. W. MELLOR's "Three Problems About Other Minds," *Mind,* LXV
(1956).

A. J. AYER also discusses some of the problems of other minds in: *The
Foundations of Empirical Knowledge* (London: Macmillan & Co. Ltd., 1940),
Chap. iii; and *The Problem of Knowledge* (London: Macmillan & Co. Ltd.,
1956), Chap. v. Ayer's views are discussed in the following: JOHN WATLING's
"Ayer on Other Minds," *Theoria,* XX (1954); V. C. CHAPPELL's "Myself and
Others," *Analysis,* Supplementary Vol. (1963); and IRVING THALBERG's "Other
Times, Other Places, Other Minds," *Philosophical Studies,* XX (1969).

A contemporary defense of behaviorism can be found in PAUL ZIFF's
"About Behaviourism," *Analysis,* XVIII (1958), reprinted in PAUL ZIFF's
Philosophic Turnings (Ithaca, N.Y.: Cornell University Press, 1966). Ziff's
article is discussed, along with a great many other things of importance to us,
in MORELAND PERKINS's "Emotion and the Concept of Behaviour: A Disproof
of Philosophical Behaviourism," *The American Philosophical Quarterly,* 3
(1966). For additional arguments against behaviorism, see H. H. PRICE's
"Some Objections to Behaviourism," *Dimensions of Mind,* edited by Sidney
Hook, (New York: The Macmillan Company, Collier Books, 1961), paperback. Price's article is discussed briefly in C. D. ROLLINS's "Price's Objections
of Behaviourism," *Journal of Philosophy,* LIX (1962).

A number of the positive claims that H. H. PRICE put forward in his essay
"Our Evidence for the Existence of Other Minds" were first suggested in his

"Our Knowledge of Other Minds," *Proceedings of the Aristotelian Society,* XXXII (1931–32). R. I. AARON expressed a view very much like Price's in "Our Knowledge of One Another," *Philosophy,* 19 (1944). Both Price's and Aaron's opinions are discussed in J. R. JONES's "Our Knowledge of Other Persons," *Philosophy,* 25 (1950).

Another view concerning the philosophical problems of other minds can be found in: JOHN WISDOM's "Other Minds," *Proceedings of the Aristotelian Society,* Supplementary Vol XX (1946). Wisdom's style is difficult and distinct. In this essay he tries to understand why anyone would think that what we ordinarily take to be a good reason for a person's believing that there are other minds or that another person is thinking or feeling some particular thing isn't really a good reason—or a good enough reason—for such knowledge. In his discussion Wisdom sets down what he takes to be good reasons for believing statements about other minds. He also expresses his views on these and related matters in "Philosophy and Psycho-Analysis"; "Philosophy, Metaphysics and Psycho-Analysis"; and "Philosophical Perplexity." These three essays are reprinted in JOHN WISDOM's *Philosophy and Psychoanalysis* (Oxford: Basil Blackwell & Mott, Ltd., 1953). Wisdom also published a series of eight essays on the problems of other minds; they are reprinted in JOHN WISDOM's, *Other Minds* (New York: Philosophical Library, Inc., 1952). His article "Other Minds," mentioned above, is discussed by A. J. AYER and J. L. AUSTIN in *Proceedings of the Aristotelian Society,* Supplementary Vol. XX (1946). And views more or less similar in spirit to Wisdom's can be found in ALFRED DUHRSSEN, "Philosophical Alienation and the Problem of Other Minds," *The Philosophical Review,* LXIX (1960); and JAMES THOMSON's "The Argument from Analogy and Our Knowledge of Other Minds," *Mind,* LX (1951).

I will mention one additional position on these problems of other minds, that expressed in P. F. STRAWSON's *Individuals* (London: Methuen & Co. Ltd., 1959) Chap. iii. Strawson argues that the relation between a person's behavior and his psychological state is never a logically necessary relation or a logically contingent one. Instead, the relation is such that, on some occasions, a person's behavior serves as logically adequate criteria for another person's thinking that he is in a psychological state of a particular sort. Strawson's views are discussed: in A. J. AYER's "The Concept of A Person," *The Concept of A Person and Other Essays* (London: Macmillan & Co. Ltd., 1963); GARY ISEMINGER's, "Meaning, Criteria, and P-predicates," *Analysis,* XXIV (1963); and TERRY FORREST's "P-predicates," *Epistemology,* edited by Avrum Stroll (New York: Harper & Row Publishers, 1967), paperback. A good critical review of Strawson's *Individuals,* as well as a discussion of his views on other minds, can be found in ALVIN PLANTINGA's "Things and Persons," *The Review of Metaphysics,* XIV (1961); and B. A. O. WILLIAM's "Mr. Strawson On Individuals," *Philosophy,* 36 (1961).

III. CONCERNING A PERSON'S KNOWLEDGE OF PHYSICAL OBJECTS IN HIS IMMEDIATE VICINITY

D. W. HAMLYN's *Sensation and Perception* (New York: Humanities Press, Inc., 1961) is a good history of the philosophy of perception. A survey of contemporary philosophical views about how we come to know anything about physical objects in our immediate vicinity can be found in: R. J. HIRST's "Perception," *The Encyclopedia of Philosophy*, edited by Paul Edwards (New York: The Macmillan Company and New York: The Free Press, 1967); JOHN PASSMORE's *A Hundred Years of Philosophy* (London: Gerald Duckworth & Co. Ltd., 1957), Chaps. ix to xii; and T. E. HILL's *Contemporary Theories of Knowledge* (New York: The Ronald Press Company, 1961). A number of anthologies have been published which contain excellent articles and excerpts from books on knowledge and perception, together with good introductions and long bibliographies. The three best are: *Realism and the Background of Phenomenology*, edited by R. M. Chisholm (New York: The Free Press, 1960); *Perception and the External World*, edited by R. J. Hirst (New York: The Macmillan Company, 1965), paperback; and *Perceiving, Sensing, and Knowing*, edited by Robert J. Swartz (Garden City, N.Y.: Doubleday & Company, Inc., 1965), paperback. Unlike the other anthologies, that by Swartz, contains only work published in the twentieth century. A good introductory book on perception written by a psychologist is M. D. VERNON's *The Psychology of Perception* (Baltimore: Penguin Books, Inc., 1962), paperback. An outstanding annotated bibliography of most of the best work in English on the philosophical problems of perception and our knowledge of the physical world is in *A Modern Introduction to Philosophy*, edited by Paul Edwards and Arthur Pap (New York: The Free Press, 1965), pp. 583–90.

Different versions of the phenomenalist theory of perception can be found in: GEORGE BERKELEY's *A Treatise Concerning the Principles of Human Knowledge*, 1710, Part I; JOHN STUART MILL's *An Examination of Sir William Hamilton's Philosophy* (London: Longmans, Green & Co., Ltd., 1899), Chap. xi and the appendix to Chap. xii; C. I. LEWIS's *An Analysis of Knowledge and Valuation* (LaSalle, Ill.: Open Court Publishing Co., 1946), Chaps. vii, viii, and ix; H. H. PRICE's *Perception* (London: Methuen & Co., Ltd., 1932); and A. J. AYER's *The Foundations of Empirical Knowledge* (London: Macmillan & Co. Ltd., 1940).

All of the works mentioned in the preceding paragraph have inspired discussion in various books and articles. The following are representative: G. J. WARNOCK's *Berkeley* (Baltimore: Penguin Books, Inc., 1953), paperback; and H. H. PRICE's "Mill's View of the External World," *Proceedings of the Aristotelian Society*, XXVII (1926–27). C. I. Lewis's views are discussed in RODERICK M. CHISHOLM's "The Problem of Empiricism," *Journal of Philosophy*, XLV (1948). LEWIS replied to Chisholm in "Professor Chisholm and Empiricism," *Journal of Philosophy*, XLV (1948). Both Chisholm's article and Lewis's reply are discussed in RODERICK FIRTH's "Radical Empiricism and Perceptual Relativity I," and "Radical Empiricism and Perceptual Relativity II," *The Philosophical Review*, LIV (1950). In *The Problems of Perception* (London: George Allen and Unwin Ltd., 1959). Chap. iv, R. J. HIRST discussed the views espoused by Price in *Perception*; while those put forth in Ayers's book are examined in J. L. AUSTIN's *Sense and Sensibilia* (London: Oxford University Press, 1962).

Various versions of a representative or causal theory of perception can be found in: JOHN LOCKE's *An Essay Concerning Human Understanding* (1960), Book II, Chaps. viii and ix and Book IV, Chap. xi; BERTRAND RUSSELL's *An Analysis of Matter* (London: George Allen and Unwin Ltd., 1927), Chap. xx; C. H. WHITELEY's "The Causal Theory of Perception," *Proceedings of the Aristotelian Society*, XL (1939–40); and A. C. EWING's "The Causal Argument for Physical Objects," *Proceedings of the Aristotelian Society*, Supplementary Vol. IXX (1945). Among the writings which discuss the foregoing are: H. A. NEWMAN's "Mr. Russell's 'Causal Theory of Perception,'" *Mind* XXXVII (1928); and MAURICE MANDELBAUM's *Philosophy, Science, and Sense Perception* (Baltimore: The Johns Hopkins Press, 1964), Chap. i. The latter includes an examination of Locke's views, whereas those of Ewing are taken up in an article authored by R. I. AARON and D. G. C. MACNABB in the *Proceedings of the Aristotelian Society*, Supplementary Vol. IXX (1945). Two additional critical discussions of the representative theory of perception can be found in: H. H. PRICE's *Perception* (Methuen and Company, Ltd., 1932), Chap. iv; A. R. WHITE, "The Causal Theory of Perception," *Proceedings of the Aristotelian Society*, Supplementary Vol. XXXV (1961).

An attack on some basic assumptions of both the phenomenalist and representative theories of perception is in A. M. QUINTON's "The Problem of Perception," *Mind*, LXIV (1955). Quinton argues that when a person perceives something he rarely, if ever, directly perceives sense data, and often directly perceives physical objects—objects which exist independently of anyone's perception of them. Quinton goes on to say that while a person's perceptual experience might be part of a causal explanation for his beliefs about a physical object in his immediate vicinity, it is not normally his reason or justification for believing some statement about the object. Quinton's article, "The Problem of Perception," is discussed in R. WILLIS, "The Phenomenalist Theory of the World," *Mind*, LXVI (1957). In this article Willis also talks about the existence, nature, and role of sense data in our knowledge of the existence of physical objects in our immediate vicinity. Additional discussions of sense data can be found in the works mentioned below: WINSTON H. F. BARNES's "The Myth of Sense Data," *Proceedings of the Aristotelian Society*, XLV (1944–45). Barnes argues that there is no good reason to think that sense data exist. In "Sense Data," *Inquiry*, 10 (1967) BENSON MATES argues that there is no good reason to think that sense data do not exist and there are good reasons to think that they do exist. "Sense-Data and Material Objects," *Mind*, LXVI (1957) is an article by NORMAN BROWN, in which he argues both that sense data do exist and that sometimes, at least, a person can directly perceive a physical object in his immediate vicinity. Sense data are discussed in more detail and with greater complexity in RODERICK FIRTH's "Sense Data and the Percept Theory," *Mind*, LVIII (1949) and LIX (1950).

A recent and difficult discussion of the general nature of and justification for inferences to the best explanation is GILBERT HARMAN's "Knowledge, Inference, and Explanation," *The American Philosophical Quarterly*, v (1968).